This Is It
2 Hemispheres, 2 People, and 1 Boat

Jackie Parry

© Copyright Jackie & Noel Parry 2024

All rights reserved.
The copyright of this book belongs to Jackie & Noel Parry.
No reproduction without permission.

ISBN: 978-1-7636458-0-6

Dedication:

To everyone brave enough to follow their dreams.

Note to reader:
At the back of this book, I've included details on *Pyewacket*, the process of checking in, the costs, and some technical aspects of the boat. This is in an attempt to maintain the flow of the story, the journey, and the experience.

At times, I refer to people travelling on boats as "cruisers" and sometimes as "boaties"; sometimes, I refer to people by their boat name – that's simply how it's done in the cruising world. I've tried to refrain from using too many boating terms; where it's unavoidable, I've included a glossary at the back of the book.

I've written the dollar amounts in USD and occasionally mention other currencies. The exchange rate is pertinent to 2009-2011.

I refer to *Pyewacket II* and *Mariah II* mostly without the *II* for ease of reading. I do the same for SV (sailing vessel) and MV (motor vessel).

Where I have included advice and details on requirements of checking in, etc., this information was correct at the time of our travels. You are responsible for your own research; governments, rules, and costs may have changed

Though this is a work of nonfiction, I have changed some names to protect the identities of the people I've written about.

If you'd like to view some pictures,, please visit: www.jackieparry.com and hover your mouse over books, there you can select which book and photo album you'd like to view.

We are constant travellers, and both Noel and I become

confused with which hemisphere we are in.

This note is for you *and* us:

- This story begins in Australia.
- We travel to America to buy the boat.
- As I write, we are living in Belgium.
- I am originally from the UK, and I am an adopted Australian.
- Noel is a true-blue Aussie.
- Where we'll be *tomorrow* is anyone's guess.

PART ONE

1. Will it be Enough?	1
2. BUY! SELL!	7
3. Diverse San Francisco and (Near) Calamities in California	15
4. Time to Scratch	29
5. Futile Thoughts, Towing Traumas, and Exploding Toms	33
6. Costa Rica's Little Gem	48
7. Escapades in Ecuador	60
8. Panama's Secrets	94
9. Sweet Stash and Not So Sweet Travel	106
10. The Home of Land-Based Cruisers	131
11. Alien Forms, Rotten Cheese, and Chooks	140
12. Occluded Fronts and Associated Stunts	148
13. Taking Stock of Locks with Smoking Clippers	161
14. No Strangers Here	168
15. Wallis Island – The Beginning of the End	191
16. Epilogue	203
17. Where Are We Now?	206

PART TWO – Bonus Material — 208
Articles, information, and further reading.

Pyewacket's Particulars	209
Buying in a Foreign County	212
Mexico: Costs, Checking In, and Supplies	214
Ecuador: Fees, Cruising Guides, and Visas	216
Pitcairn: Communication and Information of Interest	218
Gambiers: Anchoring Information and What We Could Have Done Differently	219
Suwarrow: Formalities and Costs	220

Australia: Checking In and Importing A Foreign Boat
Costs, How It Works, and Contacts 221
Steering by a Star: Fitting an Aries Wind Vane to a 51' Boat 229
Ecuador: Radio Invigilating in Ecuador
Pilot Testing the New, On-Line Exam in Ecuador 236
Flopper Stopper in a Flap 241
Route Map 244
Glossary 246
From the Author 260
Acknowledgements 261
Other Reading 262

PART ONE

1

Will it be Enough?

'I think it's what we should do.'

Leaning on the sink, I stared out the kitchen window. The sulphur-crested cockatoos broke the silence with an ear-piercing squawk.

'While we're young and fit enough,' Noel continued.

Rainbow lorikeets flitted between the plump maple trees that were dominating the postage-stamp garden behind our cottage in Greenwell Point, New South Wales.

Was I ready to leave all this again?

Could I pack up our life's possessions and leave the stability of owning a house and living in a small community?

We'd done it before, but I was in my twenties then.

Would it be vastly different in my forties?

Was Noel right? After all, what is life for if you're not wringing out every last drop?

'Come and have a look at this boat – it'd suit us.'

Twisting from the stainless basin, I peered into the interior gloom and waited for my eyes to adjust. I raised my eyebrows at my grinning husband who sat with confidence by the computer; he knew I'd agree. I wasn't going to say no to a new escapade; but another sailing adventure? I'd had my heart set on exploring Europe by barge.

Walking towards my buddy and his aura of excitement, I rolled my eyes. Convincing me was easy, and the flutter of anticipation stirred my stomach.

'Will it be enough?' I asked, thinking of all the sailing miles already under our belts.

'Enough? Enough! You don't think buying a boat in a foreign country, preparing it to cross oceans, *and* sailing back to Australia is enough?'

'That's not what I meant.'

'What do you mean, then? You know it's not an easy task.'

I wasn't sure what I was trying to say. Perhaps it was because we'd already sailed around the globe on *Mariah*, a thirty-three foot boat. I'm not saying it was easy or that I felt as though we'd *been there, done that*. I simply hadn't thought deeply enough about this new idea. I was thinking about an old steel barge on the European canals, which would be easier, but it was a different challenge – something new.

I constantly crave that kick-in-the-gut emotion from the delicious mix of fear and thrill that a new challenge offers. I must put myself out there and have a plan in motion that makes my heart jump. I need to push myself to new levels, fill my core with wonder, gasp with joy, and quake with fear!

Would another sailing trip do this? Later, this thought would come-back and slap me hard on the face.

My jumbled emotions and thoughts made little sense to me, but that was nothing new.

How challenging would a barge be? That was the second thought that'd turn around and laugh in my face much later on.

I questioned my ability to sit through night watches, though. I need eight hours of solid sleep. How would I cope with four to six hour shifts while crossing an ocean now that I was staring at my forties?

'Buck up,' I muttered to myself. 'You're not too old yet!'

But these thoughts carried me off and caused a certain amount of angst that swirled with the anticipation of sailing again.

* * *

Noel and I worked for a couple of years, squirreled away our earnings, and dashed off on another voyage – not a few weeks in a foreign land, but a living exploit. We weren't rich, just careful with our money. We had no debts; we never bought something unless it was imperative – whether it was for the house, for us, or the escapade.

Fashion wasn't important, nor was the latest phone or computer. If our gear worked fine, that was enough.

We didn't use credit cards. We steered clear of unnecessary constraints like careers and mortgages. Our life was the journey – the adventure – we spent more nomadic-time than working-for-someone-else time, and that balance was shifting even further in our wandering favour.

The buying-a-boat-in-America idea grew from living in the USA for a year (on *Mariah*, while traversing The Great Loop). We had found that boat prices in the States were less expensive than in Australia. We circumnavigated on our first boat, *Mariah*, ultimately sailing into Greenwell Point NSW, the closest safe harbour to family – and where the next escapade was taking shape.

'If we found a boat cheap enough, used our skills to transform it into a good sea-going vessel and comfortable home, when we've finished our trip, the boat sale may end up funding the entire trip.'

'You mean it pays for itself?' I asked.

'Yes, and our living on board expenses for a few years. That's pretty much what happened with *Mariah*.'

Making money on boats was not easy; it was rare to sell for a profit.

Discussions on this scheme rolled in and out of our lives like a tide across a sandy beach; at times, the tide was out and a damp beach allowed only a trickle of thoughts to seep in; other times, our ideas raged upon a flood tide with plans that rolled and bobbed on the surface.

* * *

Over the following year, while we worked at our maritime teaching jobs at Technical and Further Education (TAFE), I became an Internet widow while Noel scoured the USA for our next boat. The idea settled in my muddled mind, and I started to grasp the enormity of the undertaking.

The momentum gathered me up and swept us both along. Enthusiastically, I immersed myself in the hectic but exhilarating project of leaving Australia, renting out our home, resigning from our jobs, liberating ourselves from our possessions, and bidding farewell to family and friends once again.

With intrepid excitement and a smidgen of horror—*what on earth are we doing?* – we landed in San Francisco, hauling just the clothes on our backs and one small bag each. Our bags bulged out at awkward boat equipment angles; they acquired some odd looks. Not so apparent to our fellow passengers was the huge dollop of determination that sat squarely on our shoulders.

* * *

The idea of buying a boat in the States was also a good excuse to explore the bejewelled Pacific Ocean once again. On our last boat, we discovered a smattering of her diamonds. This time, we weren't interested in traversing the Panama Canal a second time, and we'd already sailed much of the east coast and the inland waterways of America, including the Great Lakes, the Ohio River, and the Mississippi River.

Exploring new parts of the vast ocean was top of the list.

Noel and I grew up with British history. Bligh held particular interest, because he became Australia's Governor fifteen years after the mutiny in 1789. Noel chomped through many historical books detailing HMS Bounty, the maligned Bligh, and the mutiny. I devoured Hollywood's interpretations through Mel Gibson, Marlon

Brando, Clark Gable (as Fletcher Christian), and Anthony Hopkins (playing Bligh in The Bounty).

Sailing from America towards Australia afforded us the opportunity to sail down to Pitcairn's latitude, en route sat Easter Island, the remotest inhabited island in the world. If you have sailed to one, why not visit the other?

Although, the more recent Pitcairn history supervised a portion of my mind.

Surely that black cloud has long gone.

On the lighter side, extraordinary viewpoints encouraged our aspirations.

As friends and relations caught wind of our plans and the whispers fanned out, sailing 'experts' and travelling 'specialists' declared our strategy too hard.

'They can't do that!'

'You can't anchor there!'

'It's too far!'

Self-professed authorities didn't quell our thirst for this demanding voyage. We'd dealt with nay-sayers all our travelling lives. Every time we would prove them wrong, and each negative comment stimulated our gypsy spirit with the motivation to accomplish.

It emerged that Noel's main goal was to sail to the remotest inhabited island in the world: Easter Island. I was wrapped up in that dream, so it became mine, too – but, fundamentally, my role was to support Noel in his endeavours and help make it happen. That may be why I was wondering if this was enough.

I craved the freedom of sailing and travelling with our home; home being where we belonged, a refuge from the outside world, a safe haven of comparative peace, and the ability to travel with our own bed, pillow, and favourite drinking mug. The fact that a home can, strangely enough, be a bobbing cork in the shape of a cruising boat is a remarkable concurrence.

The idea embodied our souls; it came alive, evolved, carrying us along as if it was the director and we were just the puppets. The animated scheme developed into a good excuse to return to our voyaging lives, because that was when we had a distinct purpose; besides, we were good at it. *Would we be this time, though? Or had the sailing community been on the money? Did our dreams outstretch our ability?*

2

Buy! Sell!

We landed in San Francisco mid October 2009, our limbs heavy with fatigue. Our impossible timeline between finishing work and flying out meant we had to perform miracles to organise our house and affairs in Greenwell Point, NSW. Friends were renting our home, so when the timeline squeezed down to seconds, I didn't have to worry about leaving the kettle and toaster unpacked in order to catch the plane.

San Francisco is a buzzing, colourful city crammed with vibrant characters. Roy and Chris kindly put us up (or put up with us) in their home overlooking the Golden Gate Bridge, while we tried to convince our bodies and brains that we were in another time zone.

We met Roy and Chris during our voyage on *Mariah*, while they were on board *Sol Mates*. They had saved us, with some flour, when we were running out of food in the Red Sea. After our initial encounter, we had met them at various and exotic destinations around the world, becoming great friends.

Land travel was a nightmare. First, Americans sit and drive on the wrong side as far as Australians are concerned. During the first ten minutes in the hire car, we idled at the edge of a six lane highway.

'It's clear, you can cross now.' I said to Noel as we both swung our heads left to right like inept dancers.

'Yes, but *how?*' he answered with a slight quiver in his voice.

A GPS navigator was prerequisite and kept imminent divorce at bay. We never left a car park until the next destination had been tapped in and loaded.

Despite the expense of car hire, we were comforted by having good door locks. This was one place where suitable contemplation must be taken when choosing which suburb to stop in. More than forty neighbourhoods sit around San Francisco, and no two are the same.

The city is a mix of vibrant madness that we could dip our toes into with a visit via car. But a brief trip to town was enough.

San Francisco was an interesting choice of place to search for a boat. In 1991, a firestorm destroyed almost four thousand homes, killing twenty-five people in Oakland Hills – where we were staying. We learned, with a disconcerting indifference, that our friends' house sits right on the Hayward Fault line. Nearby is the neighbouring San Andreas Fault, which caused severe earth movement in 1906 and 1989.

'If an earthquake should occur, if we manage to escape being crushed by the house, the enormous water dam over the hill will collapse and drown everyone in the valley!' they said.

Bush fires or earthquakes, San Franciscans are a hardy, tenacious lot, who divulge these horrifying stories with a shrug. For us, the forest of eucalyptus trees surrounding our accommodation – and explode in wild fires – were terrifyingly close.

Fortunately, we didn't have too much time to dwell on our safety. We wanted another boat, and we needed a home. We were vagrants once again.

Primarily, we wanted a longer boat. We had coped well on *Mariah's* thirty-three feet for nine years, but it was time to try something different. Steel construction didn't enamour either of us – working with a rusting hull held no appeal. We'd already owned a timber boat. This time we were steering a course towards fibreglass. (A more detailed list of our specifications appears at the back of this book.)

'Why are you after a bigger boat?' our hosts enquired curiously.

'Well, the idea is to accommodate guests in two cabins. Many sailing friends are keen to hop on board and sail a leg with us or just come and sit on anchor. We like that idea, and two cabins and toilets means a little extra comfort for us all.'

* * *

The first amazing insight of boat hunting in this part of the world is most boat brokers are not the slightest bit interested in selling boats. We were staggered at the lack of interest in our enquiries. In desperation, Noel wrote an email to one broker stating:

> *We are from Australia, we have cash, and we have*
> *jet-lag and a desperate stare in our eyes.*
> *In short, we are mugs ready to be led down the*
> *path of nautical slavery If you can't sell us a boat*
> *there is something very wrong.*

We didn't receive a reply. Perhaps they just didn't understand Australian humour.

Pushing open a polished door to a small building, we faced a long, narrow office. The suited broker sat at the back of his domain and shouted at us from his chair, some ten metres away. This was our second attempt to arrange a viewing on a boat he was advertising.

'I need twenty-four hours' notice,' he yelled.

We tried to give him notice, but simply grew weary of shouting.

Do the boat owners know that potential purchasers were unable to view their boats?

The first broker we pried off his bottom originated from a Hollywood movie, not because of the glamour, but because he was unbelievable.

Jed's business attire comprised orange plastic flip-flops, bright Hawaiian shorts and t-shirt. His chemical-induced watering eyes dribbled towards the smouldering cigarette that appeared to be glued to his bottom lip.

He didn't instil any confidence as he displayed a jarring ensemble of jerks and twitches, dispelling our last shred of confidence in our garishly garbed would-be broker.

The boats we viewed were on the hard in the yard. Jed smashed the ladder onto the topsides of each of the three boats that caught our eyes with a crunch that made us cringe. Noting our horror, he shrugged and sat in various cockpits, allowing the dirty ash from his smoke to fall on the cabin floor, the smoke spiralling up to stain the canvas, all while we viewed the generally beaten up boats.

'BUY! SELL!' another broker with a different set of boats yelled into his mobile phone and cleared his throat with tubercular force, while we crammed into a tiny aft cabin together. We were close to Hollywood, but this was ridiculous.

During the fiasco between decrepit boats and peculiar brokers, we commenced discussions to view a boat we stumbled across.

We became disillusioned with what we saw, which was primarily rot, delaminating decks, blisters, and mould.

It sounds like a dream to hop on a plane and spend each day viewing boats in an exhilarating foreign country. The reality is different. Our budget meant clean motel rooms, but that was all you could say about them. Car hire is a speedy way to empty your bank account (due to the insurance). Also, our desires were difficult to fulfil – centre cockpit boats were few and far between.

We toyed with going to Seattle, where we narrowly missed out on an Olympic Adventurer, but other boats sparked our interest. Ted Brewer designs caught our eye.

During the debacles with the bothersome brokers, we arranged to view a boat, without a broker, that we stumbled across. While inspecting a vessel via a broker, we spied *Pyewacket II*, an Aleutian 51, a few docks down, floating quietly, alone. The boat we had arranged to see was not for us, we stepped onto leaking decks and into a cockpit that two four-year-olds could possibly squeeze into with the aid of a crowbar, and told the broker to forget it.

With our buddies, Roy and Chris, we meandered along the dock to a proud, large monohull.

'Wow, look at the thickness of the rigging.' Her pristine, heavy duty rig included two backstays and running backstays – additional rigging was a good start.

Right then, I knew she would be our new home.

Uninvited, we rudely inspected *Pyewacket's* exterior.

Meanwhile, Roy slinked off into a neighbouring fishing shop. A few moments later, he reappeared displaying a wide, smug grin, waving a piece of paper.

'She's for sale, and here's the owner's number!'

My stomach shifted as if my organs had stood to attention and saluted.

Pyewacket's nautical slave, George, confirmed the boat was for sale. Fed up with his broker, he had terminated the contract and decided to sell her privately for a little more than we could afford.

'I've just dropped the price significantly for the third time!' A deep, exasperated sigh carried over the phone line. Meanwhile, I pressed the buttons on the calculator in my mind, cajoling and stretching the finances to agree.

Having harvested a collection of disappointments upon viewing boats below deck, I tried to curb my enthusiasm until we had seen *Pyewacket's* interior.

She did not disappoint.

A small stern cockpit provided an entrance into the aft cabin with en suite. Moving forward, we stepped into a long, narrow galley port side of the engine. On the opposite side, a long workshop caused Noel to smile. The engine room sat between the workshop and galley with the centre cockpit above. The wide and comfortable saloon led forward to a shower room facing enormous cupboards followed by the front cabin with one double and one single bed.

'It's a bit seventies.' Roy frowned.

'Paint'll fix that.' Noel smiled.

I hadn't even noticed the décor. I loved the layout – useful, practical, and comfortable. *Could we afford a boat this big?*

Over the following weeks and during several inspections, buyers and seller slowly became friends. I thought George and I were kindred spirits when he mentioned he owned horses in a previous life. Later, he revealed he was a horse dealer. The horse dealers I have met had never been friends, but George appeared upfront and honest with his boat dealings.

During the tricky negotiations, we viewed other boats – none striking us in the same way. *Pyewacket* met our needs, but we just couldn't seal the deal. Finally, frustration grabbed us by the throats, and we booked flights to Florida.

'We'll find our boat there,' we said in an ever so grown up way.

The day before flying out to commence our search on the east coast, we were back with our friends, Roy and Chris.

Two weeks had passed since we landed in San Francisco; it felt like two years.

'I'm going to call George one more time,' Noel announced in the evening. My jaw clenched, and anger bunched in my lively stomach. I had already paid for the tickets, but I couldn't hide the spark of excitement that twitched on my lips.

We didn't speak to George until we were driving to see the popular 2009 Michael Jackson movie, *This Is It,* that evening.

We increased our offer, but hadn't extended far enough to meet George's expectations. While we watched the film, George thought about the dollars.

After the inspirational story, with a spring in our step and joy in our hearts, we agreed to enjoy every waking minute of this adventure, our lives.

As we climbed into Roy's car, the phone rang. My skipping heart momentarily stopped, then took off again like a bunny in mating season.

'That's George,' I said, gulping air in an attempt to slow the hammering in my chest.

'Well, why don't you talk to him?' Noel grinned at me, raising his eyebrows in challenge. I hated negotiations. I never discussed money with anyone except Noel.

Reluctantly, I answered the call.

The collective silence hummed, intermittently the leather car seats creaked, and the interior groaned under white knuckle grips. I knew this moment would shape the rest of our cruising lives.

For several minutes, George and I bartered back and forth.

Then the stillness hung in the air as I allowed George to wrestle with his emotions and find a way to agree to our offer.

Although not directly watching me, I sensed the intense scrutiny of Noel, Roy, and Chris. This administered the motivation I needed.

'Take this as a virtual handshake,' I announced into the palpable silence.

We reached an agreement, and Roy, Chris, and Noel broke into applause; Roy offered me a job. 'My goodness, you can negotiate!'

Never did I think that a few words from Michael Jackson would inspire us and be part of the boat search. Excitement from up-and-coming live performances radiated from his dancers, and Michael softly rebuked and reminded his troupe: '*This* is it – life's happening right *now*; enjoy *this* moment.'

This became our mantra on *Pyewacket*. Steadily, the hands of time ticked by; each second added up to one less moment to relish in the long run.

We were living a great nomadic life, but installing a new head (toilet), fixing an oil leak, and many other disagreeable jobs can be hard, frustrating, and dreary. Our adopted mantra may be obvious to some, inane to others, but for us, it worked. Those unpleasant jobs occur a lot on boats, and rapidly strip the gloss from what is often perceived, by the unenlightened, as a glamorous gypsy lifestyle; but we were enjoying *everything* we were doing.

Craving the simple lifestyle once again, our plans were to go adventuring, not race home to sell the boat. Indeed, the costs of importing a foreign boat into Australia were enough to make us sail right on past!

Pyewacket came with a whole gamut of added extras. George walked off the boat with the clothes he stood in. Tools, linen, kitchenware, TV, and navigation equipment were just a few of the items left behind. I even found a spare, unused condom! He also left lengths of timber, a quantity of stainless steel, screws, nuts, and bolts – some of which were put to good use immediately – gear, grease and gauze. The boat brimmed full with bits, pieces, and doodads. We were grateful for every single item.

'What do you think about the name?' Noel asked one evening while sipping a cool Californian Pinot Grigio.

'I hadn't even thought about it. There's been no time!'

'It's a bit obscure. What shall we change it to?' The cockpit filled with silence; sometimes, the creative juices don't flow. Was it because we were exhausted? Or did we not care that much?

'Well, previously we were the *Mariahs*, perhaps we'll be the *Wackets*,' I said, smiling at the memories of *Mariah* and the hope of new friends and making new memories on this trip.

Among others, *Pyewacket* means Familiar Spirit. Familiar Spirits are human spirits in animal form – in the movie *Golden Circle*.

3

Diverse San Francisco and (Near) Calamities in California

Creeping silently, blanketing all in its path, the white swirls looked soft, but I knew the secrets it hid and the dangers that lurked beneath its cotton wool subterfuge. The legendary San Francisco fog encompassed all in its path.

Sailing in murkiness induced my fear to bubble up; upon spying its approach, my neck stiffened and my shoulders bunched up towards my ears. The rips, currents, and tides in San Francisco Bay made an interesting challenge, too, adding a great dollop of danger to the excitement of traversing these waters.

Reading the tide tables was a two-fold task. In addition to the times of the tides were the 'overruns' – the flow information. Understanding this data was essential; otherwise, you could be pushing against a five knot current.

All these thoughts and fears swirled in my mind as we viewed the great Golden Gate Bridge from land. *Would we ever sail beneath this grand structure?* From a hill, I peered into the harbour, watching the rips and overfalls bubble and whirl. Vessels stuck in nature's grip slowly lost the battle as if sailing through syrup. Those that timed it right, or were going with the flow, flew under the bridge at a speed that was just as scary.

Safety and respect of the water was imperative; it was humbling. The vast bay could kick up into a brutal chop in a heartbeat. One minute, a breath of wind tickled the sails, and the next, a twenty-five knot breeze could almost knock you over. The wind blows from the Pacific Ocean into the harbour, affecting the area from the bridge, past Alcatraz and over to the East Bay, not the entire port, which was why the current of air caught unsuspecting people.

'That's enough of reality,' Noel sighed as he pulled his eyes from the water. 'Let's go and have some fun!'

We took time out to explore the city via the ferry system that zigzags around the Bay. At the terminal, lolly, coffee, and doughnut vendors created a jungle of scintillating smells that increased the mayhem, compounding our total disorientation. Ticket sales took a poor second place behind the array of doughnuts. It took us an hour, two coffees, and several sweet sticky things to locate the ticket booth.

'Can you smell that?'

'Smells like fish to me, and not edible fish at that!' I said with my hand over my nose.

'Look, it's the sea lions; do they bring back memories or what!'

The famous *Pier 39* was packed with colourful locals and international visitors. Candy coloured pastry shops, historic hotels, and an array of tourist attractions competed for attention with the sea lions.

'Are we stopping at Galapagos? You know we haven't really thought about our route.'

Our memories of cavorting with these playful creatures in the Galapagos Islands on our last sailing trip came flooding back. Here, they were both an attraction and a pest. The fishy smell assaulted your nose before you saw the slippery creatures. Like shiny black sand bags, they flopped over each other for a prime position.

'I'm not sure yet,' Noel said, peering at our odorous friends. 'I think we'll do what we usually do: trundle along and something or someone will show us the route we're taking.'

We both smiled.

We had ideas and likes but not hard-and-fast plans. You couldn't when you were on a boat; nature was too fickle. We relied on the wind and currents to reach our 'planned' locations; sometimes the fight was too hard and dangerous, and we were forced to change routes. On board *Mariah*, we missed Turkey due to the weather. The struggle to battle into wind and waves inspired a port turn towards Greece.

The unique vista around town created a diverse vibrancy. *What people and islands will weave themselves into our lives and shape our future?* The trip on *Mariah* had changed us both. Generally, we were both more tolerant of, but paradoxically less accommodating with, people whose lives had stagnated; we had little time for negative and judgemental folk.

* * *

'It's good to be back home,' I sighed, kicking sandals off my aching feet.
'She's already home, isn't she?' Noel patted *Pyewacket* affectionately. 'Now the hard work begins!'
Within the madness of owning a new boat in a strange country, we found contentment in having our own home, our own space. On board *Pyewacket,* we stayed at Richmond Marina, a place where everyone we met told us to be home by dark.
The Richmond District is a neighbourhood in the north west corner of San Francisco; one road is lined with the wealthy, the next a ghetto, where our legs pumped that bit harder on our bicycles. A local claimed it to be one of the most dangerous cities in the States. The Marina itself was safe, with barbed wire and twenty-four-hour security. During our stay, Noel and I stayed together and did not venture out at night. That said, we did not receive one impolite word from anyone or witness any aggressive behaviour.

* * *

During our eight weeks since landing in San Francisco, we had inspected twenty two boats. We hauled *Pyewacket* out of the water, arranged a survey, sealed the deal, and moved on board. We rolled anti-foul paint onto the hull, changed anodes, fitted filters and fan belts, and freed up the spinnaker poles and sea-cocks. We fixed hanks, hosing, and housing and cleaned, wiped, scrubbed and washed everything within an inch of its life. We balanced, built, bodged, and bought tonnes of gear. On board were the builder's notes, which were read, absorbed, and regurgitated. Eating became a time-absorbing inconvenience. Burgers and soft drinks laden with salt and sugar worked at hardening our arteries. Helping to work off the consumed lard, we polished the hull and prepared to sail south.

We were preparing to bid farewell to San Francisco. For weeks, we'd pondered, studied, and worried over our decisions: a foreign boat, a few weeks' preparation before heading to sea, tumultuous waters to traverse, and a diminishing bank account. The work fended off our chaotic thoughts from becoming all absorbing, but in the back of our minds, anxiety nibbled and gnawed – until our desire to keep moving resumed control, and off we went!

We cast off from the protected marina and sailed within a soft breeze to Treasure Island, choosing to anchor overnight in a sheltered position and to catch the predicted tidal stream early the next day.

* * *

Have we done enough work? Will we fulfil our dreams as we did on Mariah? Can we prove the nay-sayers wrong? My cluttered thoughts chased off any efforts to sleep until my aching muscles, from all the preparation work, allowed my body to drift into a satisfying sleep.

As night surrendered to the lemon blush of dawn, we glided past Alcatraz.

'There are two things I don't want to bear in my life,' Noel said, staring at the sombre structure. 'I don't want to accidentally kill a person, you know, a car accident or something like that.'

'I get that.'

'And I couldn't stand to be locked up; someone taking my freedom, having complete control over me.'

Silently, we watched the prison glide by. I shuddered. I agreed with Noel – I *needed* the freedom we were so used to.

The famous bridge beckoned, and with a gentle flow, we glided beneath the splendid superstructure. The only turbulence we experienced was the unruly grins smeared across our faces. Our trip south, ultimately towards Mexico, served up two small fog patches that immediately delivered hard rocks of fear into my tummy and increased my heart rate enough to create a few more platinum highlights.

I was looking forward to exploring other parts of California, preferably quieter towns with a slower pace. Half Moon Bay sits twenty-five miles south of San Francisco. We anchored there on the first night and revelled at being on-the-road again.

We left as dawn parted the darkness. Weaving through the crab pots into deeper water, we agreed to over-night south. Storms were gathering momentum in this part of the world as winter approached, creating an edge of urgency to sail south of Point Conception before full-on winter storm season commenced. November arrived, and part of our thoughts projected forward to hurricane season commencing in June.

The conditions remained calm, and we motor-sailed much of the time, for two days, towards Morro Bay, our next destination, to avoid the forecast gale for the Point Conception area south of our location.

Point Conception is legendary; it's California's answer to Cape Horn. Rounding Point Conception is not for novice sailors. The weather is unpredictable, and this area has the reputation for some of the roughest sea conditions on the west coast – jumping from flat calm to thirty knots without notice. It's not the place to be during winter storms!

Pyewacket was going great. During our about-to-cross-the-bar check, we discovered diesel spraying over the hot engine, an engine which had been running continuously for twenty-four hours.

We had yet to install a blower in the engine bay to remove the heat and fumes. One tiny spark from the alternator or the tangled mass of wiring that festooned underneath the injectors and Blammo! Fried *Pyewackets*!

The spraying fuel was coming from the return lines that ran from the injectors back to the fuel tank; one had split, and one had come off entirely! The tubes (not rated for fuel) were common old clear plastic that, in the heat, had practically melted to soft and gooey bomb fuses.

At this point, we were ten minutes from the approach to the Morro Bar. We had been receiving weather warnings all night on the VHF radio, forecasting a gale and the onset of four to six metre swells. Morro Bar Coast Guard announced possible closure at midday – it was 11 a.m. We were a little tense.

Quickly buying a boat and sailing the strange vessel in foreign waters left me without time to think about what we were doing. We'd sailed *Mariah* around the world, but we'd spent two years cruising Australia's NSW coast, getting to know her thoroughly before venturing overseas. I still didn't have time to fret, worry, or wonder what the hell we were doing. Cruising was like having a series of minor heart-attacks that interspersed with fun. At this moment, the minor heart-attack gathered momentum.

In the panic, for fear of it not starting again, we were not game to turn off the engine; this being the fear-driven logic at the time. So there we were, replacing the split tubes with fuel dribbling everywhere and thinking about the fire potential, while trying to recall our fire-fighting training.

I steered while Noel replaced the lines. Our hearts raced, and the seas continued to build. The wind kicked the briny water into action, lifting it higher. The rigging howled in protest as *Pyewacket* slammed into the waves. Salty spray tap danced across the windshield as if seeking a weak spot. *Pyewacket* valiantly fought nature's weapons, her heaving hull throwing off water from her deck as if proving her power.

Fighting to keep *Pyewacket* steady beneath rolling waves, the adrenaline skipped through my body and along my tense arms to the wheel.

My eyes darted to companionway, searching for Noel. I'd look back up at the approaching entrance, the extremely *narrow* entrance. There, the waves were clashing with the ocean's swell, creating bouncy peaks and mountains of water that we had to traverse. We barely knew this boat or her capabilities. I didn't trust the engine yet. Although it was fine so far, we had no history with it – *was it reliable? Will it hiccup as we are crossing the bar? Then what?*

My mind had an incredible ability to make up horror scenarios. I was okay if Noel was with me. I was sure his heart was bouncing through the wall of his chest, too, but outwardly, he was cool, thoughtful. He taught me to deal with what was at hand, to ignore the drumming internal organs and leg-shaking adrenaline, and get on with what needed to be done.

'Morro Bay Coast Guard, Morro Bay Coast Guard, this is sailing boat *Pyewacket II, Pyewacket II*, over.'

Silence.

After twenty seconds, I cleared my throat, deepened my voice, and concentrated on speaking a slow, clear rhythm of words.

'Morro Bay Coast Guard, Morro Bay Coast Guard, this is sailing boat *Pyewacket II, Pyewacket II*, over.'

Still no reply.

'Great,' I muttered.

I checked our course, the dials, and the gauges to ensure all was well elsewhere on board. I scanned the horizon for other boats. We were on our own.

My heart thumped, and the wind let out a squeal of warning.

Again, I tried the radio, with no luck. Local knowledge was always useful in these situations, but we weren't going to have any.

Noel re-appeared within a haze of diesel fumes, sporting a wide grin and umpteen stained rags in his filthy hands.

'I found the spare fuel line, and I've fixed it on!'

By now, I was dancing on my toes, watching the land creep nearer.

'Well done, you! I wouldn't have had a clue where they were!' This was a turnabout in our roles. I could usually lay my hands on everything on board. However, as *Pyewacket* had a huge workshop, Noel had gleefully organised the drawers and cupboards and had remembered where he'd stowed the spare lines.

'Right, let's go!'

Over the last half an hour, my tensing shoulders had risen up towards my ears. Now I could release them a little, but only momentarily.

As Noel turned the wheel to the entrance, I readied the lines and took a few deep breaths to steady my nerves.

Port entrances usually opened up as you approached, but this one didn't. The narrow waterway, hemmed with white water, sucked the ocean over jagged rocks – one small error, engine failure, or steering problem would create disaster.

Beyond the rocks, sandy banks protected the entrance from the wind, but the erect seas were wrapping around the walls, merrily growing and racing into the opening, waiting to carry us away.

In reality, we'd both crossed many bars such as these; indeed, the Australian NSW coast was notorious for challenging entrances into protected harbours. I'd safely towed boats over vicious entrances, in seas where my crew could barely look, at the helm of rescue craft. But even though – at times – fear clutched my tummy, we motored in safely every time, for it was my responsibility. If it was too dangerous, we didn't do it. Besides, I had been trained for all conditions at sea.

With surf breaking across a bar entrance, it is critical to count the wave sets and enter on the back of the last wave. I didn't like it, but I could do it. It can be more thrilling than a fair ground ride.

To add to the excitement, America had navigation buoys on the wrong side. Wrong for us, that is. Boats entering Australian ports put green buoys to starboard and red to port. Here, it is the opposite: green to port and red to starboard. It's easy to make the switch if you're not simultaneously thinking of fires, sandbanks, six metre waves, and surfing.

With Noel's help, *Pyewacket* eased over the tumultuous water and held a steady course. The waves lost their anger, and the boat lost her tilt as if the enraged wind and rollers didn't exist. *Pyewacket* now wore white trickling water around her bow, and we turned sharply to starboard into the safe, protected port.

I did not relish the anxiety during events such as these. But I liked the adrenaline rush, the pumping heart action, and the buzz in pushing your emotions aside and getting on with what needs to be done, right in the moment. Was this living? I knew it made the easier days more enjoyable, worthwhile – we'd survived, after all. The good times were heightened by the extreme times. They were not bad times; they were scary and daunting, but they were a challenge, and one way or another, we both thrived on pushing our limits. Besides, it proved that our work had paid off. The boat was seaworthy; it could cope with adverse conditions and so could we.

Within ten minutes of tying up at the Yacht Club at Morro Bay, we were offered a beer and the use of a car. The relief of a safe port was heightened by the heart-pumping action before crossing the bar (entrance) – we had thoughts of staying forever. So we sat for a few days at Morro Bay – one day complete with a hangover after we visited the kind of bar you sit in to forget your worries instead of a port entrance bar. It would have been easy to stay and lap up the friendly town's hospitality.

Mindful of the hurricane winds forecast for the following week, we waved good-bye to Morro Bay, and upon softly textured seas, we pushed on. *What would we face next?* With the fuel line problem fixed, anything could be thrown at us. We yearned to be farther south prior to the strong winds, but predictions can change; bad weather has a habit of breaking forecast rules.

Two days later, we arrived at Newport Beach, CA. We had viewed a boat here before buying *Pyewacket* and knew we could pick up a mooring for five American dollars a night. With great protection from the stirring seas created by the enormous developing low, we were elated to be able to tether to a mooring and indulge in the shelter of the salubrious houses lining the shore.

Within a twenty minute bike ride, we found boat shop heaven – Minney's Yacht Surplus, a huge store overflowing with second hand boat gear.

'Look at all this stuff!' Noel's eyes darted around the sagging shelves and overflowing boxes, and he disappeared into the piles of marine gear for, what could be, hours. I loved these shops, too, and took off towards shiny objects I could covet.

'Here, Jack, what d'ya think about this for a new hatch? What about that for the doodah, oh, and give me a hand with these screws and bolts, will ya?' Noel didn't know which way to turn next. We were like kids in a sweetie shop, especially when we could pick 'n' mix stainless steel screws and bolts. Thrilled to score an oil tray for the engine (a legal requirement in the USA), I rummaged deeper into the 'help yourself' pile outside the front of the shop.

Every couple of days, we were back. Buying a boat wasn't the only expense. Bringing it up to seaworthy standards involved buckets of time and skip loads of money.

Slowly, we whittled down the lengthy to-do list.

As well as boat hardware, we searched for wet suits. Every boater inevitably fouls their boat propeller – we needed to be prepared. The water wouldn't always be a comfortable temperature. Noel found a couple of suits he could try and discreetly scampered off to the changing room, as one of the ladies that worked there had taken a shine to him.

'Oh, er, uh.' Odd noises came from the small fitting cubicle.

'Are you okay in there?' the shop assistant called while edging closer to the curtain.

Silence.

'I could come in and help,' she said, teasing, flirting.

'No,' he squawked. 'I'm fine, thanks, really.'

Noel continued to grunt and groan. He had tried on a tad-too-small wet suit, thinking it would stretch. With the suit three-quarters of the way on, he stretched the last part over his right shoulder, and the suit sprung back and pinned his arm to his side, trapping him helplessly.

'I danced in circles trying to get a grip on my trapped arm; meanwhile, Sherry crept closer to the curtain!' Noel's later recollection of the story made me titter; I had missed the whole episode.

'I was stuck fast and panicking; she would've had me at her mercy if she'd come in.' Noel took a breath and shuddered. 'It was quite traumatic!'

Although Noel had to negotiate the lustful assistant, the teasing and flirting played out light-heartedly with jest and good humour, and it lightened up the shopping excursion.

The shop's prices were fair; they were also world famous for international supply of second hand sails. On Saturdays, the exuberant employees ask you to join them for warm bagels washed down with bitter coffee. Often, our wallets were empty on departure. With our gear, we carried a smile – the hospitality to indulge in and the treasure trove to hunt in. The teasing seductress unwittingly helped me by persuading Noel to leave sharply.

With an intimidating selection of equipment to buy and fit, we found ourselves immersed in several dozen projects at once. With travelling and learning about a new boat, we'd had no time to reflect on our achievements or what we were doing. It's rare that Noel and I suffer from homesickness; family and friends drift in and out of our thoughts, but the intangible force to move is more powerful; it's irresistible.

Travelling makes sense to us both. We're most content when we have a home that can move and relocate anywhere. Entering a new port, we're filled with the excitement of exploring, learning, and meeting new folk. But when it's time to leave, we become edgy and fidgety with thoughts: *will the weather help or hinder?* And when it's time to go, there's no controlling the urge – an invisible force pushes us along. On the one hand, we are lucky to have the same drive, inquisitiveness, and sense to explore; on the other, I wonder why we are so unsettled. We are malcontent with letter boxes and a home that doesn't move. We find contentment in being unsettled, where nothing is the same, where locating the right shops is a skill (and figuring out how to get there), the language changes, the culture challenges.

Being nomadic is not often about being foot-loose and fancy-free; romance plays a minuscule role. Frustrations, costs, and the hardships of uncertainties and fickle weather are all part of the story. But the flip side is immense: a life that's kindred to freedom, confronting each ordeal to reap the rewards of seeing the world, and meeting people from such far-flung cultures that teach you so much. Luck plays a tiny part – it's mostly about making it happen. It is an extraordinary life, but it isn't easy. We split ourselves from our family, friends, and the comfort of day-to-day income and services. We can be up night after night in bad weather, bored listless on anchor watch, petrified of what's around the corner, and boat bound due to unsafe ports. But that's what makes it *enough*. The highs are the foundation of the lows. If we don't have something to look forward to, something to push our bodies and stretch our skills, complacency replaces joy. We choose this roaming lifestyle because of the challenge and rewards – whatever path we choose, we have to deal with crap; the particular garbage that comes hand-in-hand with travelling is the stuff we can deal with. Noel and I are woven from the same cloth, and I thank my lucky stars we found each other.

* * *

At Newport Beach, Christmas came and went. With no friends or family to visit and many boat tasks to tackle, we ignored the festivities and both our birthdays. Ironically, convenience became stronger than the pull to move. We were sourcing all we needed for our list of projects. The desire to improve the boat and reduce heart-stopping moments (like the fuel line fiasco) temporarily heralded a change in our longing to move. When work concerning our safe passage is necessary, the yearning to travel constantly had to be forced down.

When we were focused on important tasks to ocean-ready the boat, we didn't allow things like festivities to slow us down. We were blinkered, and the pressure began to bear down; we had to leave America within three months to avoid sales tax, which could be eight percent of the value of the boat. We still had work to do to create a blue-water boat. It had taken two years to bring *Mariah* up to standard to traverse oceans; three months were a mere blip – a terrifyingly short amount of time to do the necessary work, learn all we could, and gain complete confidence in the boat's abilities!

We might have ignored Christmas, but we could not ignore the town's Christmas Harbour Boat Parade. For six nights, from prime seats, we watched the 101st Christmas Parade. A kaleidoscope of colour on sixty boats floated around the harbour. Festive music bounced keenly over the water, warm reds and deep greens reflected to every corner of the bay, illuminating our faces as the parade wafted by in a thriving hum of colour and merriment.

Moments such as these allowed a brief respite. I loved Christmas as a kid; as an adult, it was an interruption to my spine-tingling, fun-filled life. As a child at Christmas, we'd been family-orientated, complete with a huge roast turkey and presents under the real tree with its unmistakable piny perfume.

Growing up in the UK, snow often came at Christmas, piling soft white flakes on the window ledges. Building plump snowmen with wonky stick arms and black stones for eyes with my sisters created joyous giggling and pink noses. I smile at the memory of bright, colourful wrapping paper scrunched up and burning on the log fire and the funny British TV comedies that our family watched together – Mum and Dad, two older sisters, a menagerie of pets, and stream of visitors. As the years creep up on me, I notice not only the silver highlights, laughter lines, sags, waning eyesight and hearing, but also short moments of melancholy for times gone by: riding horses in narrow country lanes during summer months, family Christmases, few responsibilities. I gather up those moments of blues and whip them into shape; for why should I be sad for owning wonderful memories? I'm sorry those days are forever gone, but I am blessed to have recollections that make me smile and feel so loved.

We don't have all the answers. We know what works for us – mostly. Now, Noel and I would raise a glass thinking of family across the oceans. The distance between us felt farther than miles but further binds Noel and I, our family of two, and an ocean going vessel.

4

Time to Scratch

The Golden Gate Bridge was the entrance to another world and recommencement of our cruising life. California had welcomed us and made us feel at home. Californians bore witness to our new beginning back on board, and San Diego was our next stop.

My mum and dad joined us at Newport Beach, and together, we took a leisurely sail south to San Diego – on the brightest, calmest day.

Entrance into San Diego harbour was spectacular in a peaceful way. The sun twinkled diamonds in the molten water.

'Arhhh, what's that!' my mum shrieked, leaning over the starboard handrail and pointing.

'Where?' I scanned the water.

'There! There! Look!'

A vast black shadow of a humpback whale eased its bulk out of the water to suck in a quick breath.

'It's a whale, look Roy, a whale!' My mum's excitement became contagious, and we exchanged grins. Carefully, though, Noel and I watched the mammal's route; we'd experienced a nasty run in with a whale on *Mariah* some years back.

The gliding shadow peeled off and left the playful dolphins to skim our bow.

As we approached the entrance, even the aeroplanes departing San Diego's heart looked welcoming as they strained against gravity. The famous cruisers' jungle drums had beat information our way about a Police Dock, a place to tie up at a reasonable price.

With a charming mix of mega yachts and masquerading pirates sailing on the harbour, and salubrious abodes next to squalor in town, San Diego is a melting pot of poverty and prosperity. On the edge of America, with Mexico in sight, here lies the stepping off point for cruisers. San Diego is not a cruising ground as such with its king's ransom fees and stifling regulations, but it's a gateway to the Pacific Ocean.

It was late in the season, and most cruisers were already in Mexico and beyond. But a few lurked, mainly small sailboats with no fixed agenda. Vessels that lived here are pristine. The boats ready to do miles wore a comfortable, travelled look.

Big industries here were manufacturing, military, ship repair, and construction. Tourism played its part, but for cruising-folk, there was enough to see of the watery world type. The navy base was buzzing with activity almost every day. Roaring jets vibrated the boat as they launch into space, on exercise, ready for battle. War roars of planes, ships, and helicopters mixed with the war cries from the AM/FM radio, provoking thoughts of the terrifying world we lived in. This was one of the reasons why we were on a sailboat seeking what good was left on the planet.

On board, we had our own situation to deal with: visiting parents.

We'd found that guests preferred to be active. We had a boat to prepare, so those activities took the form of work. The Aries wind vane needed a full service, new bearings, and fitting. Noel and Dad locked themselves into the workshop while mum and I tackled jobs such as making a dinghy cover, inspecting the anchor chain, and supplying copious cups of fortifying tea. We did allow my folks some time off, and San Diego offered a smorgasbord of fun.

A succession of weather lows came and finally abated, glorious warm sunny days returning. Harmony was restored on board, shedding any remains of cabin fever.

* * *

The San Diego Boat Show provided us with hopeless dreams. Discounts at chandleries, fascinating electric boats, fold up dinghies, and US Coast Guard were some of the exhibitors that held our attention, as well as the free beer and chocolate. Sail and motor boats clamoured for favour in the marina. Visitors stepped on board, and we almost drooled at the mouth-watering new boats. Returning to *Pyewacket,* we noticed not her vintage but how homely she felt.

Later, we sought a marina for a short spell, and Shelter Cove looked after us well. The Sunday morning steaming coffee, sweet doughnuts, and delectable bagels were a big hit. Nestled in America's Cup Bay, Noel and I returned to the boat one afternoon to find my parents chatting, unbeknown to them, with a celebrity: Dennis Connor of America's Cup fame. He was the first man to unsuccessfully defend the cup, much to the delight of Alan Bond's *Australia II,* skippered by John Bertrand and Australia as a whole. However, armed with numerous successes both before and after *Australia II,* he had helped form some fantastic races. Connor was spending time with Challenged America, an all-volunteer charitable program that provided adaptive sailing for adults and kids with disabilities.

'Thanks for the memories,' Noel called out as Connor eased the boat, *B Quest,* from her slip. Dennis had watched us take down and service our winches.

'I could use some of those skills over here,' he suggested forthrightly.

'Yes, we could make use of your skills, too,' Noel responded.

And some of you sponsors, I thought.

And that was the end of that conversation!

As a budget-conscious cruiser, I refused to pay the extra for WiFi. I knew with a little effort, I could find free access, even if it meant traipsing to a library. Living this way taught me tricks: laundromats usually had a good Internet connection. The one in town did, but I wondered about the marina's laundry room. Armed with determination and an open laptop, I strolled around the marina and found the connection. Washing day became a positive delight. The laundry became my office. Firm tables and soft chairs were freely supplied with warm air from the dryers and the hum of washing machines massaging the silence; wafts of clean clothes smelt of home – all within a few strides from *Pyewacket*.

* * *

With my parents back home, the sailing path of Mexico beckoned. The Spanish language we were so desperate to learn wafted around our ears via recordings, but none of it made an entrance to our brains. We were looking forward to Mexican food and tasty, cheap eats sold from the curbs in portable kitchens. We had the equipment for learning a new language, but not the time. Considerations of having a book to learn Spanish next to the toilet were discussed.

With *Pyewacket* an official Australian registered vessel, we were slowly easing into a-job-a-day on board amid the regular chores. We were ready to explore Mexico and let *Pyewacket* stretch her legs. Itching to get going, it was time to scratch.

5

Futile Thoughts, Towing Traumas, and Exploding Toms

Eager to leave the States, ditch the mobile phone, and collect more great sensual experiences, we turned the bow towards Mexico. Coastal sailing south revealed jagged rocks standing tall and proud, lining white sugar beaches that were randomly scattered between the parched earth headlands.

Following an over-nighter across the border from San Diego, we stopped in the new marina at Salinas in Mexico. The entrance was narrow, creating a strong desire to make use of a large blindfold. At thirty dollars a night, we thought the marina reasonable, but there was no running water directly to each slip. The key advantage was the assistance in the arduous process of checking in. A personal chauffeur, who knew the drill, drove us through the dusty, dilapidated streets to Ensenada, the checking in port about sixteen nautical miles south. He helped smooth the paperwork trail and translate. Once immersed into the conglomerate of officials, they desired our company for the entire day. We didn't understand much of the process; the officials wrongly assumed they were dealing with intelligent and capable listeners. We incorrectly thought everything was squared away.

With a strained smile, we mimicked nodding dogs, filled out blank boxes with personal details, and handed everyone we met vast wads of cash. In addition, we purchased fishing licences for us both – a requirement, we were told. With these permits and new fishing gear, our first (and only) fish cost about three hundred dollars!

* * *

Never venturing outside the marina complex at Salinas (aside from the Ensenada visit), we spent a gentle three days socialising with kindred spirits over coffee and home baked cakes; these delightful days were stitched together with small, simple tasks on board.

'It's time to make miles south,' I said, feeling the days slink rapidly past.

'We have to make a decision on where to hide for the hurricane season, but for now, we need to get south; the nearest place I know of is the Sea of Cortez.'

With hurricane season not far on the horizon and decisions of a hidey hole to be made, we cast off to make miles farther south. A combination of sailing and motoring amid the gentle breath of wind transported us toward Turtle Bay.

This was a good time to experiment with our spinnaker poles; they resembled telegraph poles, so we were a bit anxious about the set-up. Blending patience and prior experimentation on other vessels, the process became simple and speedy. The trick was to use plenty of lines and blocks to do the work.

Two effortless days later, we glided into Turtle Bay, its wide entrance opening before us like a big, welcoming grin. The forecast strong north westerly compelled us to the nearest north west protection, located half a mile from other local vessels.

Facing a dazzling white beach and tall rocks stretching for the sky, we seized some moments for ourselves; for three glorious days, we sat, absorbing the view, and we read and caught up on sleep, simply relishing the reasons for having a boat. *Pyewacket* had new solar panels, steering gear, paint, plumbing, and a myriad of new toys recently fitted – it was time for us.

Eventually, we upped anchor to move closer to town. Extending from the fixed jetty, a long floating dock bobbed and dipped on our arrival – it was a safe tie-up place for dinghies, not so safe for mere mortals. The rickety pontoon with gaping holes appeared to be held together with fetid guano, the pong enough to make your nostrils curl. The jump to reach the ladder to ascend up to the main quay quickened the heart rate like a shot of an adrenaline junkie's hit.

The lumbering swell, hardly detectable on board, pumped the two jetties together and apart; timing was everything. Completing the triathlon and desperate for an injection of caffeine, we coerced our shaky legs to carry us into the small settlement. Dusty streets, yapping dogs, friendly smiles, and spectacular fresh produce were in abundance. Jumbled along the dehydrated lanes, small abodes crouched around an Internet café and a miniature supermarket.

Catching up with friends and family via email, purchasing fruit and vegetables, and sneaking in a quick cup of coffee fulfilled our brief dalliance with reality. Within two hours, we were back on board, ensconced into our own mini-village, where we didn't have to wear shoes and, often, clothes. I never wore a bra on board and had difficulty putting up with one when on shore. I've been known to remove certain annoying underwear while in public – discreetly, of course!

The moon grew in tune with our longing to head south. The forecast north east fifteen knots spiralled into thirty-five. With the sails fully reefed, *Pyewacket* sliced the ocean with a hearty eight knots. We were en route to Bahia Magdalena, an enormous bay with several anchoring options; our choice was the small fishing village.

* * *

As though falling through air, I watched *Bruce* (the anchor) grab the sand in ten metres of salty water. *Clean water at last; we could swim here.* The thought had me skipping along the deck, throwing my clothes off in wild abandon.

The south setting current maintains a briny coolness, causing your skin to stretch taut against the chill. Sporting a soggy grin, I yelled to Noel, 'I feel so alive.' These are the ingredients that make me happy: freedom, travel, excitement, and my own personal swimming pool!

On arrival to a new port cruisers check in with the port captain, our sandals crunched on the stones and dried mud, breaking the silence that hung in the streets as we searched for an official. With a population of 110 ten adults and thirty kids, the peace and quiet was tangible.

Twice, we found the port office closed. No one cared, even when we settled onto the benches at a closed beach bar. The brilliant yellow ball of sun was held back by a lonesome tree that provided respite from the heat. Although not one telegraph pole marred the view, there was WiFi! Briefly, we had the most stunning office in the world: jade blue water swept across fine white sand right where we sat.

'The moon's waxing nicely.'

'Hmmm,' I agreed, relaxing in our vast cockpit on luxurious cushions. 'I can handle night sailing better with the moon in company.'

The moon becomes your buddy when sailing, especially at its peak. During cloudless nights, you can practically read by a full moon; so bright is her light we thought about switching off the red headlamps we use to maintain our night-vision. These are my favourite sailing times. You can still see other vessels' lights from miles away; it is cool; the deck and seas are bright and sparkling, and there's something magical about sailing with a large, bright heavenly body peering down on us. Night or day, we always know the moon phase when sailing.

* * *

With bright eyes and renewed energy, we watched Magdalena Bay slope off the horizon as the forecast light winds helped us continue our journey

'Our next dilemma is hurricane season.' We'd set *Pyewacket* into a comfortable sail and poured the tea.

'So, do you think we'll find somewhere here, in Mexico?'

'That's about it, I think,' Noel replied. 'We could stop at La Paz, and if we like it, find a safe place there.'

'Sounds like a plan; from what I've read, it would be a good place to stay and catch up with the travelling circuit again.'

Keen for kindred company, our next destination offered a larger town and was a milestone. Tucked inside the Sea of Cortez lies La Paz, the place to make destination decisions.

* * *

Pyewacket took on a serene, swaying motion over the next three days, the whispering breeze allowing us a smattering of four knot sailing. Catching the sun's rays, the ocean appeared to be layered with liquid silver. But the tranquillity was about to be rudely interrupted.

'There's something up in the engine room,' I called up to Noel. 'Come quick.' My voice carried a slight quiver. *What drama will unfold now?*

The battery voltmeter had hit the red.

We both stared, taking a moment to absorb the problem and figure out the remedy.

'The alternator's frying the batteries.'

'Er, that doesn't sound good; why do you sound so calm?' A tense throb shifted behind my brow. I imagined sailing into the next unknown port without the aid of an engine; possible, of course, but with the mix of an unknown port and fickle weather, it could be tricky.

'We have a spare regulator; it won't take long to swap.'

The alternator was cooking our fully charged (and new) batteries. Engine checks were part of our hourly routine when on watch, so we could pick up problems such as these before they developed into a major issue.

We had both tuned into *Pyewacket's* sailing sounds and motoring hum; any change became obvious and checked immediately.

Our homemade log book listed the date, local time, location (latitude and longitude or port), course and speed, wind speed and strength, sea state, any traffic or radio calls we encountered, and included two columns we could tick for the engine and bilge. Every hour, when we noted our position on the paper chart and in the log book, with the additional space for ticks, we were motivated to check the bilge (for any water creeping in) and engine (for problems such as frying batteries). We had a comment section, too, and often in bad weather, the scribbled notes could be colourful. Frequently, we'd leave messages of encouragement or endearment for each other, especially during night watches.

Fortunately, Noel dug out an old, spare regulator – a relatively easy and temporary fix. However, this was a mere trifling affair. Thirty-six hours of stressful sea-time lay in wait, where we'd take terrifying risks to save a boat and its crew.

***

As we turned north into the Sea of Cortez, a light and unusual southerly breeze teased our sails but didn't help much. The hazy dawn cleared to reveal a sixteen metre sailboat adrift with engine trouble. We had seen *Windsong* in San Diego.

'We have engine trouble; we can't use it,' the skipper explained.

'Well, the wind's picking up today, so you should be fine to sail north later.' Noel wasn't being heartless; he was doing what any good skipper should, weighing up all the elements of what towing a large vessel meant.

'We've been adrift for two days.' The forlorn voice was losing hope. Swathed by guilt, we threw together a bridled tow line, agreeing to tow them until the wind picked up. We were 120 miles from La Paz.

Maritime law states that all skippers must help a vessel in distress. *Windsong* and her crew were not happy, but they weren't in distress; we were not legally obliged to help.

But why would we hesitate in helping out a fellow sailor? Well, there was our fuel capacity; would we have enough diesel to manoeuvre and drive two large vessels? Did we have the right equipment on board? Enough people to carry out the tow safely? All these elements and many more had to be considered. Our safety had to be taken into account, too.

Our robust Chrysler engine propelled the combined mass of thirty-five tonnes for several hours. Fifteen nautical miles from Canal Cerralvo (prior to the relatively narrow Canal de San Lorenzo's passage), the wind grew to twelve knots. Envisaging a fun race with a similar sized boat, we freed the constraints and hauled up all our canvas, and *Pyewacket* shot away from the static *Windsong*.

'What're they doing?' Noel said. Fed up with the responsibility and delays, his hand rubbed the back of his tense neck.

'I've no idea; they look dead in the water; we were hardly racing!'

'Christ!' Noel muttered. 'We'll have to slow down and see if they catch up.'

We were tired; with two on board, it worked well, but we were always busy, and care had to be taken when managing our fatigue with the extra responsibility; four people crewed on *Windsong*.

As they shrunk on the horizon, we reefed down our sails to mere handkerchiefs. When we reached Lorenzo's constricted passage, we had to turn back for them; they were too slow, and we needed to be nearby to re-connect when the wind died and for when we reached harbour.

As the two boats, back in tandem, pushed their noses into Lorenzo's passage, the wind and thirty of his mates lifted the seas. Fighting to keep our feet beneath us, we hauled up part of the mainsail to assist *Pyewacket* and her grunting engine. *Windsong* could not do the same; their in-mast furled mainsail was jammed. They were now disabled, no motor and no sails. I'm sure I heard Neptune snigger under the cover of the blackest night in history.

I felt every minute of that night. Noel and I stayed in the cockpit together; for when you are towing a boat, one person stays on the helm and the other has to watch the tow, the line, and the boat to ensure nothing is going wrong. Occasionally, though, we did take turns to doze in the cockpit for a few minutes.

With immense relief, dawn tinted the sky a light blue, and at a critical moment in the clutches of gusting wind and the narrowest part of the canal, the tow line parted. Engulfed with fatigue, the nervous energy galvanised me into action.

The dawn turned grey as if angry with the fracas beneath it. The unforgiving currents picked up *Windsong* and guided them, side on, to the quintessence of jagged rocks. Meanwhile, opposing winds lifted the flowing currents, turning a placid passageway into an angry, frothing nightmare.

With no time for a text book tow, we leaped into action.

'I'll tie a fender to the end of this line,' I yelled into the whipping wind, while putting my knot training to good use. 'We can drag the line off our stern to see if they can pick it up with their boat hook'

'Good work,' Noel agreed, while concentrating on the safety of our own vessel.

With winds strong enough to lift and twist our boats sideways and the solid, bumpy waves bashing against the hull, we had to manoeuvre far enough away from *Windsong* for safety, but drive close enough so they could pick up the line.

Fenders float; therefore, it kept the line on the surface of the water. When boats' propellers rotate, they can easily suck lines in and around the propeller shaft, stalling the engine and potentially causing expensive damage. Many possibilities and dangers existed and had to be considered and accounted for.

'I'll come around again,' Noel called out while the wind viciously whipped away his words. 'Haul in the line for a minute.'

'Okay,' I yelled back, and *Pyewacket* bumped and heaved in a circle, while I prepared the line to sweep it past their bow once again.

We watched the crew of *Windsong* valiantly try and fail to retrieve their life-line as we swept by their bow, time after time. Their taut faces matched those of an athlete, poised for the starter's gun. On board *Pyewacket*, our concerns for our own safety deepened; the engine strained against its mounts as we asked for the almost impossible. As *Windsong* slid closer to the awaiting rocks, we had no choice but to keep our distance. We couldn't risk our boat and us.

We stood by helplessly, watching a fine boat surely become dashed on unforgiving boulders.

In desperation, and at the last second, they started *Windsong's* motor. A broken engine mount (amongst many other problems) meant the shaft could snap at any moment, if a fire didn't break out first. Between white knuckle grips and a collective sucking of breath, we all waited for the flailing boat's propeller to bite into the tumultuous water.

We followed them into a safe anchorage, Puerto Balandra. Turquoise blues edged along white sand, but the beauty was lost to lethargy in the aftermath of stampeding adrenaline. After a brief rest and re-grouping, we hooked up once again, and the entourage made for La Paz. The winds were kindly easing.

With instant mollification, we cast them off into the safety of a marina. A meal out and two hundred dollars for fuel barely covered our losses; although, I received plenty of gains: stress lines, grey hairs.

I noticed our rescuees were strangely relaxed about the ordeal.

'That night passed quickly for us; we had DVDs playing. There's a really good series about—'

'No, I don't want to know,' I interrupted sharply. 'Noel and I were up all night; neither of us could sleep while towing a boat. It wasn't so easy for us.'

Fatigue obliterated what little patience I had left.

* * *

La Paz has a fascinating cruiser's community and club. It also has concrete stairs haphazardly strewn intermittently along the pavements ready to break an unsuspecting ankle. The odd, jagged pipe, thoughtfully cut off with a blunt instrument, stuck up six inches above the path, waiting to pierce soft body tissue. If these obstacles don't get you, the air conditioners that are considerately located at head height will.

While traversing the streets became second nature, more relaxed times were to be had at Club Cruceros. Run by volunteers, it is brimming with assistance and affability. A daily VHF radio network welcomes or farewells fellow travellers and assists in pointing you in the right direction for that specific doodad you *have* to find.

We timed our arrival perfectly with the commencement of Bay Fest, a week full of seminars provided freely by cruisers with the know-how. Bread making, photography, painting, volleyball, jewellery making, knot tying, dinghy racing, and safety were some of the seminars on offer. With our new membership, we attended many professional talks. At the top of our list: The Hurricane Seminar.

It was the exploding tins of tomatoes in the heat that had us squirming in our seats, coupled with terrifying pictures of a violent hurricane barrelling up the centre of the Sea of Cortez.

During the hurricane seminar, I turned to Noel and whispered, 'D'ya think we ought to get out of here, perhaps sell the boat, take up knitting?'

Accompanied by a sickening feeling, we knew we had to leave; for us, the risk was too great. When the stories unravelled of all three marinas being wiped out in previous years, El Niño in full force assisting the water temperature prime for a humdoohey of a cyclone, experts predicting a bad year, and being told that at least one of the attendees would lose their electronics during a storm, we struggled with the urge to shriek, leap up, and gallop back to the boat.

While neighbouring cruisers, playing cyclone sweepstake, took notes to remember the importance of removing tinned tomatoes, Noel and I tried not to whimper aloud.

'So, does anyone know the nearest port that is outside of the cyclone area?' Noel asked at the end of the talks.

'Ecuador,' someone piped up. 'They don't get them down there.'

'Ecuador? Blimey, I was thinking of Panama!'

'No, don't go there. Costa Rica and Panama are the lightning capitals of the world. Costa Rica has something crazy like eleven hundred lightning strikes a day!'

'And you're still in a cyclone area until you get near the equator, and Ecuador is the nearest safe port you can anchor in,' someone else chimed in.

'Ecuador looks good!' I grinned at Noel.

'Yup, and I think we'd melt in the heat here.'

With weighty weariness, we stowed our gear; replenished food, fuel, and water; and squared our shoulders in preparation for facing around 2,300 sea miles.

* * *

'Anyone on board?' someone asked as we were readying the boat.

Rob on board *Pachuca*, a fellow Australian, who we'd met in San Diego, hopped on board, and we discussed our plans.

'You know about Isla del Coco?'

'No,' Noel and I said together.

'Well, it's a possible stop between here and Ecuador. I don't know much about it, but I know it's possible to pull in there if you need to; it's worth bearing in mind.'

Noel and I hadn't checked our charts at this point, so Noel jumped below decks.

'Let's have a look.'

'It's right there.' Rob pointed to a minuscule rock, the tiny Costa Rican Island, three hundred nautical miles south west of Costa Rica.

'It's directly in our pathway; well, pretty much. Thanks, Rob.' It would offer us a short reprieve.

We still had around one thousand sea miles to reach the possible stop en route to Ecuador.

It was all too much to digest, but we had to go. Our bodies had already relaxed with the thought of a break from night watches. Heat, apathy, and convincing our limbs to become alert and ready again was a tiresome drag, but we became instantly motivated with the fear-driven thoughts of a facing a cyclone.

We still had to check out of Mexico, though.

'What do you reckon about checking out at Acapulco?' Noel asked while studying our charts and pilot books.

'Well, it'll beat going loco.' We laughed. 'It sounds like a good plan.'

'It's the last jumping off point where we can check out; we can top up with fuel and water there, too.'

'Okay, let's work on the waypoints.' Noel leaned over the navigation table to plot our route on paper charts. Later, I'd check them, and together, we'd input the latitude and longitude into our handheld GPS.

'At least we've another stop before facing all those sea miles.' I was a bit anxious about a long haul. We were heading for the Intertropical Convergence Zone (ITCZ); we expected to do a fair amount of motoring; there would be fickle weather.

Having become more familiar with *Pyewacket,* I either ignored the endless nights we were about to undertake or I knew we'd be okay. *Pyewacket* had proven herself to a degree, but mostly, we didn't have time to reflect or worry. Once we'd made the decision to leave the area, the hurricane season drew nearer at an alarming rate.

We bade farewell to La Paz, kindred spirits, and, no doubt, lots of fun.

My emotions evolved into an odd mix of relief and trust in our decision, but also concern and unease with facing another long journey traversing a tough stretch of water.

The arrival into the deep, land-locked bay was impressive with vivid green cliffs looking down upon the narrow entrance, a contrast to the dry, dusty deserts farther north. Acapulco is a fairly large industrial bay that's also lined with soaring hotels vying for prime position on the shoreline.

It's best known for its 1950s glitzy heyday when Acapulco was the getaway location for Hollywood stars like John Wayne. It's not lost its sizzle either; numerous night clubs compete for supremacy in town next to motels neighbouring the sandy beaches, the night-time would be alive and swaying like it used to.

'I feel like we should be listening to Frank Sinatra.' Noel hummed a tune as we puttered around to find a safe place to anchor. 'He used to live here, too, you know.' We both enjoyed the dulcet tones of Sinatra, mixed with the heady sense of achievement of making port, and a thrilling one at that, and belted out tunes, utterly caught up in the moment.

Acapulco was crammed full of events, tours, and spectacles, but we were here to complete a task: the final preparations for our voyage to a safe port and conclude the necessary paperwork. Not every destination can be explored; it isn't possible. Cruising is a continual map of decision making, which is equally as important to seeing the world.

'We've got a few pesos left. I'm going to pick up more fruit while I can.' We were refuelling at the opulent marina's dock.

'Why don't you buy yourself something?' Noel said. 'We don't need any more supplies.'

I peered at the coins in my hands and skipped the short distance into town like a kid out to buy penny sweets. Huge trees unfolded their branches across the market place, shading the plaza. Six thousand taxis hooted around the city while I negotiated for a small top as a cherished memento.

I rarely think of myself; the journey and our needs as a travelling couple come first. On a wedding anniversary several years ago, Noel had led me into a jewellery shop.

'Pick something, anything you like,' he'd said. We don't possess endless pots of money; Noel knew I wouldn't spend much, because I hate spending money.

The ladies behind the counter perked up and nearly rubbed their hands together.

'Er, well,' I muttered, trying to figure out what caught my eye.

'Come on, there must be something you like.'

The women followed me as I skirted the glass counter that dripped with shiny objects; my circular wandering brought me and my entourage back to where I started.

'We need a new windlass for the boat; I'd rather have one of them.'

Noel laughed and sighed; the shop's assistants looked at me in disbelief. We left empty handed.

That day, Noel made me buy a new coat.

'It's about time you had something new.'

That about sums me up: the important things in my life weave through my *entire* life, not just for instant gratification. It's about the big picture: having money and gear to continue living the adventure, not booking a holiday for two weeks. Make-up, hairdressers, nail technicians, expensive shows, and restaurants are not part of our lives, and I don't miss them one bit. I've cut my hair for years and am far happier with it. Charity shops supply great clothes, often with vastly reduced pricing on new items, too. We still visit restaurants, of course, but only from time to time, not every week, not even every month. They are a special treat and always chosen carefully.

That's how I like it.

* * *

I couldn't wear my new top to check out; a singlet with a glistening turtle and 'Acapulco' written across the front in sparkling sequins would be my memento from our short stay here – not appropriate attire to face dower officials.

Checking out was simple, good humoured, and courteous, even amid the problems. Immigration, during check in, had issued the correct papers but failed to stamp the part confirming we had paid – we paid again. Coupled with a small exit fee, we spent less than sixty dollars. When we finally spied the Zarpe (exit papers), the sweeping relief was immense.

'We must check our paperwork more thoroughly when we receive it,' I muttered, put out about the extra cost.

'Right, if we can decipher it,' Noel snorted. The paperwork was not in English; it could have stated a breakfast order for all we knew.

Replenished with food, water, and fuel, we pointed south, traversing the ITCZ, the Pacific Vortex, and into the next throng of problems.

6

Costa Rica's Little Gem

Armed with the Zarpe and way too much food, we were eager to be southward bound. Other than craving succulent roast chicken and gooey ice cream while away from shops, there was nothing to worry about.

We sliced through the ocean, enjoying the stuff of which dreams are made. The concerns of motoring much of the way were temporarily held at bay. Leaving Acapulco, Mexico for Isla del Coco, we were blessed with perfect sailing for four whole days.

On the fifth day, ignoring our plaintiff cries about fairness, the wind inevitably clocked around to the south. The deep blue, cream flecked waves transformed into roller-coasters of water. The head winds delivered dark grey skies and seas that harmonised nicely with my green face.

In my head, I could hear our sailing buddies back home calling us wimps.

A jolting hull meant jerking beds; restful sleep was impossible. It was a relief to be back on watch with a purpose, but that was when the random thought demons appeared.

Have we made the right decision?

Why did I say such a stupid thing twenty years ago?

Thoughts of what we'd achieved so far helped cradle my busy mind while battling angry seas. The judgements we'd received along the way came back to haunt me, though. On *Mariah*, a raging storm had bashed the boat and our bodies for many endless days en route to Fiji; with safety and survival in mind, we turned for home, to run with the weather. Our greatest critics had spread the word that we weren't ready for the trip, but sometimes you just can't argue with Mother Nature.

Arguing with the weather en route to Cocos, equipment hiccups, and disappointments added to our current misery. In our hurry to tack onto a better course, my salt water shower ended abruptly, and I forgot the fresh rinse. For twenty-four hours, sticky salt plagued my skin.

'We may have to consider the Marquesas,' Noel mentioned to me gently. 'Either that or turning back to Mexico.'

'Neither are appealing.' I frowned while scratching my saline-soaked head. 'I don't think we have the supplies for the distance to the Marquesas, especially if we encounter delays.'

We had sufficient food and water, but I didn't want to go there. I craved a new journey, different sights and sounds; there is so much to see.

Noel's focus on sailing to Easter Island had become my quest.

'Turning back to Mexico worries me; we're already running out of time.' We were both quiet while we pondered the situation. Cyclone season was on its way; we were running short on time if we wanted to be clear of the area the ferocious winds could potentially mutilate.

For a few hours, we allowed the wind to carry us wherever it pleased while we weighed the pros and cons of altering course to the Marquesas, over three thousand nautical miles away. Eventually, the wind backed slightly, pointing us toward the Galapagos group of Islands – a definite improvement.

'We could go to Galapagos now,' Noel said, keen on the idea.

'D'you think we really have to? I'm happy to push on.' I wasn't ready to revisit the islands again – not yet. My heart was firmly set on Cocos.

We flapped and farted about for a day, rethinking plan A and B, developing plan C and D.

We're going to work our way through the entire alphabet!

Finally, at 3 a.m, we agreed to motor to Cocos Island. Necessary repairs were now a major factor in our decision.

The wind helped us to decide, too. The north east and south east trade winds meet around five degrees north and south of the equator, respectively. *Pyewacket* joined their gathering, and we had a brief taste of the ITCZ (Intertropical Convergence Zone aka The Doldrums). Squalls loomed on the horizon, large and lively. Lightning burst from the sky, playing games with my unruly imagination. But it didn't unsettle us too much – that would come later.

Two days from Cocos, blue sky pushed back the ballooning black and molten clouds, the winds eased, and the ruffled sea became as sleek and shiny as a new coin. We relaxed our muscles and luxuriated in level water.

The last two days were so calm; it enabled Noel to install two small hatches into our hard dodger. He sat on the wooden structure, sawing holes, his buttocks clenched to prevent him from sliding. Although the water appeared smooth, a lumbering swell still rolled *Pyewacket* in a lazy, swaying motion.

The ocean beneath was the colour of indigo as Isla del Coco loomed out of the white, hazy mist. Racing the approaching night, our eyes strained to locate the mooring buoy, the exquisite surrounds lost on the practicality of safety and sleep. As darkness swept over the island, our radio continued to stay silent upon requests for permission to enter the bay and advice on mooring.

* * *

A concert of tides and rapid currents synchronised nicely with hauling up the mooring. A battle ensued with boat, buoy, and brute strength. I lost, gifting a boat hook to Neptune. Swapping roles, Noel took on the heavy heaving, and with much effort, he folded lines into quick knots that held us fast.

Battling to lift our heavy limbs, we covered sails, furled lines, and organised *Pyewacket* into apple-pie order. Before we could indulge in the delicious satisfaction of a successful voyage, the Park Ranger puttered over in a small timber boat.

'Hello, welcome, you have to move.'

My shoulders dropped; I put the bottle of wine back on the counter. The freedom to sit and enjoy quiet contemplation snaked away. I sighed, but my shoulders straightened.

The sooner we move, the sooner we can relax.

'I'm sorry, this mooring buoy is not good; please follow me to another.' Noel and I peered into the black, our vision penetrating only a metre into the void, but we could hear waves breaking. Noticing our reluctance, the ranger continued, 'It's okay; I'll put my light on, follow it, it's not far.'

We let go of our mooring and followed a swinging glow that eerily hovered within the dark abyss. Not one sliver of natural illumination broke through the tangible black that night, not a star blinked. With the knowledge of hard and invisible rocks nearby, we followed the ranger's swaying light deeper into the small bay to pick up the new mooring.

Calmer currents allowed us to tie up in a few short moments. The ranger waved farewell.

'See you in the morning to go through the paperwork.'

With a smooth chardonnay, thirst-quenching beer, and crunchy chips, we dined on deck in awe of the surroundings we couldn't see. The breaking waves were now a soothing background melody and not a worry.

'I can't be bothered to switch the gas bottle over,' Noel said, relaxing on the deck. We kept two nine kilo bottles of gas on board. When one finished, the swap involved a heavy job with shifters to exchange them over.

'Nah, neither can I; this'll do for dinner.' I grinned, sipping a mouthful of wine and collecting another fistful of crisps.

Amid wide yawns and the sense of accomplishment, sound and smell were heightened. Silence sat on the blackness, tranquillity washing over us. The night air carried the tang of moist green.

I'm addicted to that sense of success – a successful voyage, feeling safe, the pride in reaching our goal, and the dizzy feeling of depleting energy after working hard to reach a bay prior to dark and moving within the deep black.

I'd learned on *Mariah* that a successful voyage means different things to different people. To me, it wasn't only about reaching our goal; it was Noel, me, and *Pyewacket* being in one piece. Goodness knows there are enough variables on the water to cause untold mayhem. Even if we set out and had to turn back – providing we did so safely – that was a success.

* * *

Nestled in the small Bay de Wafer were six boats: three ranger boats, a tourist dive boat, a local fishing vessel, and *Pyewacket*. The rolling anchorage deterred any thoughts of sleep, which allowed me to watch dawn push through the black, revealing a striking spectacle. The damp dewy smell transformed into a visual of lush growth cascading down the sheer rock face. Waterfalls tumbled between the leafy vegetation to the craggy shoreline. Hundreds of frigates swirled overhead, singing the song of freedom. Above the birds, great clouds rolled off the tips of the small cliffs.

With intrigue tugging, I could hardly wait to explore and search for treasure.

According to legend, in the nineteenth century, pirates used Cocos to bury their plunder in the remote hills. Dying first from disease, execution, or battles, the pirates never returned to collect. I didn't like my chances, though; over the years, numerous expeditions armed with treasure maps had left the island empty handed. Through the centuries, since its discovery in the sixteen hundreds, the 'Island of

Coconuts' has been a resting and replenishing point for ships, whalers, and a temporary home to pirates and exploration parties.

Back to the present, with our homemade Costa Rican courtesy flag and yellow customs Q flag idly flapping in the breeze, we welcomed the Park Rangers on board with cool cola and dry biscuits. Our Spanish was still shamefully scant, so we were grateful for a translator. The two rangers sat in our cockpit and played good cop, bad cop. The good guy translated, while the other acted austere and exacting. The usual paperwork was required and studied, together with proof of our marine qualifications.

Our request for refuge to fashion repairs was met with an intense frown.

'Our mainsail needs re-stitching, and our furler is jammed,' Noel explained. 'I can show you if you like.'

Negotiations ensued; the cost of our stay was a budget-breaking eighty-five dollars a day, whether venturing ashore or staying on board. The tightening of worry lines and jerking down of mouths became an Oscar winning performance for Noel and me. But we were not partaking in amateur dramatics; we had had a difficult journey, and now, we needed to repair imperative equipment. Only after we proved beyond any doubt that we had bona fide repairs did the rangers agree we could stay.

'Many sailboats seek sanctuary here, claiming false problems,' they explained.

The rangers inspected our problems and watched us make repairs, puttering past several times to ensure no theatrics. They didn't want visiting sailboats here; they received better fees from the dive boats. We were told that the island was declared a Marine National Park in the seventies and a World Heritage Site by the United Nations Educational, Scientific and Cultural Organisation (UNESCO) in 1997. The water is teeming with rich marine life and divers flock here to glimpse the large frenzy of hammerhead sharks that cruise these waters.

Our bodies were still in the rhythm of the shift sleep pattern and refused to let us rest well. At sea, one of us is always awake. We generally start with four hours on, four hours off, like a tag team match, and gradually extend this to six hours. It's important to have treats during the night. I make delicious chocolate muffins that are snacked on through the long, lonely hours. When I'm tired, I tend to eat more; needless to say baking muffins became a regular job; the simple baking process helped wile away the endless dark minutes through the night, too.

For the first day at Cocos, we sewed sails, freed the furler, baked bread, and made yoghurt. The second day, we explored. Having used up most of our diesel, we were also keen to replenish. Our prior Internet research revealed that diesel was available here. However, things had changed. Going green meant the island now uses a Pelton wheel water turbine to extract energy from the impulse of moving water to generate electricity; this meant no diesel for us from on shore.

Discovering that the large tourist dive boat had spare fuel filled us with hope. They would sell us some if the rangers granted permission for the transaction to go ahead. As we explored the island, the rangers and the tour boat skipper sought permission from their supervisors.

* * *

The pumping Pacific swell wraps around the island and rolls into the bay, making landfall via our fibreglass dinghy an interesting prospect. Weaving in our trickling wake, a dozen or so small sharks followed our progress. As the beach loomed, we steadied our rowing dinghy, waiting for calm amid the circling sharks. With a practised eye, collectively, we usually knew the right time. Noel propelled the oars into action atop of the flat water. With fear of a roller taking us for a sandy ride, I hopped out of the dinghy too early, hoping my inelegant gait scared off anything lurking below with sharp teeth. Without thought or care, I was soaked to the thigh, a mere trifle and often soggy occurrence in our watery way of life.

On shore, diesel may not have been available but Internet was. Modern computers and radios adorned the offices. With regular staff changes, the island's keepers have everything they need, including magazines and books. Culinary treats were no longer a useful bargaining chip for cruisers.

An unexpected buzz of activity circled around the base. A dozen volunteers were scattered between partially constructed wooden huts.

The Coast Guard have a presence here, as well. Amid the work, one guy snoozes in a rocking hammock while another is folding his laundry. The rangers multi-task; they protect their island from illegal fishing, and they fix, repair, and maintain the site. Their most dangerous activity is fighting off the Japanese in their cruel catching of sharks, slicing off fins and throwing the mutilated bodies back in the ocean, alive; another compromise of seeing the world, you hear of ghastly tales from locals with first-hand experience. They work eight weeks on, four weeks off, which allows time for maritime study back on the mainland.

The purposeful community is nestled within ideal surroundings; waves crunch onto the beach, frigates call from above, and large coconuts and plump limes plop onto the compacted sand. Hidden beside the main base are mountains of confiscated fishing gear, not bullion. Piles of snap connectors, plastic buoys, and hooks and miles of line and heavy rope lay in neat, abandoned heaps. Even buoys with high tech radio signalling equipment are scattered amid the debris.

After a brief escort around the functioning part of the island, we were pointed in the direction of a swimming hole, about an hour's walk away. With sweat coursing over our salty skin and darkening our shirts under the arm, we trekked through the verdant jungle, our wobbly sea legs struggling to balance on the tilting land. Deer and boar apparently roam the island, too shy to reveal themselves. A dinosaur had yet to be sighted – the locals proudly told us that the opening sequence of the movie Jurassic Park was shot here. Oddly, mosquitoes were not a problem.

Our hike took us over an extraordinary home-made bridge, fashioned from confiscated fishing gear.

'You go first,' I giggled. I liked volunteering Noel.

'Ya big chicken.'

Gingerly stepping on the swaying structure, the bridge jingled, bobbed, and emitted a little groan. It was a unique and oddly fitting structure, linking two pretty paths. After the bridge, we climbed for what felt like a fortnight until we came across a dam of fresh water and gratefully peeled off our light summer clothes that felt like winter woollies. The cool water almost triggered our hot bodies to hiss off steam.

On return to the base, treasure-less, the diesel situation had not moved on. Radio calls finally revealed that we had to compose a letter to the rangers, seeking permission for fuel. Within ten minutes, we were armed with appropriate prose. Still, we waited. Finally, as it started to rain, we were granted permission to purchase the fuel from the tourist boat. With two twenty litre jerry cans, Noel stoically rowed back and forth five times, the rain cooling and the satisfaction of replenishment calming.

Although the clouds persistently hung around the peaks, it didn't rain much where we were moored. Happy to be there, our three days encompassed repairs, rest, exploration, and re-fuelling. Prior to leaving, I cooked up a large pan of spaghetti bolognaise; we'd eaten all the meat, so I used lentils instead. I could easily heat it up; it would feed us for several days after we allowed our bodies to accustom to the relentless movement when underway once again. The lentils would do their job, too, supplying a good dose of roughage until we were able to let our muscles go and relax properly.

As we departed from the secret island that we would never see again, we peeked around the corner to the other anchoring location, Chatham Bay. There sat another solitary sailboat; we had no idea they were there and would have enjoyed kindred spirit company. But it was time to go; hurricane season was verging on arrival.

With renewed enthusiasm, we set our course for Ecuador and further traversing of the Intertropical Convergence Zone. As we approached the ITCZ, it greeted us with a bewildering array of layered greys, cracking winds, and streaking lightning.

* * *

'Something's caught in our line,' I called out. As we were clear of Costa Rican territorial waters, I'd thrown out the trolling lines. Almost immediately, a large brown booby had swooped down, searching for food and became snagged.

'Stupid thing!' Noel muttered as we gently pulled in our lines with the squawking bird attached.

Sea folk believe that the spirits of dead sailors live on in the albatross. Samuel Taylor Coleridge's 'The Rime Of The Ancient Mariner' is about the fate of the ancient mariner and his condemnation after killing an albatross – to harm them was to harm a sailor. We hoped this didn't apply to the booby!

I've met a sailor with such fear-driven superstition they claimed to have had given mouth to mouth to a bird that had stopped breathing on their boat!

'Grab a towel; it'll calm it down.' We heaved the heavy, flapping bird on board as quickly and gently as possible and threw the towel over it. Although this wasn't an albatross, the bird was still hurt and needing help, and we didn't wanted to tempt any fate.

Immediately, it stilled. With the odd wriggle, Noel cautiously extracted the hook from its leg.

'There are only a few spots of blood; it'll be okay,' he said, wiping his hands.

The bird sat quietly on the deck for a while, trying to assimilate what had occurred; we left him in peace. Suddenly, he sat up, performing a full body shake and launched off *Pyewacket* and into the air.

We tried to settle down while watching the great breasts of clouds grow, putting the sound of the squawking bird behind us. With hundreds of miles to traverse, leaving Mexico unsettled us. We'd had a brief rest at Cocos, but we still had over five hundred miles to go. I wasn't as fit and slim as I'd been on *Mariah*, on our previous trip. My chocolate muffins were not helping; middle-age spread had something to do with it, too. But although we planned well, had a good boat, and knew our stuff, I still sensed the occasional clench in my stomach. *Pyewacket* was new to us in comparison with the years we spent on *Mariah*; that made a difference. However, I was far more educated now. After the trip on our first boat, we'd both become commercial skippers and eventually nautical teachers – ignorance is bliss and, for me, a certain amount of that saying was true during the first part of our trip on *Mariah*. Now, the list of things that could go wrong was in the front of my mind, especially as we were traversing routes that few sailors ventured down. I'd shown students endless horror movies of fires, sinking, collisions, drowning, storms… I had faith in us, but my knowledge did cause some worry. Tiredness through lack of sleep during shifts and elements of fear led to me eating more, becoming less fit, and, consequently, less happy.

We needed encouragement and reassurance, which we gave to each other. But we were slightly perturbed when the radio 'weather guru' for this area stated, 'You are doing the wrong thing; you are heading deeper into the cyclone area. I wouldn't do that.'

We were trying to reach the safety of Ecuador, where cyclones never tread, but first, we had to traverse the waters that we wanted to get away from. The lengthy trip, the quick decision, and the unknown boat were enough to worry about. *What was this guy thinking?* Why say such negative statements to people who are out there alone in a vast ocean? Offer support, or maybe make recommendations. It was a phenomenon and still is – this need to criticise and scare-monger. We come up against it time after time, and nine out of ten times, we realise it is people's own fears that are revealed, and our decisions and journeys are so often right.

7

Escapades in Ecuador

At four in the morning, the odd pitching motion spun our compass in a dance; I was hand-steering, because the electronic autopilot 'talked' to the spinning compass and therefore took us on unnecessary jaunts; the Aries wind vane hung idly in the limp breeze.

Hanging lanterns suddenly swayed out from deep within the black void. The yellow pin pricks jiggled alongside and slowly vanished.

'What the...' I muttered, while trying to force my eyes to pierce the dark.

Manning the lanterns on board the local boats, known as Pangas, the fishermen hoped we would see them in time; I hoped so, too.

Steering a course towards the rocks, the black ominous shapes felt closer than my instruments indicated. The sheer cliffs watched our approach. The radar, GPS, and paper chart confirmed we were in safe water. But the shallows were scattered all around, waiting to bite. I held course and tried to unwind my shoulders down from my ears as we glided towards Bahia de Caraquez.

'Okay?' Noel popped his head up into the cockpit.

'Bugger off,' I said. This was not my usual choice of vocabulary. However, Noel had constantly thought of something else he *had* to do; he was off-watch and supposed to sleep. With two on board, taking rest when not on shift was imperative. He had become tired, tetchy, and simply annoying. I wasn't physically tired; I was husbandly tired! Constant reminders of the safety of resting and recuperating had, unusually, fallen on deaf ears.

I heard him mutter, 'See if I care if we run aground!' Lack of sleep generated this out-of-character comment.

The time ticked by; I stayed at the helm, gradually easing into contentment with the gentle breeze and smooth sailing, watching the silent lighthouse sweep its beam in never-ending arcs, breaking up the black, pressing sky. The silence on board indicated that Noel had finally followed my advice.

As dawn fought its way through the billowing bleak clouds, the shallows mutated from paper and ink on the charts to a visual sign of coffee-coloured water laced with white froth. The Waiting Room (official anchor site) co-ordinates we gleaned from our pilot books were spot on.

Noel appeared with a sleep creased face and a peace offering: a steaming cup of tea. 'I felt vulnerable being so close to shallows,' he admitted and grinned when I said I'd heard his comment about running aground. 'I couldn't settle. I became so tired I was past caring.'

'You also knew, deep down, that I had everything under control.'

We sat in silence for a while, enjoying an easy ride until it was time to organise our entrance.

'Puerto Amistad, this is the sailing vessel *Pyewacket II*,' I called on our VHF.

It was 6 a.m., and the radio stayed as silent as the calm sea; at 7 a.m., it crackled to life; by then, we had missed the necessary high tide by an impossibly tiny thirty minutes.

The entrance to Bahia de Caraquez is through an unmarked channel, uncomfortably close to the shoreline and shallow in places. It is cheap insurance at thirty dollars to hire a pilot.

Anchoring in the exposed Waiting Room was our only option.

For twenty-three hours, we impatiently hung around for high tide and daylight to synchronise. With visions of upping anchor during the night while riding the building swells, we tried to sleep in the afternoon. The 1,500 nautical miles from Acapulco (via a brief stop at Isla del Coco) had taken its toll. Dirty steel-coloured water beneath persistent squalls and looming black clouds streaked with lightning had been our constant companions. It was often too cold to shower. We had a hot shower on board, heated by gas, but I didn't want wet hair on watch during the night or when I was off shift and trying to sleep. Now, wrapped in the comfort of my own dirt, I tried to summon the motivation for a wash. My thoughts were on sleep; Noel's thoughts tunnelled deeper, rigging up a flopper stopper to ease the rolling.

A flopper stopper is a simple device that helps dampen the boat's roll while anchored in swells. With the flopper stopper in play, the wind miraculously eased to a soft breath, hardly enough to dimple the sea. The anticipated blending of deep water and day was forgotten, reliance resting on the GPS anchor alarm. Burgers and beer were tantalisingly close.

Twenty-three hours later, our pilot spoke as much English as we did Spanish (*nada*), but with hand signals and lots of great white smiles, he guided us through the narrow, windy channel into the river that wrapped around the peninsular on which Bahia sits.

We'd been advised to use an agent to check in. The owner of Puerto Amistad (Friendly Port), Tripp, was an agent who knew the process thoroughly and spoke Spanish (Tripp hails from Alabama, USA).

Tucked snugly behind the peninsular Bahia sits upon are the moorings and anchor area. Safe on a buoy, we put *Pyewacket* to bed (thanking her as per the ritual) and opened a beer. It was half past seven in the morning. While self-congratulatory comments flowed over the decks, we reminisced at the journey, which we'd decided wasn't so bad; the beer instantly softened the memory.

'Most of the boats look empty,' I said, swallowing the amber liquid and becoming acquainted with our new neighbourhood.

About a dozen boats sat idly in the gentle breeze. With one beer, a light head, and awaiting the officials, another dinghy puttered past and stopped when they spotted our Australian flag. 'G'day.'

Never had a sound felt so much like home. Sandy and Max on board *Volo* are seasoned cruisers, but home is Australia.

Prior to the officials' arrival, we launched the dinghy and snuck into the small town to the Banco, scarfing a burger, the staff at Puerto Amistad begging us to be back within an hour before the bureaucrats arrived.

Health, customs, and immigration travel via taxi from the town of Manta, we paid all their expenses. They stamp passports, shuffle paper, and present invoices. We were free in Ecuador. But first we needed sleep.

* * *

The wave struck at midnight, jarring us from dreamy sleep.

'Why?' I mumbled. 'It makes no sense.' The boat thrummed; I heard someone scream... in delight.

The music swelled and pumped loud, as if on personal headphones. Ecuadorians liked loud anything, but this was obscene. As rashly as it started, the careless, ear splitting beat stopped. We supposed the tiny town of Bahia de Caraquez was in a spin with the President visiting tomorrow. He was here to open the new bridge that spanned the river. It was the longest bridge in Ecuador and prevented sailboats going farther upstream to moorings that were kinder on the wallet.

Despite the noise of preparation for the esteemed visitor and the pumping music from the yacht club, the anchorage and mooring site was safe and secure for leaving your boat and travelling inland; this being why many of the boats were temporarily empty.

As a transient boat, we could only stay in Ecuador for three months, so we applied for a visa extension. With form filling and money, the process would be easy – or so we thought. As our passports were returned with the visa stuck on a page, we were told that to finalise the validity of the visa, we had to obtain an 'official stamp.' Then we'd be furnished with a secondary, essential document.

South Americans love their paperwork!

This stamp could only be obtained in a town that was a nine hour bus trip (one way) away. However, after some gently offered 'grease,' the officials at a town one hour away were happy to do the deed. The bribe was insignificant compared with the bus ride and accommodation costs that we could have incurred. Our taxi driver figured out the acceptable amount of ten dollars and performed the transaction as a regular part of his hire services.

With the extended visa, we could relax. To keep our stretched budget more flexible, after a couple weeks on a mooring, we decided to move onto anchor. The employees at Puerto Amistad were an absolute credit to the place. Juan and Raymondo took care of boat jobs, gas, water, diesel, maintenance, cleaning, and even cooking.

They helped us move. But we all had our own ideas how best to do this. We wanted a bow and stern anchor out, so we had to give the process some thought. After I tied-off the line from the bow anchor, *Pyewacket* decided to swing towards our neighbour.

'Use this.' Juan held out a short line to me.

'It's not long enough.'

'Use this,' he said, frowning.

'No long enough!' I repeated, with my stupid fake Spanish accent and gesticulating; I tried to get the message across.

'Use this!' Juan was on the verge of yelling at me.

Noel kept busy by manoeuvring the boat between other lines, moorings, and boats.

Anxiety started creeping through my innards.

In desperation, and inches from our new neighbour, I shouted, 'Just take *this* fucking rope!' Again, this isn't normally my usual language, especially to people who were trying to help, but the international language of desperation has its use!

At the same time, a couple in an inflatable dinghy were heading our way.

'Excuse me; could you give me a hand?' I smiled sweetly, swallowing my alter ego, the deranged woman who had just sworn like a – *ahem* – sailor.

They puttered over.

'Could you just push on our starboard quarter? We needed to manoeuvre the stern to port.'

'Not a problem.'

Juan and Raymondo worked their little behinds off for us, and soon, we had two anchors aft and a large Bruce anchor off the bow, safely buried into the thick mud; we were all wondering what all the fuss was about.

Juan and Raymondo hopped on board, following our invitation, and I offered a tentative smile and a warm handshake.

'Okay? Indicating I had no hard feelings and hoped he didn't.

He laughed and grinned into the cold beer and tip I'd handed to him.

Earnings here are slimmer than a Weight Watchers biscuit, so a decent tip secured these guys as our buddies.

* * *

In South America, the buses are the cheapest way to travel... if you don't mind putting your life in the hands of strangers.

Ecuadorian buses range from new-ish to bone-rattling, head-spinningly ancient.

In the city of Guayaquil (south of Bahia), we hopped on a bus to venture into the city centre for sightseeing and promptly became engulfed in giggles. The bus came straight out of an old movie, and we, the characters, had stepped into the set of *Alice in Wonderland*.

While my right buttock became intimate with a crinkly, sun-beaten grandad, who appeared to be enjoying himself far too much,

Noel looked as though he had eaten one of the 'eat me' cookies and grown into a giant; standing up, he held his head bent at ninety degrees to squeeze beneath the low roof.

Like most large cities, personal awareness is important. At the place we alighted in the morning, after shopping and sightseeing, we stood and waited for a bus to take us home.

Suddenly, police appeared from every direction and surrounded us with large evil guns in hand, fingers near triggers.

'What are you doing here?' they demanded; their concerned eyes scanning the road and pathway.

'We're catching the bus back to our hostel.'

'It's too dangerous for you; get in a taxi,' they commanded.

'Thanks, we're fine; we caught this bus this morning.' But their hands were twitching near their guns, their eyes flicking in every direction. Receiving presidential protection was slightly unnerving.

They stopped a taxi, man-handled us into the dilapidated car, and sent us packing back to our accommodation – our cupboard sized room with no windows, where far more danger existed. If a fire broke out, we would have undoubtedly been turned into little people chips.

Scattered throughout the cities, outside the main hub, numerous signs warned tourists: *Danger, tourists! Do not walk in this area.*

How much danger could we be in as tourists?

* * *

It was time for visitors. My dad arrived from England with my thirteen-year-old nephew, Kieran.

We met the bewildered and tired travellers at Manta airport after some sight-seeing along the way. This was their first trip together, and Kieran's first trip abroad. From the airport, we taxied from one bus terminal to another, seeking the right bus to transport us to Bahia, about eighty kilometres away.

At one station the four of us stood in a huddle, disorientated. Noel and I were embarrassed by our lack of Spanish, Dad and Kieran worried that they were in a strange country, in the care of two so-called travellers who couldn't find their way home!

As we shuffled on our feet, kicking up dust and lost within our own desperate thoughts, suddenly, the four of us were grabbed by the scruff of our necks and manhandled into a taxi. Meanwhile, the driver's accomplice loaded the suitcases into the boot. Hurtling through anonymous streets, the boys asked me what was happening.

I wasn't really sure, but I felt comfortable enough to indulge in some fun.

'Well, we've been kidnapped, and I think they'll be sending Mum a ransom note!' I was the only one who appreciated this humour.

A few moments later, all at once, we were propelled forward as the car screeched to a halt.

I watched my wide-eyed nephew, hoping that my joke wasn't the truth; my dad fidgeted in his seat, his responsibility for his grandson weighing on his shoulders.

Lurching to a halt, behind us we swung our heads around in unison to watch another large vehicle skid to an emergency stop; exchanging nervous smiles, pretending we weren't frightened. As the dust settled we climbed out of the car and saw a square yellow bus with the words across the front: BAHIA.

The taxi driver at the bus station had figured it out; he knew where to find the bus. His English was as bad as our Spanish so he didn't waste time with words and simply shoved us in his car, tracked down the bus that was already en route to Bahia, and flagged the driver to a stop!

Feeling like extras in a James Bond movie, we lugged our cases into the bus's hold and hopped on board, bemused and thankful.

'We're on the 'chook bus' Noel laughed.

'How lovely,' I said, nudging a chicken away with my foot as it filled the bus with an indignant squawk.

The bus rattled us to pieces for the next hour-and-a-half, while chickens fought to steal our seats.

This is our life; our day-to-day existence is unconventional and stimulating, but that is normal to us. While this suits us perfectly, it's not for everyone. Kieran stoically suffered through nibbling on unidentified foods. At times, he left a whole meal because the chicken looked so different – there was little in the way of McDonalds. My dad is a meat-potato-and-two-veg guy; a meal like this is tricky to find in Ecuador.

Some people like the idea of travelling but don't like all that goes with it. To survive financially and mentally, and to experience the culture as a whole, you must eat what the locals eat. For me, that is crucial to soaking up everything a new country offers. I also hate waste; many people couldn't afford the cheap meals we purchased. But despite different views on how to travel, the four of us packed-in plenty of fun. In a two-week-dash, we jumped on buses driven by race-drivers, rafted in the Amazon, lazed in thermal pools, wore jungle war paint, and perused Quito. We ventured up into the clouds to gaze at snow-capped mountains and came to friendly blows over card games by a crackling fire.

All too soon, it was just Noel and me once again.

Travelling and exploring can become addictive – it certainly has for us. The daily life of a nomad is sometimes not enough for me; I constantly crave more, new challenges to stretch my abilities. I am most comfortable when out of my comfort zone. Something drives me to experience everything within my reach, financially and time-wise. The continuous adrenaline buzz is my drug. So, I still sought adventures within our escapades, but I didn't realise the next exploit would tattoo our hearts with such precious memories.

* * *

'Are you still keen on this teaching idea?'

'Yup,' I replied. 'I may have found something.' I smirked as Noel rolled his eyes.

I've always wanted to teach English, and I knew opportunities existed in South America.

When I researched teaching English, the details horrified me. You had to pay huge amounts of money to volunteer! *We're not qualified English teachers, but we're still offering to help out.*

I'd flicked off a half dozen enquiries on email before I hit the jackpot.

'Listen to this,' I said to Noel. 'This guy's just written to us:

Hi Jackie, Noel, we'd love your help.
I'm running a programme to teach young adults
Salsa dancing so they can eventually teach the tourists
and make a living We need some help bringing
their English up to speed.

'Hmmm, right,' Noel muttered.

I continued reading the email.

All you need do to is get yourselves here and pay
a small contribution for accommodation,
which includes three meals a day – the current
teacher is leaving in a week, can you come then?

'Brilliant,' I beamed. 'I'd love to do it!' I searched Noel's eyes, hopeful.

'Then it looks like we are.' Noel knows when it's pointless to argue.

We offered six weeks of our time, arranged the bus trip, and squared *Pyewacket* away.

***

'For goodness sake!' Noel peered out the window and down at a two hundred foot drop.

'My buttocks are clenched so tight I swear they are the only thing preventing us from going over the side!'

I stifled a giggle under my blanket. I'd bunched up the thin material over my nose to avoid breathing the vomit smells – young, delicate stomachs new to bus travel couldn't handle the swaying motion. But, the cover also helped control my mirth. My laughter had the knack of enveloping my body in hilarity so completely I lost control and started crying – especially in unique situations such as these, where death was just a sneeze away. Within my own little emotional roller-coaster, I could keep myself amused for hours.

The thirteen hour bus trip, over the Andes and into Peru, left us vowing to catch a flight back. Not one barrier stood between us and certain death down a cliff – not one driver knew the meaning of safe speed.

Crossing the border into Peru meant an armed guard riding shotgun with the driver. Noel and I exchanged worried glances, but we shuffled down in our seats and kept quiet.

By some miracle, we didn't die in the mountains of South America, but we were sick of buses. In the vehicle, we were sitting with two young lads who were excited to be coming home to Lima. I stared out the window; the hotch-potch homes fought for space where there was none, grey, listless streets carried beggars and thousands of scurrying feet – we couldn't wait to leave.

In our cheap back-packers accommodation, where we could listen to everyone's intimate conversation from our room, we sourced reasonable prices for flights from Lima, Peru to Cusco via the Internet. Happy to be sitting on a plane, I welcomed the respite; my tummy did a little flip-flop in anticipation as we landed.

The short car ride commenced along cobble streets. Our hosts spoke little English, and our Spanish hadn't improved. We alighted from the dusty car and an olive-skinned woman with beautiful dark hair opened an unremarkable shabby green door. After a few steps along a dark cement-floored corridor, we stepped out into a courtyard. Dark brown brick rooms sat in a circle above our heads with a small balcony hemming the walls. Downstairs, a woman worked purposely in a laundry room; the kitchen lay idle; a few doors were firmly shut. We were shown to our room.

'There must be camel hooves in these pillows.' Our accommodation left a lot to be desired.

The lumpy pillows were cast aside, and we folded jumpers to use instead.

We were pinned to the bed beneath the extraordinarily heavy, animal-hair blankets.

'I'm not sure they got rid of the entire animal!' Noel groaned, trying to turn over.

When we did manage to roll over, the blankets rolled with us and straight onto the floor with a loud crump.

'I'm sure they are about to walk off when they hit the floor!'

Each evening, we played Russian roulette in the shower, as the bare, electrified wires were sited directly in the stream.

'If you keep your head and hands at least a foot away from the shower head, you get less of a shock.' Noel tested the 'safe zone' of the shower head! The nearer our body got to the equipment, the stronger the shock.

The process to achieve a hot shower changed each night. Usually, the water stopped when you were at your most foamy!

We hadn't reached the challenge of teaching yet, but other obstacles had to be dealt with first.

Evening strolls around the old stone roads soon became a battle of wits. Skinny dogs snarled as we strode passed; neighbouring dogs would join the melee, so a small pack of three or four teeth-baring dogs would often threaten us.

'Go-oooorn, get out.' Noel yelled, forcefully trying to show the dogs we weren't scared.

'I could almost see the rabies dripping from their mouths,' I said to Noel, horrified.

'Right, come with me.' Noel promptly marched off the road and down a bank. 'Come and give me a hand.' A few moments later, after some grunting and groaning using the Leatherman saw attachment, we both grasped a handy, solid stick. 'Just whack 'em with that if they get too close.'

I felt better, but less inclined to walk around the back streets.

* * *

'I feel crappy.' I sneezed again. I rarely fell ill, but somehow, I had picked up a head cold. 'I can't get warm, and I'd love a hot shower.'

'Right, I'm off to find somewhere else to stay.' Noel left me whimpering beneath the dead animals.

Several hours later, he returned, positively bouncing through the door.

'Pack up. I've found the perfect place.'

I had already organised our gear – two back-packs – in anticipation of the move.

'It's not far, but we'll jump in a taxi.'

'Well done, and thanks; it's a relief to get out of here.'

'I'll settle up; let's go.' Our hosts were a bit perplexed that we left their accommodation, but I'm sure it's a regular occurrence. We couldn't be the only ones to find the cheaper and superior accommodation.

The taxi dropped us fifty metres from our new front door. We strode up a narrow, shaded alley, hemmed in by crumbling stone walls. Noel turned toward a small wooden door and rang the bell.

'How on earth did you find this place?'

'Well, I tried all the obvious hotels and hostels. I asked them if they had hot water. They said they did, so I turned on the taps and waited and waited, and they were all cold! So, I explored the back streets.'

The door opened into a private courtyard that glowed beneath the trapped sun; vivid pinks and juicy orange blooms bordered the cheery garden. Birds twittered in welcome, and I instantly felt better.

The large, clean, and airy room made me sign in relief. The brand new bathroom had not one bare wire in sight. The enormous stone built family kitchen was offered for our use.

'Please use our kitchen anytime you like,' our hosts offered. The family kitchen housed a large stone, domed pizza oven, and a long, sturdy dining table. I imagined boisterous family meals and plenty of food.

'Perfect,' I sighed.

We soon settled into a routine, and we found a wonderful fresh market that we frequented daily; barrels of plump olives caught our eyes, and piles of freshly cut lettuce stood to attention. Fruit and vegetables positively gleamed without the supermarkets' tricks of spraying a fine mist of fresh water and clever lighting.

'I love this market.' The Mediterranean diet suits us perfectly. Noel and I could eat the fresh produce in our room, at a small dining table, or while boiling eggs and making tea in the kitchen, all the time admiring the huge dome of the pizza oven.

**

'I'm so glad you've done so much preparation,' Noel said.

'I thought you might be.'

For our first session, we put the seven girls and five boys into two teams and arranged an assault course of tables and chairs. The students were blindfolded and one of the team – with no blindfold – had the job to guide the rest of their team through the obstacles, while speaking English.

The entire small complex of admins, organisers, and the owner stopped their work to watch the mayhem.

'I had a good feeling about you two,' said David, the proprietor. 'That was amazing.'

The next day, he told us that during the dancing lesson, the students talked incessantly about their next English lesson; they couldn't wait.

Beautiful girls with long dark hair and handsome boys with chiselled features and strong bodies of youth laughed, played, and learned. Laughing, they attempted to teach us a few Salsa steps.

'You're doing well on the creative side of lessons,' Noel said.

'I try; it's tricky as they're all at different levels. Hey, how about this for an idea? We could use that song "put your left leg in, your left leg out..." remember the one, what's it called?'

'I can't remember, but that'd be good.'

'It's "The Hokey Cokey!"'

'Oh, that's right, but don't you mean "Hokey Pokey?"'

'We call it "Cokey" in the UK!'

At the next lesson, we gathered the group into a circle, and Noel took the lead.

'*You* put your left leg in, your left leg out, in, out, in, out, you shake it all about, you do the hokey cokey and you turn around, that's what it's all about. HEY!'

We grabbed their hands and pulled them all into the middle, merrily singing loudly and badly.

'*Oh*, Aussie Dancing, *oh*, Aussie Dancing, *oh*, Aussie Dancing, knees bent, arms stretched rah, rah, rah!'

Dazed and a little embarrassed, the students followed, looking at each other wondering if they should be left in a room with two lunatics. They didn't know, though, that we'd altered the song words.

I sang again, using my right arm.

Next to me, Sandra widened her eyes as I urged her to have a go. Helping her with English she managed a verse. Without warning, Noel and I were grabbed, propelled into the middle in a rush, while the students belted out, '*oh*, Aussie dancing, *oh*, Aussie dancing...'

As they left for their Salsa lesson, the whispered words to 'Aussie Dancing' floated around the complex; the song played in their heads, and they sang under their breaths.

I still worry that our students will travel to Australia one day and belt out The Hokey Cokey, thinking it's our national anthem!

The youth of the group struck us. Early twenties was a distant memory and spending a few hours a day with the students highlighted the difference. It wasn't thoughts or ideals that we noticed, but the aging of our hands. We'd lean on their desks, pointing to a word or their writing, and our hands would be close to theirs. You don't see how old your own hands are until they are next to young ones. Reminiscent of gift bag stuffing, our crêpey skin gave the game away. Prominent veins stuck out and almost yelled, 'Hey! Look how old I am!' The sight of a youthful hand next to my crinklies made me tuck them away in pockets. I felt like I had been young forever; that's an odd thing to say, I know. Age creeps up on us. It doesn't happen gradually. Suddenly, we wake up and have grey hairs, slackening jowls, and old hands! It's that pesky gravity; one way or another, it will get us – first by pulling us down, tugging at your skin, and eventually pressing us into a coffin.

Mixing with the young helped us lie to ourselves, convincing our older bodies that we were back in our twenties, too; we felt young and full of energy. Conversely, it also highlighted that we had left our twenties well and truly behind – especially when glancing at my reflection in the mirror.

I find it a bit astonishing to be in a new group of people, the middle-aged lot, which I never thought I'd reach. Fortunately, Noel and I are young in mind and believe we are young in body. Sailing helps us stay supple and fit. We're away from city pollution most of the time, exercising regularly via the movement of the boat, and, more importantly, enjoying life and living how we want to live.

* * *

The six weeks flew by. We missed one day of teaching when I suffered a mild, but amusing, inner-ear infection. I am sure the altitude assisted my temporary foray with the floor. One morning, as Noel made a cup of tea up in the large kitchen, I stepped out of bed and crumpled to the floor. The room span as if I'd consumed several large whiskies.

'Well, that's interesting,' I said, needing to speak aloud even though I was alone. I giggled. I knew I had an ear problem, and my balance was out of whack. I decided to enjoy feeling drunk without the pain of an impending hangover!

I hauled myself up and clutched the wall as I made for the bathroom on unsteady legs. The shower quickly disgorged wonderful hot water, and I stepped beneath the stinging spray and promptly fell in a heap again. I laughed and sat for a while. I knew it would pass.

'What are you laughing at?' Noel stepped back into our room, clutching two mugs of tea; he popped his head around the door, 'What on earth are you doing?' He snorted a laugh and continued to put breakfast together on the table.

'I'm dizzy. I've fallen twice,' I called into the bedroom. 'It's an inner ear infection, set off by altitude, I'm sure.'

'Do you want a hand?'

'Nah, it's okay, I might skip today, though; can you send a quick email?'

I spent the morning in bed reading. Noel sat in the sunny courtyard; we basked in a gentle day all to ourselves.

I promised myself, and anyone who listened, that I wouldn't cry when we bade farewell to our class. I am sensitive – emotions come too easily; I also like to see the good in everyone I meet; in fact, I like everyone I meet until they give me a reason not to like them. Noel pegs people instantly; it's an incredible ability. Even if the person's true side doesn't reveal itself for some weeks, even months, Noel has sussed them out within ten minutes. It takes me a fair bit longer! But our students were good, kind people, and I knew the last day would be emotional for us all.

During the twenty minute walk to the classroom, we made a habit of stopping to buy some munchies. The street vendor pushed along her rickety wooden cart that buckled under the weight of muffins, lollies, sweeties, and all sorts of scrumptious treats, and parked beside the curb.

On our last day, we approached the smiling lady who had no qualms about showing us her bare gums, and as usual, she shoved the school kids aside. We purchased several dollars of treats and many unidentifiable items for the students. It must have been the vendor's biggest sale ever. I think she slinked off home after we'd left.

Noel and I filled the table with yummy treats; the girls cried, which made me cry. They presented us with gifts and clasped my arms and hands, not letting go for a moment.

Those six weeks were a thrilling and unique experience that created international friendships we still hold dear.

* * *

With the teaching complete, we planned a bit of sightseeing, hopping on more buses to Machu Picchu and Lake Titicaca. The incredible sites of Machu Picchu left us with gaping mouths and sore knees.

We'd hiked up the hill in a bid to see the deserted village, atop a mountain, at dawn. Surprisingly, we strode past twenty-year-olds who'd all but given up the tough climb – our sailing legs were stronger than theirs. Our protective batons that we'd cut from a tree when threatened by rabid dogs were now handy walking sticks.

Throughout the morning, while the tingly misty air cooled our red skin, we witnessed an eerie haze and dynamic hues of blue. The glorious sunrise burned off remaining wafts of clouds, revealing the strikingly clear sky. Amid roaming llamas, we spent the morning stepping in the footprints of the Incas while strolling through their ghostly fifteenth century village.

As part of our tour from Cusco to Machu Picchu, we coasted down the steep mountain on bicycles – an adventure that was irritatingly cut short due to road work.

An interesting mix of four made up our group: two blonde twenty-year-olds (our guide who couldn't take his eyes off the girls) and Noel and me. They were lovely young women and all was fine until they said, 'It's so great being with you two. We don't have to worry about what we look like!'

It's nice to know that if you look that bad, people around you can avoid brushing their hair, washing, and putting their clothes on correctly; I was happy to help. Topping that comment, the girls said, 'It's like being with our very own travelling Mum and Dad; our parents are really happy we are with you guys.' I am sure there was a compliment in there somewhere.

During parts of the trip, we linked up with other small groups and traversed the dusty countryside via a small twelve-seated van. Unfortunately, thirteen bottoms needed seats.

'Just letting you know when I'm asked to move over again, I'm not doing it,' I said to a startled young man sitting next to me.

'Don't involve me!' he said.

Coward!

For the next hour and a half, the people on our row of four seats were shunted across to allow the humpty-dumpty female guide to sit. She took a complete seat while our row sat between seats. My back complained.

The guy next to me fidgeted. Noel sat the other side of him.

The guide leaped on board in a surprisingly agile manner for her size and tried to shunt us all across.

I stayed put.

'Move over,' she commanded.

'No.'

She scowled. 'Move over!'

'I've paid for this seat. I'm not sitting between two seats again.'

The people in the rows behind us tutted, and I could hear the dull murmur of protest.

I swung around. 'Well, why don't you move across so she can sit in your row?'

They stared at me blankly.

The guide chose another row and made them move over.

Noel smirked. He'd always stood up for what he thought was right and doesn't let anyone rail-road him into something he needn't do. I usually give in too easily. I guess that is part and parcel of becoming older; I don't allow people walk all over me anymore. I have a right to certain things, and I am able to stand up for myself. The bus of twenty-year-olds will understand that in a decade or two!

The tour continued with an eye-pleasing walk of dry vistas broken up with pretty creeks running through the bottom of a deep valley; we hiked over rocks to the fast-running waters of a ravine.

Many of my brave decisions came back to bite, and the choice to stand up for myself would be no different.

'Oh, this is going to be interesting.'

'What's that?' I said, following Noel's line of sight. 'Oh.'

As part of our walk, we had to cross the gaping ravine littered with large boulders. A wide snake of a deep, cold stream rushed over the rocks, creating a froth of white, treacherous water.

Our group stood in a line; we would cross the gap via a wooden tray, like a cable car, but with no car! The tour guide helped each couple climb onto the flat piece of timber.

Noel and I reached the head of the queue, and instead of holding the equipment steady, the guide let it go, so Noel and I flapped and fumbled, struggling to lift our bodies onto a moving platform. The desired effect of making us look silly didn't work. We giggled, relishing challenges such as these. Team work is what we were good at; when the situation was not life or death, we saw the funny side.

The ropes and pulleys swayed as we coaxed our legs into a crossed position. Noel sat behind me; I looked over my shoulder, and he grinned. 'This'll be fun. Let's hope we make it to the other side.' With that, my nemesis shoved us away from the safety of land, shooting us over the precarious drop.

'*Weeeeeeeeeeeeeeeee!*' We chuckled like kids, exhilarated. The guide on the other side pulled us in the rest of the way.

* * *

Tristan Jones was an inspiration for us both. The English author and mariner wrote numerous books and articles about sailing. His stories tended to be a combination of fact and fiction. Apparently, he was the consummate story-teller. But if his stories included fiction, some part would also be fact. He was a remarkable man. His challenges and quests made ours look like child's play.

Growing up in orphanages, with little education, after a stint in the navy, he purchased a sailboat. He taught himself to sail, and thereafter, his adventures included whiskey smuggling and taking a sailboat to the Dead Sea, the surface of which is said to be over 1,300 feet *below* sea level.

He trucked his boat to Lake Titicaca, said to be 12,500 feet *above* sea level, and hauled it across to Bolivia and sailed down to Paraguay and Argentina. It is the story recounted in *The Incredible Voyage* that urged us to make the journey ourselves – not by boat, though!

We found Lake Titicaca marred by the locals' desperate need to sell knick-knacks to tourists. Useless trinkets were the main focus. Doing our best to ignore the Disney-effect creeping in, we marvelled at the process of island building. They'd gather the reeds and weave them on the top; at the bottom, the reeds slowly rotted. It was a continual process to keep their feet dry, but it worked.

Our accommodation on the muddy island was wrapped in a restful ambience. Locals were welcoming, but not nagging, with the intention of selling their wares, and the expanse of vegetable plots that were lovingly cared for rolled over the meandering hills, much like a drier version of England. We stayed with a family: Mum, Dad and their daughter. We reached our room by teetering on narrow steps towards a door that was four feet high. We were back in the *Alice in Wonderland* story.

Our lumpy mattresses must have been made out of llama hooves, and with no electricity, we played cards by candle light, sipping freshly bought cool beers. Phones, Internet, and television were blissfully absent; a call for dinner was the only interruption.

We ate in our room. I don't know where the family slept; the only other space we came upon was the kitchen, and this was not a kitchen as we know it. The mud-packed floor was surrounded by four walls of stone, one with a large opening where a door would usually hang. Mum sat on the floor in her wool dress, woven in a selection of patterns and dyed in bright colours to differentiate her from the lower class; a cotton pinafore protected her clothing, like an apron would, as she peeled vegetables. On the fire sat a large cauldron, the daughter worried the contents with a stick snapped off a nearby tree. A couple wonky wooden shelves clutched the wall. Dinner must always be before dark; no hint of light brightened the gloom.

With no room inside for anyone else, we peered in from outside, took a picture, and received a scowl from Mum; her daughter had given us permission to take photos. We gratefully took our plates that were piled high with steaming plain rice and vegetables.

We planned to stay more than one night on the main island but had to leave suddenly.

'I can't breathe!' Noel gasped. He sat bolt upright.

'Can I help in any way?'

'Every time I fall asleep, I stop breathing!' Altitude sickness is indiscriminate, rotten, and a bit frightening. 'I can't stay here another night.'

* * *

I longed to head east over to Bolivia, but Noel had had enough of sleeping in strange beds.

'Besides, we have to get the boat organised; we can't stay in Ecuador forever.'

He was right; there'd be other trips. I constantly had to remind myself that we couldn't see everything.

In Cusco, we found two bus companies with wonderful, large, comfortable buses and decided to bus home despite our promises of flying. On the whole, the return journey was far better until I encountered visa problems.

'This isn't right.' The sombre official peered out of his wooden hut, shook his head, and flicked through my passport once again.

'What's the problem? I have a visa to allow me to return to Ecuador.' I shuffled nervously.

Noel had already been stamped and allowed through, meaning being able to leave the dusty path to climb back onto the bus.

I could hear the queue tutting and fidgeting behind me as if I was causing the problem.

The silence hung in the air, and I refused to move, despite pressure from every angle.

Noel handed his passport over to the official once again, and he compared the two visas.

He peered at my passport for an agonising minute, shrugged, and stamped a page.

'What was all that about?' Noel asked.

'Buggered if I know.' We stalked back to the bus, relieved I hadn't been stuck in Peru!

'You know, I think the official thought you were on your own. We've got different national passports, so he didn't twig we were together.'

'How's that make a difference?' I shuffled in my seat, making a nest, glad the episode was over.

'Well, they're always on the take; he'd have made you wait and demanded a payment to allow you on the bus.'

I thought about that for a moment. 'You're right; if I was on my own, ten or twenty bucks would be nothing to be allowed back into Ecuador!'

That's the reality of this part of the world. I used my UK passport; Noel had his Australian passport. The official may have assumed we were not together. A woman alone was an easy target to make a few dollars.

After travelling and sightseeing, it was always a relief to arrive back to our home port, the Yacht Club. Smooth-faced, olive-skinned girls kept the bar in order and all the cruisers entertained. They tried to improve our poor Spanish, but most days, they folded themselves in half, clutching their tummies in agony with laughter.

On tranquil evenings accompanied by the song of cicadas, Noel and I would take advantage of the two dollar beers.

'*Dos vasos, por favour.*'

Snigger.

'*Baso? Vaso?*' Noel blustered. 'Not kisses!'

As we'd share a bottle of beer, Noel asked for two glasses. Glasses and kisses (*vasos* and *besos*) sounded the same to our untrained ears. It became a standing joke that Noel asked for two beers and two kisses. He claimed that he tried to say 'glasses.' The 'b' in Spanish is pronounced similar to a 'v.'

To add to the joviality Janet, the bar-maid named Noel 'Papa Noel.' Every evening she ran to Noel and flung her arms around his belly, she made a production of energetically rubbing his tummy while singing, 'Papa Noel! Papa Noel! Ho! Ho! Ho!'

* * *

With greetings of wide, friendly smiles whenever we walked into town, Ecuadorians, and especially Bahians, are a welcoming bunch. They are small people, averaging around five feet, which made me, at five feet three, feel tall. It's an unusual sensation to suddenly be taller than everyone, as if I'd eaten the 'grow' cookie.

I felt pretty good, but my clothes brought me back down. Ecuadorians take great pride in their appearance: wrapped up in smart jeans that cling to their sexy curves, topped off with ballooning breasts. Popping into the supermarket for cornflakes and cheese, their clean, crisp appearance contrasted with my cruising clothes.

'Fashion' was deleted from my vocabulary. I wore tatty t-shirts and jeans that were neat and tidy fifteen years ago; living on board meant that most of my clothes had their own unique branding (aka boat-stain).

Launching the dinghy each day guaranteed my clean attire finding the grease that lubricated the derrick – usually on the breast or bottom. But, if I wanted to be involved in the day-to-day running of the boat, I had to accept this – it was better than changing several times a day. The tenacious marks were there to stay, even when I laboured like a demented laundry lady with a brush as hard as wire.

I scrubbed our clothes in the aft cockpit, utilising several buckets of soapy water, which I then sloshed across the decks. Minimal detergent, a warm day, and an idle mind made this job an enjoyable experience rather than a chore.

It is an odd phenomenon, as most long-term cruisers have a similar look. Their clothes may not be as ill-fitting as mine, and they may have less 'homemade patterns' on their garments, but a universal crumpled look is part of this lifestyle. Boats are generally lacking in space, and apparel is not as important as all the gear you need to prevent the boat from sinking. Inevitably, our garb was squished and stuffed into tiny cupboards. As for ironing, I was there to live, not press clothes!

Having been on land for around two years prior to this escapade, the weight crept on; sneaky bulges appeared here and there. My clothes were appropriately up-sized. However, usually the cruising life meant an instant diet: seasickness curbed my healthy appetite. When in port, we lugged water, shopping, gas bottles, and parts, walking endlessly or cycling miles to find a right-handed doodad. Consequently, my body shrunk in width, and my clothes hung in an embarrassing, lumpy arrangement. Although I'd trimmed down a bit on this trip, I'd not lost as much weight as I did on *Mariah*. Life felt simpler on that journey. I was more settled, and that made a difference. As I've said, we knew *Mariah* much better than we knew *Pyewacket*. Age changed things, too; bruises, accumulated while sailing, caused me to suck in my cheeks with pain more frequently. And this escapade was tougher. Or perhaps when I look back at *Mariah*, I only remember the good parts. The simplicity of owning a boat and nothing else endowed us with a better sense of freedom back then, even though, on this trip, our house in Greenwell Point caused no concerns. I thought this tour would be effortless. My sailing knowledge had vastly improved, and I appreciated life far more as time was noticeably slipping away. Looking back, I don't know why I thought it would be easier this time around; we were heading to remote parts of the ocean, and we were still only on a tiny boat in comparison to the vast, deep sea.

It's not sensible to compare journeys; besides, I was still doing everything I wanted and basking in my fun life.

Getting on with this existence – right now – is what's important. I realised that if I'm not happy with myself in a crappy house, I won't be happy with myself on an ocean voyage – it all starts with me and my mindset.

* * *

On board was a lovely gas-heated shower, but in Ecuador, we had to pay for all our water. It wasn't expensive, but we could save a few dollars and a bit of effort by showering on shore. Coming ashore each evening, in Bahia, for a shower, we couldn't help but fire up the laptop while we waited for our turn.

Via the Internet, we were, of course, sourcing equipment at the same time, but we didn't need to be online every day. We were trying to break the habit by limiting it to every other day, skipping weekends altogether. Of course, this failed miserably since we searched for quotes and ordered new sails.

In Brisbane in 1998, we were moored on the pilings, and I remember receiving a large package from my family in England. As I opened the envelope, cards, notes, tiny gifts, photos, and a long, hand-written letter spilled onto the table; everyone in the family had contributed. For two blissful hours, Noel and I sat in a coffee shop, glued to the messages and updates.

The joy of receiving a hand-written letter is a rare experience these days; everything is so instant, so electronic.

Cruising changes to the degree we allow it. Once upon a time, we'd row ashore and talk about boats, books, life, and likes. Admittedly, back then, the fabric of our sailing lives was stitched together with frustrating international calls, costly faxes, and untrustworthy snail mail.

Now, the pattern is different. No blame or accusations lie with anyone; it is the world changing, and Noel and I are becoming the worst offenders. The Internet has changed everyone's lives, but for cruisers, it is a ruder invasion.

Everyone has their reasons for sailing; one of our motives is the freedom from communication. We are all bombarded with ads selling us stuff we simply do not need. I am as guilty as the next person, but I have drawn the line with Internet on board. I simply don't want it; it kills a little of the reason for going cruising. I find it thrilling that land folk don't know where we are or what we're doing; it's all mine and private, and I decide what to share. It's not control or secrecy; it's that delicious sense of freedom.

Power via solar panels and catching our own water is a type of freedom and independence. We don't have to rely on marinas, and we avoid starting the engine every day for power. Life moves on, but technology advancement gallops ahead and doesn't stop for anyone, and freedom comes in different forms. Having paid for water, it inspired us to create a simple solution to catch rain water. Many cruisers have varied and wild ideas about how to do this. Our water deck fill points were nearly flush with the deck; so we constructed a simple dam out of a piece of timber and held it in place with two dive weights behind it and one on top. Once the decks had had a good clean beneath the downpour, we'd put the dam in place and the water became trapped between the toe rail and our dam before flowing into our tanks.

Freedom is maintained by living carefully on a budget. That's why I loved the markets at Bahia. Daily fresh, cheap produce meant I became a regular. The downstairs market brimmed with a host of delectable items like blood red and lush green fruit and vegetables, chicken, and cheeses. Meanwhile, upstairs, Noel regularly purchased bunches of flowers from the first floor florist; they were a few cents and brightened up the boat. The butchers, with uncovered meat upon a concrete bench, were off-putting – but not to the flies; the vendor always threw us a wide smile and a happy wave as we passed by. Semi-sweet pastries were sold from a plain worktop with no frills.

'These are delicious; do you have coffee?' Noel loves his coffee and cake.

'One moment please.' The baker pulled out her personal thermos and poured the rich, black liquid into thin plastic cups.

'We can't take your coffee!' I said.

But she was delighted to share her drink while we purchased more sweet treats for just a few cents each!

Food was simple in Bahia, and our diet consisted of rice, vegetables, and chicken; often, small cafés offered a starter of soup and main meal for a couple dollars, including a fruit drink. But hot drinks were an eye opener. Take coffee, for example. One would think that because Ecuador grows coffee, they would produce magnificent beverages. Coffee was served in the form of processed fine granules in a plastic bag (You knew you'd hit the big time when that bag was a Ziploc!). Usually, every person prior to you had dunked their wet spoon into the powder and clogged it into a lumpy quagmire. The waitress dumped the instant-coffee bag on the table before you with a lukewarm cup of water – deliciously revolting! Although I think of Ecuador and coffee in the same sentence, it appears coffee crops are declining and have been for a while. Apparently, Ecuadorian coffee barons found it more profitable to import cheap, low quality coffee from Vietnam than to pay a fair price to local Ecuadorian farmers; a bizarre decision, but greed often creates short-sighted decisions. On the positive side, their hot chocolate is pure creamy delicious heaven. Known as Black Gold, much of Ecuador's fine cocoa beans are used in gourmet products because of their superior taste. Much like wine, chocolate reflects the flavours of the region where cocoa beans are grown and how they are dried and fermented. They tailor-make their chocolate according to the cocoa beans they harvest.

* * *

I thought that we had developed a good resistance to bugs, but on return to Bahia, we suffered severely. For several weeks, we fought various kinds of flu viruses. It turned the experience from enjoyment to a desperate need to leave. But Noel's additional fight with a nasty fever provided a whole gamut of interesting challenges for me.

He spent four hours on a drip in the hospital, but it felt like several days to me.

Cluttered together within the cool, clinical infirmary, a dozen green rooms branched out from the grey corridor. Nurses quietly squeaked past on their soft shoes, as if little hamsters were warming their toes and squealed when trodden on. With most rooms sitting empty, Bahians must be healthy people.

Short on modern technology, the hospital didn't accept credit cards. I needed to organise a cash payment of about one hundred dollars. Noel spent the afternoon in his air-conditioned room with TV and the rehydrating drip. I marched the fifteen minute walk back to the boat in suffocating humidity to collect Noel's credit card to take to the bank to withdraw money.

I rarely use my card, so I had forgotten the number. I was the last one to use Noel's card, and I had put it in a safe place. I tore the boat apart looking for his card. Then I panicked, thinking it must have been stolen. I jumped in the dinghy, trying to ignore the sweat running between my breasts and drove back to shore frantically, nursing our temperamental engine.

This sounds a simple task, but handling our large inflatable dinghy and naughty outboard motor was a battle. Starting an eight horse power outboard takes a fair amount of arm-pulling grunt. The cord needed to be yanked hard with great speed and in one movement to cause the right parts to spin. Arm muscles grew rapidly and lopsidedly. I could only pull with my right arm; my left hand hung on to the motor in an attempt to stop me flicking myself over the side in the violent manoeuvring. More problems arose as the outboard wouldn't idle, so I had to start it with high revs and be quick enough to bring them down as the engine fired into a deafening screech.

It's tricky to pull it all off. You need to be tied on to the boat as the current would carry you half way out to sea if you didn't start the motor on first pull. I never started it on first go, and to whip my arm back and stay balanced with that jerky movement, while the dinghy lurched forwards and backwards due to the taut line, was a feat. After balancing in a standing position while untying the line from the fighting dinghy, you had to keep the motor going until you reached the dinghy dock.

I needed to sit farther forward to help balance the craft, but couldn't leave the throttle; it needed constant nurturing – too fast and the bow shot in the air, and I couldn't see where I was going; too slow and the motor would cut, causing a wild and frantic cord pulling-balancing act to save myself from being swept away out into the ocean.

One day, the workmen in the bar rescued me. Luckily, they spotted me frantically pulling and cussing while floating down stream towards the open sea! The small oars we kept in the dinghy were no match for the current.

If all went accordingly, as I approached the dock, I needed to time the slowing of the engine (and therefore it cutting out) at exactly the right moment – too soon and I didn't make it to land and the whole process commenced all over again; too fast and I rammed the jetty with a red face, bounced off and began the entire process once again! Life wasn't dull.

Safely on shore, using Skype, I cancelled Noel's card. While waiting on the line for confirmation, I fiddled with my small camera case.

'Okay, that's it. I've cancelled Noel's card—' the helpful lady at the bank said.

'Wait! Hang on! I've just found... Blast,' I muttered as the line disconnected. I don't carry a bag or wallet, but I do carry my camera in its case, which is a great place to stash a credit card temporarily!

'Hello, hello again, I was just speaking to someone there, just a moment ago, I cancelled my husband's card, but I've just found it!' I blathered, feeling sure they'd trust me.

'Sorry, we can't reinstate it.'

'But you must, we're in Ecuador, he's in hospital, I have to pay the bill.' Sounding a little desperate, I hoped they would feel sorry for me.

'Sorry, only Noel can reactivate it, just pop him on the phone.'

'I can't, he's in hospital, we are in a small town in Ecuador, there's one place in the entire town that has Internet, and therefore Skype, and that's in a bar!'

The line when silent.

'We can send some emergency money to a bank or via another card.' They listed the help they could provide. They were fabulous. My agitation calmed as I reminded myself that they have these rules to protect people. They were trying to figure out ways to help.

'Thank you, it's good to know my options. Let me think about it, and I'll call you back if I need to.' I said with my mind galloping in four directions. Meanwhile, I pictured the nurse fluffing Noel's pillow.

I trudged back to the hospital.

There was no phone or mobile coverage from his room.

After explaining our dilemma, two orderlies took charge. In a pale green hospital gown and with his bottom peeking out behind, we walked Noel down the road, wheeling his drip contraption alongside.

Of all places, we found an Internet connection in a gym. The computer itself sat on a table on the kerb. Noel flicked an annoyed look at me, embarrassed by his attire.

As he rang the credit card company to reinstate his card, I snapped off half a dozen pictures, much to his irritation, which only made me chuckle more!

'G'day, how can I help you?'

'G'day, it's lovely to hear such a strong Australian accent; you're making me homesick!'

'Okay, how can I help you?' The bank's customer services employee was a bit taken back with Noel's comment.

'My *wife* cancelled my credit card, and I need to reinstate it, please.'

'No problem, we can sort that out for you.' The conversation continued. Noel's pronunciation of 'wife' sounded as though he'd bitten into a lemon; this made me laugh more. It was odd to stand in a dusty street next to half-naked-Noel while he sat at a computer; his accent had strengthened as accents do when you talk to your own.

With Noel back in his air-conditioned room and me filthy dirty, sweaty, and heavy with fatigue, I trundled back to the boat to restore some order.

'G'day.' I tapped on *Volo's* hull to explain to Max and Sandy why we'd not be around for drinks that evening. I laid out the day's events.

'Why the bloody-hell didn't you tell us?' they asked.

'Er....' I felt disconcerted. Why were they annoyed at me?

'We could have lent you the money, run you to and from shore, helped you! You didn't need to do that all yourself.'

I flagged a bit and giggled. I did, at one stage, think of enlisting help, but I was such a fool with losing a card and then finding it; I am fiercely independent, as well. But now I had to get back to the hospital to see if Noel could come home.

'We'll catch up another time,' they said as I spun off in the dinghy.

Completing the preparations to leave Ecuador for Panama fuelled my passion to embark on our next journey.

Noel was improving by the minute, and although the hospital lacked modern technology in payment terms, they were outstanding with tests. Many and varied tests were performed on Noel and sent off for analysis; we received all the results (all clear) on the same day!

At the same time as measuring and ordering sails, coping with Noel's hospital stay and losing things, I did battle with our tax returns. What with Salsa dancing, teaching English, ordering and receiving boat parts from New York and England, having visitors, buying a truck (another idea that didn't develop – thankfully!), my brain was overloaded. I was being pulled in eight different directions at once.

The Spanish wouldn't stick in my head, and I could no longer store or retain vital information such as where I put the putty five minutes ago. From my crammed head, I turfed unimportant information as you would delete old files from a computer. The trouble was some of the important bits were starting to go missing, too. *If my brain deleted the good stuff, what was filling the void?* Thoughts such as these helpfully popped into my head at 3 a.m. when my brain box decided it didn't want to lie idle any longer.

Perhaps useless thoughts were filling the void!

People asked me the simplest questions, and I'd stare at them blankly, highlighting the empty space between my ears.

Am I heading for a mid-life crisis? My brain couldn't perform the gymnastics it used to.

But all those thoughts would be erased soon, as we hurtled towards devastating news.

8

Panama's Secrets

Ecuador was an opulent feast of events from visitors to fevers, and *Pyewacket* needed constant attention. Her sails were tired and thin.

We were planning to traverse the great Pacific Ocean; torn sails during the voyage would leave us stranded and at the mercy of currents. We couldn't carry enough diesel to motor several thousand nautical miles.

With reluctance and creating a huge blip on the bank statements, we ordered new sails from Hong Kong. In Ecuador, the quoted import duty of between 45-100 percent (depending on the genre of the item and the mood of the customs officer) inspired us to take delivery in Panama.

We did take delivery of other equipment in Ecuador, though, via the great camaraderie of cruisers. Jill and Doug on board *Compañera* (Spanish for 'partner or companion.') offered to transport goods back to the boats. They were flying home to Maryland, and then their parents' home to collect the variety of boat equipment for many cruisers within the anchorage. The Internet, the USA address, and the offer of help had been gratefully utilised.

Jill introduced herself to me as an author, which immediately caught my attention, but her extraordinary subject matter made me sit up straight. Jill and Doug spent every summer for fifteen years – in all weather – on the water, not on a sailboat, but on a fifteen foot Kevlar rowing shell. The hull one-eighth of an inch thick! They rowed around Norway, down the west coast of Greenland, around Spitsbergen, and much more, logging over twenty thousand miles. Detailing their courageous trip in *Rowing to Latitude: Journeys Along the Arctic's Edge*, their lives do not start and end on the water. They are both avalanche experts and co-directors of the Alaska Mountain Safety Center.

Although our interlude was brief and helpful, meeting people such as these enriched our experience.

* * *

We aimed to leave December 10; we'd spent a total of eight months in Ecuador. Noel had made a complete recovery, and we turned our attention to departure planning.

The bridge building stirred up a lot of dirt. Decks and lines needed constant washing. The muddy grey river runs fast and is never clean. On our hull, weed and barnacles grew faster than the national debt.

Shopkeepers, café owners, and locals welcomed us with open arms and made our life of goodbyes that much harder, but an unexpected and final farewell waited for us around the corner.

In the meantime, we moved *Pyewacket* to a mooring in readiness for our voyage. Hauling in our three anchors, we found a serious two-day problem.

'My goodness, would you look at that.' Noel put his hands on his hips and rubbed his forehead.

Our lines were festooned with sharp, tenacious barnacles. The rope's diameter grew to twice the size.

We hauled the sharp, mucky lines on board, moved to a mooring and discussed the dilemma.

'I think we need hammers and chisels,' Noel said.

'Yup, bring the paint scrapers and a broom, too.'

It took two long, exhausting days to chip the alien shells and their gooey residents off our lines. The lines would never be the same again; tiny shards were embedded in the strands, gradually cutting through and fraying fibres, weakening the rope's breaking strain.

* * *

Chatting to my dad in the UK, I said, 'We plan to sail to Panama to collect our new sails.'

'You talk about it as though you're popping to the supermarket,' he said with amusement. With only 560 nautical miles to traverse, we thought the journey a breeze. But the trip grew to epic proportions, even before we started.

Farewells are a continuous part of the cruising life and can pitch and roll the equilibrium sailing bestows. Anchored for eight months in Bahia de Caraquez, Ecuador, we had collected many friends; most we would never see again. But tipping the scales into a whole new level of sadness was the news of the unexpected death of a local lady, new cruiser, and my friend.

Margarita had fallen in love with Phil, a sailor from America. Over the years, they planned numerous adventures, starting in the Perlas Islands, sailing out of Bahia two weeks before us.

Margarita valiantly tried to teach me Spanish, and I attempted to teach her English.

'No, don't ask the shopkeeper if they have any eggs in Spanish,' Margarita would clutch her stomach, trying to hold in the giggles.

'Why not? I asked. A warm blush crept along my cheeks.

'It's like asking for balls, men's.... you know!' With that, she squawked with laughter. No wonder the shop keeper in our favourite little shop always grinned at me.

I'm not entirely sure what I asked for, but I understood it to be inappropriate.

Margarita and I exercised together by walking each morning; she invited me in to her home, where I met her loving family, and she taught me how to cook muesli, which I now call *Margarita Muesli*.

Margarita had this magnetism and a charming charisma that was the pathway for us to form an immediate deep bond. I don't click with many people, but I sensed I could trust Margarita instantly.

We were two women with a lust for life and two kindred spirits. We shared much laughter. I couldn't wait for our planned girl-shopping excursion in Panama.

The Perlas Islands are a small clutch of atolls south of Panama. This was Margarita's first time away from Ecuador. Free of the grey skies and dirty river, Perlas Islands revel in sparkling, clear water.

Here, she played off the stern of Phil's boat, languishing in the translucent, crisp briny. While swimming and relishing in her new life, without obvious reason or sound, she left this world.

The news reached us the day before we left Bahia; the emotions emptied our stomachs, leaving a void that hurt.

Much of the town stared vacantly into space for the following days. Margarita was loved by everyone in the small community.

The autopsy revealed a cerebral aneurism.

Our tearful goodbyes in this small, close-knit town left us red-eyed and exhausted.

We couldn't comprehend the emotions, trauma, and explanations that Phil endured, transporting her body into Panama and all that goes with a devastating tragedy in a foreign port. Fortunately, Tripp, the marina proprietor and Phil's friend, dropped everything and flew to his aid.

Phil remains our friend and has managed to pull himself from the black hole that follows losing someone so special. He misses her every day.

'For what it's worth,' Phil said, 'I did tell her that I would love to spend the rest of my life with her, which to me was a declaration of commitment stronger than any civil or religious institution could establish.'

* * *

Amid a jumbled blend of the sadness of a loss, excitement for a new journey, and fear of what may happen at sea, the following three days we were driven onwards by full billowing canvas.

Life's like that; when I've suffered the loss of someone dear to me, I'm always astounded that the world carries on as per normal. Why doesn't the universe acknowledge the devastation in our hearts? Everything and everyone should stop momentarily out of respect and acknowledgement. But reality is different; the harsh world continues on, and we all have to deal with our pockets of misery. *Pyewacket* confirmed this point as she sliced through the water.

Our next test was hovering on the horizon, luckily, we had slept well.

As we entered the Gulf of Panama, the traffic thickened to an extent that made us feel as though we were playing Space Invaders on the radar screen at night.

Within fifty nautical miles of Las Perlas, one of the great processions of squalls did not dissipate; instead, it folded itself into a galloping gale. Thirty-five knot winds raised a heavy sea which beat us back. Squalls exploded amid the flurry, creating noticeable forty-four knot gusts, and reconfirmed our contempt for the ITCZ that separates the north and south hemisphere trade winds.

This area was shadowed by determined and eternally infuriating squalls; relentless armies of clouds marched across the sky, accompanied by heavy rain. *A 747 must be landing on our decks.* Visibility often became zero within the busy highway of vessels arriving to and departing from the Panama Canal. It was a tense time and compounded our dislike of this area and passion for radar.

On *Mariah,* we did not have radar; she was a simple boat, and we were quietly smug with our lack of gadgets and suffering from fewer equipment break-downs. Now, through gaining radar equipment that came with *Pyewacket,* we couldn't imagine sailing without one!

Blending into our frustration of sailing so close to Panama City without reaching the port, maddening weather, and emotional exhaustion, our lifeline to the outside world decided to lock itself into an unusable state.

'What do you think it means?'

'I dunno, but I've read the manual twice, and it doesn't give a hint,' Noel said.

'I'll have a read,' I offered, while stabbing at the buttons. 'Nothing works.'

Our SSB radio (long range), on which we speak to friends, partake in radio networks (or radio schedules), and receive weather updates, had started to flash 'UNLOCK.' Of a vintage similar to me, we were quietly satisfied with the SEA222 unit; it had worked fine until now.

Both manuals for the radio provided no clue as to its choice of words on the screen. We could not receive or transmit.

For the first time ever, we had no access to weather while underway and were slamming about in aggressive winds, wondering what would happen next.

* * *

'Can we go over the plan?'

'Yup,' I called back. 'Kettle's almost boiled.'

'Here's where we are: we can hove-to and wait it out, turn back, or head west.' Noel pulled another chart to the top of the pile with more detail of western Panama.

As we scanned the charts, we crunched into another wave, and every item below decks that wasn't in a tight space jumped two feet in the air.

'Let's get out of here. I don't want to wait it out, and I'd rather not turn back. Why don't we try west? The anchor sites look good,' I said.

'I'm happy with that. It makes sense.'

After the mid ocean meeting, we turned *Pyewacket's* bow west and endured twenty-four hours of boisterous beam on sailing.

At midnight, I eased her behind the headland of Punta Mariato, west of Punta Mala, and could not decide whether the wind had suddenly died because of the protection or if it happened to blow itself out at that point. Either way, I didn't care; we were safe.

The sea smoothed. Instead of heaving decks and great fountains of surf from our stem, the bow wave now chuckled contentedly. The twelve knot winds blew us silently into what felt like Heaven.

'What's going on?' With bleary eyes, Noel staggered up into the cockpit. I had let him sleep as the sailing had turned pleasant. I savoured much of the night alone.

'What have you done? I can't believe we're in the same ocean!'

Usually, if Noel comes off-watch on his own accord, it's to work together in bad weather. This time, he'd woken to perfect sailing. The discord he fell asleep in was a distant memory.

At 3 a.m., we puttered into an anchorage, the radar picking up tiny fishing buoys that flashed a welcome.

Weariness engulfed us both, and after anchoring and the traditional beer at 5 a.m., we slipped into blissful slumber.

Six years prior, we had traversed the Panama Canal on our last boat, *Mariah II*. At that time, we had given no thought to the Perlas Archipelago or other areas of mainland Panama; our sights were firmly fixed on the Pacific Islands.

On board *Pyewacket II* in April 2010, we sailed right past from Acapulco to Isla del Coco, and then on to Ecuador, to avoid impending hurricane season. By Mother Nature's hand, once again, we missed the Perlas and found ourselves in a place we had never considered cruising before.

Despite frantic button pushing, knob twiddling, and a mixed bag of kind and nasty words, the SSB radio stayed resolutely locked.

We were in the protection of Ensenada Naranjo and had no means of communication and no idea whether the gale persisted or had died out. That led us to meandering around islands and up rivers for four blissfully silent days. *The world must have ended.* We did not spy another living soul – not even bugs or garbage. We only spotted a party of enormous dolphins, who twisted in our gurgling bow wave. Surrounded by mangroves at night, we slept in the cockpit, watching Orion's Belt and the Southern Cross carve arcs in the heavens, while the soft breeze stroked our skin. The quiet pressed on our ears, causing us to whisper. Clothes were unnecessary, and even up the narrow river to Boca de la Trinidad, the water remained clear. It was balm to our battle weary souls, both mentally and physically.

We had left Bahia the same time as *Dana*. Lena and Henrique hail from Denmark and had quickly become people we liked spending time with. They built *Dana* themselves many years before; she's a Ferro-cement construction and kept in immaculate condition inside and out. Like my Dutch friend 'Tash, who we did much travelling with (and her partner Den on board *SV Frodo*), Lena is a strong woman and says what she thinks. I gravitate towards such women; they make sense. You know where you stand, and it gives me something to aspire to – although all my female friends agree I am just as strong… maybe outwardly; inwardly, I'm not so sure.

We had VHF radio contact for the first day, and luckily, the SSB had locked while we were still in VHF range, so we had let them know we'd be out of touch on the SSB. They, too, were heading for the Perlas, and we planned to spend Christmas together, greedily anticipating a Danish Christmas on December twenty-fourth and our traditional Christmas on the twenty-fifth. Wrapped around these events was Noel's birthday on December twenty-first and mine (heralding a new decade) on the December twenty-sixth.

After four blissful days of tangible silence, broken only by the odd, hidden keening of birds and no weather report, we left western Panama, bound east for the Perlas and Balboa. Northerlies do build in the Gulf of Panama this time of year, gaining strength as December matures.

In the lee of the land for the first twelve hours, we enjoyed riding on currents, a fifteen knot breeze, and a whopping eight and nine knots of speed over the ground. During the moonlit night, the wind eased, and we motored, fearful of being caught in the Gulf again.

In the final twelve hours of the thirty-six hour passage, we encountered northeast head winds, but with a feeble fight of ten knots. Often though, we saw patches of meringue-tipped water as it jumped vertically when swirling currents opposed the wind. We persisted with the motor, shoulders hunched, watchful of the wind speed.

What should have been four easy days to Las Perlas had been fraught with emotions and delays. Ten days after departing Ecuador, we finally made our destination. *Dana* was not at our agreed meeting anchorage. We had no idea what tactics they deployed.

'I wonder if they hoved-to?' I said, looking forward to their company and worrying about them slightly, even though *Dana* was a marvellously strong boat and they had endured far rougher sailing previously.

'They might've run with it as we did,' Noel suggested. 'Maybe they sought shelter at eastern Panama?'

They could have headed back to Bahia, as well.

Periodically, we tried our VHF to locate Henrique and Lena.

After a refreshing swim and a good night's rest, we agreed to up anchor and find more protection than Isle de Rey. Whilst it wasn't untenable, a slight roll meandered across the water; we wanted complete protection and, therefore, complete rest.

As we discussed the following day's activities of Noel's birthday, our VHF radio, which had been left on channel sixteen, jumped into life.

'*Pyewacket, Pyewacket*, this is *Dana, Dana*.' Lena's voice came booming through the radio.

'*Dana, Dana*, this is *Pyewacket*, go to channel seven-two, seventy two.' I squealed with joy at hearing Lena's voice.

'Going up.' Radio protocol dictates using channel sixteen as a distress and/or calling frequency; it is etiquette and vitally important to switch to a working channel as soon as hooking up.

What a welcome and joy to hear our friends were safe around the corner in a tranquil anchorage.

We continued chatting on the new channel.

'We've been in western Panama for a few days. What did you guys do?'

'We hoved-to; it wasn't much fun, but we managed to wait it out. It was okay, really.' The Danish, like the Dutch, are a tough race and shrug off the most trying times.

'We're pulling up anchor now. See you in a few hours. Put the wine on ice!'

Spurred on by the thought of a voyage debrief over chilled wine and good food with kindred folk, we upped anchor to move fifteen nautical miles to the west side of Isla de Caña.

Here, we shared tactics. *Dana* had hoved-to, but had been pushed many miles back south east, arriving at the Perlas two days before us. The gale had persisted for four days, giving us satisfaction in our decision to head so far west and hide out.

Sparkling water, all round protection, and sandy beaches; only the squawk from wildlife, athletic fish splashing, and the muffled rumble of distant surf broke the hush. Fresh water trickling down ancient rocks created mini pools at low tide, granting us a serene, shady setting to catch up on laundry, with drying bushes thoughtfully growing nearby.

But what the books and other cruisers do not mention about Las Perlas is the bugs. Small mosquitoes and sandflies would squeeze through gaps in the nets on board. The next line of defence was mozzie coils; they slowed down the critters a little. Spraying the nets with repellent eased their feasting for a few hours. I am convinced they shut their eyes and held their noses to fly through the smoke. Announcing their arrival by dive bombing uncovered skin, they turned me into some sort of self-slapping lunatic. One still night, I suffered so many bites I could have arranged several join-the-dots competitions on my legs. Waking during fitful nights to find I had torn at my limbs until they bled took the polish off the place. Admittedly, other, more open anchorages had fewer bugs; a good example was the west side of Isla del Espiritu Santo.

The other eye opener not mentioned in discussions or prose is the rubbish. In the immediate vicinity of the popular anchorages, locals clean up plastic into piles to bury under the foliage, leaving the three-sixty degree view at anchor pristine. However, hop in the dinghy and undertake a little adventure to windward beaches, and the piles of garbage are stunning. We could only assume that the currents create eddies that suck in the rubbish from the Pacific, and the string of islands act as a sieve, collecting great chunks of one of humanities great embarrassments, of which we are all to blame.

Compromise appears in every avenue: in sailing, living on board, and visiting 'ideal' destinations. We had a good time at the Perlas with protected anchorages, fascinating wildlife, and a tranquil rest. The tenacious bugs were like nothing we had ever experienced before and the amount of garbage was something we'd not witnessed since the South China Sea (while on *Mariah*). The Danish Christmas on board *Dana* with Lena and Henrique was delicious, fun, and excruciatingly hot – not a breath of breeze eased the pain. My birthday, at a more exposed, but suitably protected anchorage, was in twenty-five knots of wind and driving rain, making dinner a task to get over with before separating to our respective anchor watch duties. Still, much laughter carried off into the squalls.

This is the reality of cruising. We are truly blessed with a life full of adventure, fun, and love. Within all aspects of sailing and escapade, both joy and fear reside in the same neighbourhood.

Reality is the result. Witnessing fascinating wildlife means enduring hungry bugs.

The loss of someone who was becoming a good friend helped me exchange depressing thoughts of farewelling my thirties to a joy of being alive and able to experience places others cannot.

We were about to return to Balboa, the scene of our successful Canal passage on board *Mariah* with Noel's brother, Colin, and my dad, Roy, six years ago. We made lifelong friends there. We wondered what was in store for us this time.

9

Sweet Stash and Not So Sweet Travel

Three important tasks occur on board *Pyewacket*.

Firstly, Noel hides a stash of chocolate in the workshop – concealed to curtail my usual 'see-food' diet. It'd been close, but so far, I'd not resorted to rummaging. If I develop a desperate stare in my eyes, he had the immediate answer for my instant mollification.

Secondly, prior to a voyage, I buy a variety of small sweets, sort them into petite portions, and squirrel them away in corners of cupboards and places of sporadic scrutiny. While sailing the lonely expanse of sea, we sometimes stumble upon these unexpected treats.

Thirdly, and most importantly, I sort through the bewildering array of scrumptious treats in foreign ports. Several years ago. we bought chocolate in Eritrea; it tasted like cardboard, and for the first time in my life, I threw out chocolate! Here in Panama, the local branded confectionery is cheap, but like foreign, tinned food, before stockpiling, we sample a selection. With chocolate, I'd volunteer for this job again; it's something I feel I *have* to do.

Despite these odd challenges and aside from my eating enjoyment, luck accompanied us most of the way. I believe I have a guardian angel; I like to think she is my great grandmother, Daisy, a remarkable woman who died a few months before her hundredth birthday.

Living to be a grand age is becoming more common these days; however, Nana kept her smarts right up to the end. In her nineties, she taught me an easier way to tackle long-division sums. I'd come home from school frustrated with my lack of understanding, and Nana sorted me out. She listened to my guitar playing and singing with a small smile and nod; my tuneless notes must surely have hurt her ears. Anyway, that's who I like to imagine does little things to guide us safely through life. I'm positive she's prevented major injuries on board, leaving us with only minor purple bruises and tender bumps.

When at sea, injury is a big concern; the worst we have suffered in our fourteen years of cruising is seasickness, vivid bruising, fever, and food poisoning. Toe damage is a given fact; we are barefooted most of the time, and inevitably, a block, rope, or track will jump into the path of our feet and snag a toe. I am amazed at how hardy our little feet appendages are, especially the wee one at the end. It can take a hammering. You can ram the toe into a metal structure, wrenching it to ninety degrees, and it pings back, pink and throbbing but pert again and ready to go.

There have been a few odd injuries, too. I pulled on my wetsuit one day, and the zip at the back flipped up and bit my right buttock. Goodness knows how it happened, but a big purple welt, flap of skin, and yellow bruising kept me sitting on my left buttock for several days.

Bruising is part and parcel of life when cruising; I am better at it than Noel. Deep, vibrant purples appear days later after the offending item has attacked me, and by that time, I have forgotten how it happened. Bruises also appear for no reason. Swearing at inanimate objects is cathartic. When you've bounced your head off that shelf for the fourth time in a week, it relieves the pent up anger born from idiocy (don't you realise it's been there for years!). A quick slap at the shelf and a few impressive expletives goes a long way to ease the pain. I'd taken to blaming the boat. 'It jumped out and bit me,' I'd whine. Stupid, really, but I felt so clumsy to keep accumulating knocks from objects that simply don't move. I felt better if I could blame something else, rather than face my lack of spatial awareness!

We weren't stupid as far as our sails were concerned. Having ordered them in Ecuador, we eagerly awaited delivery in Panama.

Panama is the cross-roads for cruisers. A positive hive of activity buzzes around the marina, moorings, and anchor sites. Beginnings and endings meet here – some cruisers are about to meet their first ocean, while others are listing their boat for sale. It's a gateway to adventure in the Pacific Ocean, or the Caribbean Sea.

Charts, pilot books, and equipment were bartered and traded over the radio; information was sought and swapped during the weekly pizza and beer night on shore. Savvy owners of second-hand shops sourced equipment. The morning radio sched was perfect for off-loading gear or finding exactly what you were searching for.

'We have the charts for the Galapagos.' These were offered as they were heading east and had already been there. 'We'll exchange them for five coconuts.' Officially, we were not allowed to buy and sell items for dollars, but we were allowed to exchange gear. The proper negotiations on the price would occur privately and not on public radio.

It was an ideal place to take delivery of our sails, but we still had to check in first.

We chose the nearest anchor site. As we approached, I dropped our sails, and I promptly put my hand straight through our mainsail.

'Well that was good timing!' I explained to Noel what happened on deck. He'd been spot on with us needing new sails. If that damage had occurred miles from land, it would have caused problems. The mainsail provides most of the 'drive' on sailing boats. It is imperative to have good sails over long distances. We carried strips of sail patches we could stick and sew, but if the sails were that bad – and putting your hand through it gives the game away – the only solution is new ones.

We arrived on New Year's Eve, anchored on the south side of the causeway, a short bus ride from town, dropped the dinghy in the water, and drove to shore clutching our paperwork. We knew the rules had changed since our last visit, but the conflicting information drove us nuts. The first change was limited anchorage space and that we had to pay the Causeway marina thirty-five dollars per week to tie our dinghy on their dock.

The new immigration office sat near the town marina, and we waited outside a closed door. A creased, olive-skinned, but sprightly, gentleman offered me a cracked plastic seat. Around the row of doors that lined a concrete walkway sat six or so workmen who quietly sipped beer from a battered cool box, enjoying knock-off time. The portable radio sang songs of hope, loud enough to fill the quiet moments, but not obtrusive. The makeshift veranda over-looked the boats in the marina. We smiled at each other, and eventually with broken English and Noel's little Spanish, he explained what we were doing there.

'Here, today, arrived?' the youngest of the old group asked.

'Yes, we've just arrived. Is it bad that we are here on New Year's Eve?' Noel tried to keep to simple English words.

'No, it's good. Please have a beer!' With that, they passed us a cold beer each and turned up the music.

Everyone relaxed and smiled, and a groovy tune came on.

'Come on, dance?' Old crinkly offered me his hand and showed me up with his dance moves. He left me for dead with his swaying hips and funky beat. His mates cheered us on as we danced outside the officials' office!

'Relax, relax,' my new dancing partner said. 'Feel the music.' We finished our show to the accompaniment of a round of applause.

After two beers each and much fun, the officials opened their doors and checked us in. But permitting us a stay of seventy two hours only, we were required to visit a different office in January to gain permission to stay longer. We needed a mariner's visa, not a tourist visa.

A few days later, *Dana* anchored near us, and we arranged to locate the second office together. We are reasonably adept at navigating strange environments, but the day we searched for the right office, we felt inept. Hours of traipsing around hot streets, misinformation, closed offices, and re-directions to out-of-the-way places left us all cranky and tired. When the distance became too far to walk, we jumped into taxis; the drivers became lost and couldn't help. Finally, we found the right office, but we had to persuade the officials to grant us permission to stay and issue the correct paperwork. They usually deal with commercial vessels, and recreational vessels were a burden and irritating for them. Noel was on the verge of giving up, but I persisted, as I knew we needed our Zarpe, and we wouldn't have been granted that if we stayed longer with the wrong paperwork. *What if they impounded our boat?* They liked making an example out of people!

* * *

The mail receiving depot was a short ride away from where we were anchored. Each morning, we'd switch on the radio to listen to the daily announcement about incoming parcels.

'I'm a bit tetchy about delivery,' Noel admitted. 'They could hold the sails to ransom, too.'

Ecuadorian officials had caused sailing friends of ours considerable stress by not releasing their delivery to them. They demanded inordinate amounts of money to hand over the goods; solicitors became involved, and ultimately, they had to forget that large, expensive packet of sails and start again.

In Panama, the delivery and importation of large items were handled by a company that specifically deals with foreign objects, but we still had to collect the large boxes of sails from customs.

Upon arrival, with nervous excitement, we puttered over to the depot and handed over one of the numerous pieces of paper relating to the order and delivery of the sails.

'Here's your delivery now,' the receptionist said, pointing outside to where the bulky guy ferried over the boxes. 'That's twenty dollars, please, ten for each box.'

While we paused to translate the Spanish, she made an eating gesture. '*Comer, comer!*'

'Ah! I get it, *comer*, to eat, that's what the extra money's for.'

'Eh,' I uttered at Noel's light-bulb moment. 'What do you mean?'

'It's their word for 'tip' or a 'bribe,' or how they earn a semi-decent wage. She's trying to tell us they will be able to afford to eat if we pay the charge.'

I've never seen Noel whip his wallet out so quickly and hand over the cash. The lady stamped the delivery receipt and left our boxes for us to carry back. We loaded them onto our trolley, which creaked beneath the weight, and trotted back to the dinghy.

'Quick, hurry up – I want to get out of here,' Noel said, glancing back towards the depot. 'I can't believe we got off so lightly. They could have charged us fifty, a hundred, two hundred, and I would have paid it!'

Back on board, we hoisted up the large boxes and stood on deck, making a production out of the gleaming white canvas. We'd never had a wardrobe of new sails before.

The time in Panama flew, as well as the new sails; we purchased a second hand SSB radio to replace the dead one on board. We also bought masses of navy blue canvas and a sewing machine. We spent many days making a huge cover for the entire boat; the Pacific islands could become scorching hot, and these tarps would help cool the boat and maintain our sanity.

As well as an ideal location to prepare for ocean miles, Panama is a place of friendship – for both new friendships and picking up the threads of others. We were both saddened and delighted to see Phil, from Ecuador, once again. The heart-wrenching story of Margarita passing away was still so raw; only a few weeks had passed. Nothing we could say would make things better; wrapping our arms around Phil for a brief moment was all we could do.

By chance, Noel had met Amy from *SV Shango*. Our time in Panama was spent dashing from one shop to the next between boat preparations and throwing vast amounts of cash at everyone we met.

During a three hour bus ride while searching for parts, Noel listened in to a conversation by two cruisers. Amy sat next to an older guy, talking boats. Noel became caught up in the chatter and shuffled next to Amy, passing the time discussing all things nautical.

'It was like we had known each other for some time,' Noel said when he was back on board. 'Amy was so easy to talk to. I hope we see them along the way.'

Characters from all walks of life met here, but it was a sobering moment meeting the brawny skipper of a beaten-up Russian sailboat.

'I tried to sail down to Easter Island,' the whiskered captain said. 'You can see the state of my boat.' He had puttered over to us on his dinghy to say hello, and we all turned to view his vessel anchored nearby. Shredded sails hung morosely, the stainless steel dinghy davits bent and twisted at odd angles like obscure artwork; the metal frame of his dodger contorted and bowed in all the wrong places; and the canvas had torn. 'It's a lot rougher down there than most people think,' he said. 'I had to turn back to Panama to make repairs. Take great care and gain as much easting as you can on your way south.'

Noel and I were silent while we digested the images. Large overhangs, like davits, that support a heavy dinghy on the stern could become a problem. Powerful, following-seas can damage this equipment and potentially cause structural damage to the boat. The heavy weight of the small boat, up high, alters the trim and stability of the sailboat. We've heard plenty of horror stories about protruding equipment causing problems that have snowballed into disasters – in the ocean, we are so terribly alone.

Are we doing the right thing? Can Pyewacket handle those seas; can I?

In a curious way, this knowledge made the challenge more appealing. Not to prove ourselves to those who believed we couldn't do it, but to verify our abilities for us and to confirm we made the right decision, test and demonstrate our preparations and work on board, and validate our research and knowledge.

***

With the bright white canvas aloft (we could have stared in a laundry soap advertisement), we bade farewell to Panama. Both times, our visits had been long, expensive, but satisfying. We know the city fairly well, and it held an intriguing appeal. Full of kindred spirits and all we needed to complete the next leg of our voyage, we felt an affinity with the place. We were lucky enough to visit twice; this was the final farewell.

For a few days, we revisited Las Perlas Archipelago once again. This presented us the opportunity to clean *Pyewacket's* bottom to ensure she slipped through the water during the long ocean miles. We'd purchased a dive hookah in Newport Beach, and already, it had paid us back tenfold. Keeping the growth from building up on the hull is an important job. At anchor, the weed and barnacles take hold and can slow the boat to such an extent you can lose all steerage! The dive hookah is a petrol (or electric) powered airline diving system that allows you to dive without tanks. With *Pyewacket's* two metre draft, we could no longer do the job with a snorkel.

Between final preparations, Amy and Roger invited us on board *SV Shango* for a pleasant evening of soft sunsets and sailing stories. We would be crossing to Galapagos at a similar time. We were anchored near each other, but Roger still gallantly picked us up in their dinghy and drove us home, too. We'd already stowed our dinghy away – we appreciated not having to swim, especially as a creature from the deep triggered our hearts to jump in fright.

On the return trip beneath moonlight, as Roger glided beside *Pyewacket*, a large animal kicked up a stir making us all jump.

'What on earth was that?' I said with my heart stampeding around my chest.

'I dunno, but it was big,' Roger said, his eyes scanning the water.

'Right, bye then!' In true friendship style, Noel and I vaulted onto *Pyewacket*. 'And good luck!' We laughed, but we all kept one eye on the water.

We still don't know what creature lurked – a dolphin perhaps? It was big and had a good game scaring the pants off us all!

The following day, a puff of air supplied a hint of a continued soft breeze, and a few boats lifted their anchors in anticipation of a sail.

I felt fortunate to visit Panama twice, but I was truly privileged to see the Galapagos Islands again. We were in company with a few American boats. Leaving at roughly the same time, we were able to enjoy radio scheds each day to compare progress and weather.

Dana had stayed at Panama longer, sourcing different equipment and managing different repairs; we all hoped we'd get together again in the Gambiers.

Noel and I were adept at holding radio scheds. We'd been the Sched Co-ordinator on many occasions when on board *Mariah*. Noel had organised a daily chat with the small fleet of boats sailing from Panama to Galapagos. He also arranged a Musketeers Rally Passage Awards nearing the end of the trip. Many boat rallies are organised all over the world for different stretches of water. They are not normally done on a whim in mid-ocean, but inspiration hit Noel, and he created a bit of fun to relieve looking at the same vista day in, day out.

SV Reality won line honours and a case of beer, which they had to forfeit for not rounding the windward mark (Isla Malpelo). *Shango* won handicap honours and a bottle of scotch, which they forfeited for admitting on the radio that they had turned their engine on during the trip. An Australian boat that joined the sched was awarded the bravery award for admitting, on the radio, to being from Melbourne! Of course, Noel awarded himself the best husband honours! But one way or another, we were all proud; we'd all sailed to a unique and inspiring island; more than that, we'd all had a successful voyage, as well as five easy days sailing in great company.

The last night before landfall, we watched the tricolour lights of *Shango* sway at the top of their mast; I know they were watching ours. As the night swept away, we all embarked on a photography frenzy, snapping shots of each other as we sailed alongside. It's not often you have these opportunities. *I'm sure Roger and Amy have slowed their progress for us.* My thoughts proved right when we put the cameras away as hard rock of the island approached and vigilance became the priority. *Shango* streamed off in front.

At a few hundred American dollars, the cost of visiting Galapagos a few years ago was hard enough to swallow. Now, it cost a thousand and more for larger boats. We had toured around the island for three weeks a few years ago, and as wonderful as Galapagos is, this time, we only wanted to rest, replenish, and set sail towards our next destination – our minds were on Easter Island and the fickle ocean at those latitudes.

We asked for, and were granted, a twenty-four hour stay.

The temperature doesn't peak, and trough here, the Humboldt Current helps it remain a steady twenty-three degrees centigrade – a pleasant condition to complete several jobs in a short time. I topped up with a few fresh items from the makeshift market. The locals hike the prices for foreigners, but now I could negotiate with ease.

In town, I noticed the tourism growing, the locals considerably diluted with photo-snapping visitors.

You don't have to be a biologist to appreciate the showcase of biodiversity on Galapagos. We weren't excursion hunting this time, but sailing back here for the second time reminded me of the life-changing incidents and wonderful memories we collected before.

I had physically played with the sea lions – an experience that still overwhelms me today when I think back. Blue-footed booby's posed for pictures; their vivid feet framed by the moon-rock back drop, devoid of vegetation.

We ate where the locals dined, where a set meal was served for a couple of dollars, a few streets back from the tourist burger joints; a simple meal no choices to detract you from the unique surroundings.

Galapagos is the opening scene of the great extravaganza that is the Pacific Ocean. Most boats sail from Panama to these islands before experiencing the vast, lonely ocean and exotic, remote islands. An international blend of kindred spirits meet, mix, arrange radio scheds, and create a contagious buzz of excitement – we were all explorers and voyagers and all nervous, excited, and carrying the weight of responsibility to achieve a safe passage.

We managed to have lunch with sailing friends, refuel, and take water on board. We should have left that evening, but under the cover of a blushing dawn, we left the next day.

We bade farewell to the group we had sailed to Galapagos with; we were becoming friendly with these people – particularly Amy and Roger on board *SV Shango*, a forty-foot Pacific Seacraft. The kind couple had invited us for drinks in Las Perlas, so we'd sailed in company to Galapagos. We spoke often and sensed the stirrings of a deep, rewarding friendship. However, they were on their first Pacific crossing and would visit the islands we had sailed to before on *Mariah*. We weren't destined to spend more time with them at this point, but we still keep in touch via email; who knows where our paths will cross again? In June 2015, they completed their circumnavigation.

＊＊＊

Easter Island is the world's most isolated, inhabited island and boasts many intriguing names. The moniker 'Easter Island' was bestowed upon it by the first recorded European visitor. Officially, the Spanish name is Isla de Pascua, which also means 'Easter Island.' My favourite is Te pito o te henua, meaning 'The Navel of the World.' Rapa Nui is the name used on our charts and is most commonly used on the island.

The three weeks and two thousand nautical miles from Galapagos to Rapa Nui were anything but easy: twenty to thirty knots of wind and forward of the beam for fifteen days followed six days of almost becalming stillness.

During the endless days, we chatted to different boats on the radio, swapping positions, conditions, and general welfare. *SV Bobbie*, with Emily on board, was experiencing difficulties.

'The forestay has snapped, and there's a leak,' she gasped, stopping for breath. 'I don't know where it is.'

Pyewacket led the bouncing troupe. Wrapped within the drama were an international cast of vessels from Canada and America, namely *Silas Crosby, Ainia,* and *Curare*.

'*Pyewacket* is a fair distance in front. I think they should push on and see what help Easter Island can offer. We're happy to stay close to Emily.'

'Us too.'

'And us.' *Silas Crosby, Ainia,* and *Curare* would keep within sight of *Bobbie* and Emily and be on hand if the situation became desperate.

The strong, predicted south easterlies had materialised. We had all laboured hard to battle some way east to compensate for the inevitable south easterlies that would blow us in a westerly direction. Emily was farther west and fighting to work her way east, testing her rigging to breaking point.

Sailing to remote locations, in vigorous winds, and with precious little diesel, is a great recipe to miss landfall. If you are blown past an island, backtracking is not as simple as turning around. Wind, waves, and swell can make it impossible to make way forward – forethought and planning is prerequisite for good seamanship and navigation.

At this stage, *Bobbie's* water intake was increasing; the enormous rolling swells topped with waves fed the doubt to the type of the assistance that could be offered. But if the leak could not be fixed, boats were nearby for a rescue.

At times, Emily's voice would break, her anxiousness heartbreakingly carried along by radio waves.

'Sorry, team, we're changing course directly for Easter Island.' Amid angry weather, *Ainia's* inner forestay had snapped, confirming the combative component of sailing these latitudes. The rest of the team valiantly made way for *Bobbie*.

In the meantime, the leak on board Emily's boat was blindly analysed by radio, enabling her to courageously repair the identified stuffing box problem in unkind seas. Emily was out of immediate trouble and found comfort within the company of *Silas Crosby* and *Curare*.

To gain better easting (i.e. to make way in a south east direction), and therefore achieve a better angle once we had gained a more southerly position, meant bashing into the swell, the waves, and the wind. The briny water slammed into the hull, creating a jerky, violent motion that caused tea to jump from our cups and books to leap off the shelf. Our movements had to be carefully choreographed. Traversing the companionway stairs, moving forward from saloon to bathroom, at every step, we clasped handholds; a smooth moment would be rudely interrupted with a slam, bump, and – what felt like – *Pyewacket* leaping vertically in the air with disdain. Lethargy crowded our minds and muscles; exhaustion nipped at our extremities. We had to stay alert. Sleeping in the bunks became a struggle; the rolling, lurching, and hull-shudders crudely yanked us awake.

'I hate this!' I said to no one in particular while cooking in the galley, trying to catch sliding plates, tame clanging utensils, and pin down skating food.

Pyewacket tilted at a forty-five degree angle; the gimballed cooker slanted away from me. My muscles bunched as I tried to counter-balance the lean to stay upright. This caused the galley and my body to be at odds – angle wise, everything was out of kilter.

While the cupboards leaned one way, I leaned the other to stay up right – a bizarre fair ground ride complete with tummy somersaults and threatening seasickness.

'Whose bloody stupid idea was this?' I continued muttering. 'I said I didn't want to go sailing again.' I stopped short. I had said no such thing, but that annoyed me more. I needed to blame someone, and right then, it was all Noel's fault.

'Bloody boats, bloody weather,' I continued my grumpy, ungrateful tirade. We were okay, though. The boat was coping; we were uncomfortable, but managing. I was grouchy because I was tired. I took a moment to calm down. *This won't last forever.*

'It bloody better not,' I said as if the horrid me was talking to the nice me!

I fought my way around the galley, trying to ignore the water dripping on my head and the floor tilting, jumping with each new wave. All the boats on this leg were finding new leaks. The constant pumping into walls of frothy ocean meant water forced its way through every minuscule gap and all the vents. While standing at the stove, I didn't need an icy, salt water shower, too.

Although I was cranky, I wasn't scared. Not once did I fear the boat sinking, us drowning, or hypothermia claiming our bodies. I had complete faith in Noel and me. *Pyewacket* continued to earn our faith moment by moment. She had successfully answered every challenge. The only doubt that niggled was the engine. That was because we had had a brand new one on *Mariah*.

In the middle of the ocean, we were under sail, and I didn't dwell on how insignificantly tiny we were or the 'thousands of containers lurking beneath the surface, waiting to sink a boat.' This is a common worry and discussion between cruisers, but many people have a perverse joy in reminding you of this rumour prior to a voyage.

Noel stood watch in the cockpit; we usually tried to have one meal a day together.

'What the fuck!' I yelled from the galley. My feet were soaking wet. I looked down. Brown, filthy water swirled around my ankles. At that moment, a wave slammed into port side and shoved *Pyewacket* over and onto her starboard side momentarily. The disgusting water that caused me to pinch my nose gleefully ran to the other side of the galley, washing its mucky trail all over the floor.

'What the effing-hell is going on!' I looked in the sink. Another shot of water came up and over the sink's edge as we lurched back onto our port side, my feet desperately trying to grip the sloping, slimy floor.

I peered through the window that led to the cockpit and watched Noel merrily chirping a pretty song with a hose in his hand.

'Whatever you're doing, STOP!' I yelled.

I knew we weren't sinking; the brown muck had come via an internal system.

'What's going on?' Noel sauntered into the galley and sharply stopped. 'Oh dear.'

'Oh dear! Oh bloody dear,' I screeched as the foul water sloshed around the gyrating floor, and I tried to sponge it into a sliding bucket. I skidded on my hands and knees within the quagmire as if on ice, cursing as each bump on *Pyewacket's* bow caused the odorous water to leap up and splash the cupboards.

'It's from the cockpit drain,' Noel explained sheepishly.

'Never mind, help me clean up.'

In the galley floor were four boards that lifted. Beneath the floor were large bilge cupboards, where we stowed items in plastic containers in case water came in. While scooping and sponging up the marsh-like water, we hauled out cartons of pasta and rice and tried to find an alternative place to stow them in the tilting, squirming boat.

Half an hour later, we were drying out; the smell eased back to a wafty pong, and we sat in the cockpit, unaware of the jarring boat, glad to relax for a minute.

'The rain wasn't draining from the cockpit, so I connected up the deck wash hose to flush out the drains.'

'Hmm.' I allowed myself a small grin.

'The pressure must have forced all that shit up through the kitchen sink. What a stupid way to arrange the plumbing... I should have looked at that before we left,' he admitted.

I wasn't upset or angry any more. Noel was simply trying to make a repair; he didn't intend to cause such mayhem. We don't blame or hold grudges – we're both working to achieve the same thing: a safe passage. Recrimination is such a damaging emotion; it can follow you around like a shadow, sit with you at dinner, and cast a depressing grey over all you do. We had no room for that in our lives.

'I wondered what the hell you were squawking at!' Noel said. 'I thought I'd been so good, clearing it all out. It seemed such a smart idea. You should've seen all the cigarette butt ends that gurgled out – and a crisp packet!'

We both had a good chuckle, making the journey easier. *Pyewacket* continued to battle through seas, but we were okay. We were dry (mostly), safe, and relatively comfortable. We had suffered no damage or injuries. There was nothing to worry about – things were good. Our foray with the putrid water in the boat had put things back into perspective for me.

This is it, and we will do it!

* * *

We approached the island as night yielded to dawn; lush green rolling hills claimed the horizon. Sea, sky, and cloud had been our only vista for three weeks while we sailed over 2,500 nautical miles from Panama. Scattered around the small town, large trees came into focus. Verdant plants and vibrant pinks with the back drop of pacific blue sky felt fresh and enticing, our emotions heartened by the lack of western buildings.

Entering the anchorage area, we called up Pascua Radio. Between my infantile Spanish and their reasonable English, they confirmed the time our *recepción* would arrive at the boat. We had heard horror stories of the rolling anchorage that is exposed to thousands of miles of swell, but it was surprisingly still. We could see the sand beneath us, some fifteen to twenty metres deep. After dropping the anchor, I dived in and checked its setting; the refreshing chill of salt water instantly washed away the angst of the last three weeks at sea. Bruce, the anchor, settled beneath the fine sand; the clear water was breathtaking.

Satisfaction replaced stress; our contentment levels were easily met once again. The ability to relax our buttocks when sitting and eat a meal without spilling it suddenly became immensely pleasing.

A seven metre fibreglass boat, called a panga, approached with six men on board: Navy, health, customs, immigration, and unidentified others. The talk and laughter swelled the cockpit to bursting point; biscuits, drinks, pens, paper, and chaos reigned for thirty minutes. Never had checking into a country been so much fun. With no real idea of what took place, Noel and I felt half dazed by the abundance of forms. We felt as though we had partaken in a local fiesta; sincere and pleasant officials were a breath of fresh air.

As the last of the papers were shuffled into order, the official closest to me dropped the corners of his mouth and peered at me intently.

'You are being searched for.'

'I don't understand,' I replied. Why would we be searched for when we were safe?

'Your family is looking for you. You must contact them,' the official replied seriously.

Noel and I frowned.

'Alerts have been sent out to every country around this area – Galapagos, Easter Island, Pitcairn, everywhere – let your family know you are safe.'

The officials puttered ashore, leaving a silent void on board. Perplexed, Noel and I couldn't understand what was going on. We understood what happened when sailors were lost at sea; Australia is the greatest country for alerting the area and carrying out a search.

'Do you think there's a problem at home?' I asked Noel, with a worm of worry tugging at my tummy.

'I don't think so. It sounds like they were worried for our welfare.'

It was strange. We made a point of not providing a date of our arrival; we'd learned our lesson on *Mariah* many years ago during our first off shore trip. We'd tried to reach Fiji and were driven back by an unrelenting storm. Now, we kept our ETA to family and friends vague and over exaggerated. 'No news is good news' was our motto that we tried to instil in everyone.

Noel released my anxiousness by pouring a glass of wine and reminding me of our achievements.

'Look where we are; we've sailed to the remotest inhabited island in the world! Congratulations!'

* * *

The rolling swell prevented us from heading to shore for two days; our dinghy would struggle in the small harbour entrance because of breaking waves.

A few days later, we found Internet and learned of the reason for the search. A tsunami alert followed a devastating earthquake in Japan.

'It was heading your way. I was worried.' We read Colin's email. Noel's brother had set up the search for our location and welfare.

This was a stark reminder of how our families worried for us.

We'd heard about the tsunami via radio. The boats at Galapagos had been moved from anchor to deeper water – the tsunami there reached two centimetres high, but precautions were imperative. We were atop the ocean's deepest waters. We may have lifted slightly, but we knew nothing of it.

The nearest piece of land to Easter Island was Pitcairn, which happened to be over a thousand nautical miles away. This inspired us to drop two anchors; it's a long way for a boat to drift if she broke free! Feeling reasonably comfortable our home was safe, we hired a car in company with June and Bruce on board *Ainia*. We spent one day exploring the entire island. The majestic, silent, stone sentinels are humbling in size, skill, and obscurity, their purpose only guessed upon; they stand proud, arrogantly staring out along the eye-calming vistas.

'What do you think they built them for?' Noel asked our small group.

'Gods?'

'Revered members of family?'

'Boredom?'

Many theories were tossed around as to their purpose. Several giant statues were lying on their faces; apparently, in the seventeenth century, they were toppled as a result of tribal warfare. Sadly, in 1960, an earthquake caused a tsunami that scattered more statues from their bases. The highlight for me was the quarry. Witnessing a statue frozen in progress left me wondering how the devil they stood them up, perched their hats atop, and tackled their transport. The movie *Rapa Nui* depicts the natives using trees as elongated wheels to roll the stone statues to their desired destination. Most logs were crushed under the tremendous weight, until finally, and inevitably, the forest vanished.

The magnificent line of fifteen tall statues took my breath away. Quiet contemplation occurred naturally within our small group of four; our minds reaching out to the echoes of history.

The ride around the island awakened emotions of home, similarities to NSW country roads creating a rare sense of longing. Contrary to the endless fields dotted with huge stone people are the numerous cars in the town centre, interspersed with galloping horses ridden by locals opting for the cheaper mode of transport. Fit, invigorated islanders live with a sense of purpose. They are proud of their Amador (Chilean Navy), who sport mirror-polished boots and dapper uniforms.

Supermarket fruit and vegetables are in need of Viagra unless you are early enough to catch the private enterprises selling produce from their cars. Shop items are extremely expensive – a down side for the remoteness. Fortunately, we were well-stocked with dry and fresh produce – even after weeks at sea.

Many days of communication ensued with Leonardo from the Amador. He ferried us to hardware stores and other harbours to glean information for Emily. *Bobbie's* and Emily's prospects of making landfall at Rapa were increasing each hour thanks to efficient repairs, persistence, and the help of other boats. The Navy was incredibly helpful; we discussed towing, rigging, and engine repairs, stretching our limited Spanish to the extreme.

We could only spend a week at Easter Island. For two days, we were boat bound as the waves intensified, marshalled, and broke loose like galloping horses slamming into the dock. Once inside the tiny harbour, the surge maintained its formidable power.

The day before departure, our water jerry cans needed a top up, so we took our dinghy ashore. The breaking waves were not inviting; adrenaline-seeking surfers claimed the white water that seamed either side of the entrance. The frothing rapids nearly possessed us. Returning to *Pyewacket*, a breaking wave caught us out; the dinghy stood on its stern, and I released an uncontrolled yelp. With Noel's knowledge and courage, he throttled over the standing wave moments before it broke. My heart punched my chest as though it was trying to escape.

Easter Island is a magnificent destination and by far exceeded our expectations, making the arduous journey worthwhile. You can sense why the islanders felt their island was the centre of universe (Navel).

An island in the middle of nowhere – with its unexplained phenomena, vast puddles of lonely sea, and a seemingly eternal environment in the middle of an ocean – and the fact our home, our boat, hung onto a scrap of sand via a piece of metal on a chain caused us to marvel.

Taking three tough weeks to travel south to spend one week on a remote island makes the visit extra special, unique – it's also the nature of sailing. It's the event as a whole, not only the experience of a new culture and land, of course, but the entire wrapping is part of the gift – the complex journey from lounge room Internet to the euphoria of digging the anchor into the sands of Rapa Nui.

After a herculean effort and much support, Emily made it safely to Easter Island. Arriving after we had left, Emily never met Noel and me. *Silas Crosby, Ainia, Curare,* and *Pyewacket* only just managed a brief get together before we left; we hoped to see *Ainia* again in the Gambiers, while the other boats were headed east.

* * *

With a mix of relief and melancholy, we left Easter Island. The rolling swell of the ocean had rocked *Pyewacket* relentlessly. We'd never sail here again, and we were missing the island already.

The weather window indicated fair wind on our stern, and we were looking forward to a steady boat via a rhythmic movement and, as always, moving on. We both find it hard to stay in one place for long.

I often reflect on how lucky I am to find someone so similar to me: content to move with an element of discontentedness, too; perhaps that creates the impulse to see what's around the next corner (or cloud!). After twelve years of being together (nine of those on a small boat), Noel and I had become best buddies. As long as we are together, life is fun; as long as we are planning to move, life is interesting. Whether it's a curse or a blessing, this life is constantly exciting.

We're motivated by exploration, and neither of us can settle; that has its good and bad points. There's an unknown force driving us that we have no control over. We reconcile with work and groan when that worm of escape nips at the corner of our minds. Noel and I are in sync, and we've never had trouble moving as one into the next vortex of travel plans.

With over a thousand nautical miles to Pitcairn, we fell into our 'at sea' routine quickly. The wind behaved and blew steadily against *Pyewacket's* quarter. In deeper water, the ocean became gentle and kind, carrying the three of us across placid ocean swells. We hardly noticed the lift and fall of fifteen tonnes of fibreglass and all her supplies, our worldly possessions, our mini-city.

Our bodies easily fell into the rhythm of watches, especially in calm weather and good sailing. With the wind near our stern, but not directly behind where it can make a boat roll, our boat-beat – our patterns on board, improved – until the wind rudely changed direction.

Half way to Pitcairn, the wind sneaked around to our port beam and then forward of the beam, pushing us against it. Apart from slowing us down, it also meant we were bashing into the waves and the disorientated swell that had to shift its tempo in another direction, creating messy seas and an uncomfortable boat.

The jarring motion pulled at our limbs, and our legs became heavy with the weariness of constantly bracing beneath the jerks and jolts; extreme forces hounded the boat and our bodies – twenty-four hours a day, hour after hour, minute after minute.

'I don't want to switch the engine on yet,' Noel said. 'We're still so remote.'

I agreed. 'Yup, we need to save our diesel for emergencies, port entrances, and other eventualities.'

'We do, but we're heading for the wrong island at the moment!' Noel surveyed the charts. 'We're pointing to Henderson Island. We can't point to Pitcairn in this wind.'

Pyewacket pushed through the bubbling and malcontent water, and despite being uncomfortable, all was well on board. Henderson Island is part of the Pitcairn group, but uninhabited. It sits north of where we wanted to go, where people live, but the wind had other ideas.

We were in clear water, several hundred miles away from any land, which was comforting as, for five days, we watched, via weatherfaxes, an enormous angry weather frontal system approach; it was gaining on us. We were glad we'd meet it before we made it to Pitcairn – we didn't need strong winds buffeting us about near a lump of rock.

'Hey, Noel, that weather system is now on radar. It'll reach us soon.'

'What's it look like?' Noel called up from the galley, the kettle's whistle shrieked for attention, as if caught up in the excitement.

'A huge, red, angry splash of colour right across the picture, no matter what scale I set the screen to.'

'It's several hundred miles long. It's a biggy!' Noel grinned through the small hatch from the kitchen that opened into the cockpit. 'There's no chance of missing it.'

The red stain on the screen, denoting a thick band of cloud, slowly crept towards us.

Finally, the electronic cold front smudged the sky in deep, dark grey streaks, and black swirls bored down on us.

'Time to reef,' Noel called to me. I'd taken a moment to put my feet up in the saloon. We didn't know how long we'd battle the elements.

We reefed the sails; stowed items such as books and computers; and checked our equipment, lines, rigging, and all parts of the boat that were regularly monitored. We had no way of knowing how strong those winds would be until they hit, but we knew they'd be big.

'Let's turn up the music!' Funky Caribbean sounds blared out from our cockpit speakers, and the heavens opened with rain that flattened the waves and tempered the swells.

'*Yeehaw*,' Noel called out. 'Shake, shake, shake, Senora, shake your body line. Shake, shake, shake, Senora, shake it all the time.' Noel belted out the Harry Belafonte lyrics as I tried to film the phenomenal rain and black clouds.

'Ah!' As the boat lurched, I flew across the cockpit – more worried about the camera than myself. I caught a handhold on the boat to stop me flipping over the side.

'For goodness sake, put that bloody camera down and concentrate on staying on the boat, would you, please!' Noel frowned, but I laughed. It's a great video.

The Aries wind vane that steered the boat via wind, gears, rope, and a paddle kept us steady while fifty knots buffeted around our home for only an hour. As the spiralling front passed over, we had turned in a complete circle.

'Which way are we pointing now?'

'No idea,' I yelled back. The wind howled in protest. 'I can't see the compass right now, pass me another towel.' The rain dripped into the cockpit and onto our equipment.

'Don't worry too much,' Noel said. 'It's made to cope with a bit of water.'

'A bit, yes, but there's a blinkin' swimming pool in here!'

The rain had penetrated the safety and covers of our seating area, our cushions floated in small puddles.

The atmosphere thickened. Impenetrable blankets of rain cleaned the decks, and the wind howled around the rigging, trying to dislodge those inside the boat.

The storm system passed quickly, searching for its next victim, but we were not hurt; the three of us could cope with a burst of high wind for a short time. It hadn't hung around enough to create big, uncomfortable seas.

As we watched the system dissipate, we unfurled the sails and continued on our merry way to our destination – toward the right island this time! Relief pulled my shoulders back down, knowing that while we'd dealt with that one, there would be more. But right now, all was well.

10

The Home of Land-Based Cruisers

The broad British accent boomed into our cockpit via the VHF radio thirty nautical miles from Pitcairn. Noel and I smiled, listening to the voice that felt a little like home.

'Do I sound like that?' I asked.

'Sometimes.'

It did sound funny, but accents do when you haven't heard them for a while.

The Pitcairn Islands are in British Overseas Territory. They comprise the islands of Pitcairn, Henderson, Ducie, and Oeno. Pitcairn is the only inhabited island, with a population of around fifty. Its highest point stands at 346 metres. We watched the island grow bigger as we slowly crept towards her. She was just one mile long and two miles wide; we felt grateful we hadn't missed her. Not that we doubted our navigation or the GPS, but we'd battled opposing winds for many days; the promised easterlies were keeping well-hidden.

The mental and psychological strain of variable weather for over ten days was something that could require repeated and oft administered therapy at a bar!

As the anchor site became visible, we watched a solitary sailboat leave, stirring the islanders and us with a message of thanks, good wishes, and heartfelt farewells as they raised their canvas and pointed west. Alone, we dropped our sails and puttered towards the waypoints passed on through the marvellous cruising grapevine.

Approaching the island, I sensed its mystery, legend, and history. The atmosphere of shrouding secrets and fear of judgements was not just because of what I'd read. But there were also proud descendants who were making a go at a unique lifestyle. I firmly put the distasteful history to the back of my mind and lived in the moment, absorbing the unique lump of rock that is the location of intense, fascinating, and heart-breaking stories.

Pyewacket launched into a gunwale to gunwale lurch as we motored nearer. She would continue to heave in this way at the anchorage site, for it was open, near the land, and with nothing to stop the thousands of miles of undulating water.

It was 4 p.m., and Simon, the deputy mayor, and quarantine officer, on Pitcairn had gracefully received and answered our numerous questions.

'Do we have the right co-ordinates for the best anchor site?' We needed to check that our proposed location was right.

'Yes, that's the best spot.'

'Is there more protection on the other side of the island?' The swell would create an uncomfortable anchorage.

'Possibly,' came the reply, 'but it can change quickly, and it would be a very dangerous lee shore. I wouldn't recommend it.'

'Okay, thanks. Is it possible to purchase some fuel and top up with water? We have jerry cans.' A radio schedule had revealed our next destination, Iles de Gambier, to be in drought and have no fuel.

'Yes, that shouldn't be a problem.'

He offered advice and answers 'at any time.' The anchor waypoint was perfect, allowing our anchor to settle in a big patch of sand between coral patches. *Pyewacket* continued her un-gamely dance. With the anchor tested several times, we enjoyed a cool glass of Chardonnay, set the anchor alarm, and tried our luck sleeping in the cockpit. The tall, craggy land stood close. With a lee shore, we wanted to be ready in an instant. Before closing our eyes, we spent several minutes assigning duties should the anchor alarm go off.

'You go forward and haul in the anchor,' Noel explained. 'I'll start the engine and manage this end of the boat.' These were our usual tasks, but we'd regularly change roles to keep our skills current and useful. You had no idea when you'd need to switch, or do both!

The alarm bleeped a few times throughout the night. We weren't dragging anchor; we were swinging around. Noel and I spent a hideous night awake. With eight different bunk options, we played musical beds, but when the alarm started, we moved! Rolling around kept sleep at bay. Eventually, I threw cushions on the floor and tried to wedge myself in the companion way. Noel tried sleeping athwartships in a double bunk, with little success.

* * *

Fraught with breaking waves, the entrance to the small harbour looked daunting. We opted for the fifty dollar boat taxi to collect and return. Having come uncomfortably close to flipping the dinghy in Easter Island, we thought it a fair price.

We asked to be picked up at 8 a.m., which caused some re-arranging on shore, but they were happy to oblige. Our plan was to spend the entire day on the island, experiencing this unique little place before returning to the boat around 4 p.m. to immediately leave. We would sleep better under sail and didn't want to push our luck in such an exposed anchorage.

'I thought they'd pick us up in a decent boat, not a Kayak,' I said as two burly guys headed towards us; but as the boat neared, it morphed into something more substantial than my imagination had conjured up. It was my fear of safely jumping off a fifteen tonne, violently rolling vessel into a tender that rolled even more manically... Timing was everything.

With no time for polite introductions, jerry cans were loaded along with a large Dorado fish we caught the day before, books for swapping, laundry, and our two sea-battled bodies.

We didn't pay much attention to the entrance; I'm not sure which enthralled us more: the locals on the dock lined up in welcome or the jagged peaks of the island tearing through the clouds.

We were sent straight into the hands of Heather, the tourist manager. Between information and logistics, we checked in, completing two small forms, and handed over thirty-five dollars checking in fees and fifty dollars for the taxi. No Zarpe was required. Andrew and Geoff (Geoff was the Policeman on the island), our taxi-drivers, gathered up our jerry cans to fill with diesel and water for our return.

The four-wheel buggies that hummed to life with an impending sense of escapade whisked us off into an adventure park with buggies and no other traffic to spoil the fun; the weariness fell away, excitement settling in its place. It all happened so quickly. We were still trying to enjoy the fact that the weather had allowed us to make this brief stop. With a few knots more breeze and travelling swell, the anchorage could so easily be untenable.

* * *

The mutinous history is a well-known story, and although Fletcher Christian ran The Bounty aground at what is now called Bounty Bay and set it alight for fear of detection, I can understand him not wanting to leave his boat on anchor for too long! This, of course, was after the most famous of all mutinies where Bligh and eighteen loyal sailors were set adrift in a twenty-three foot open boat. Miraculously, they survived the 3,600 miles voyage over seven weeks in the tiny boat, reaching the island of Timor.

Meanwhile, Christian and his crew returned to Tahiti, where over half the men decided to remain. Christian, with eight others, their women, and a few Tahitian men, searched the South Pacific for a safe haven, settling on Pitcairn.

The history intrigues me. We 'popped' over to different islands hundreds of miles apart, and they did, too; but we were far better equipped with GPS, depth sounders, and radar. It's fascinating, and quite remarkable, that they achieved so many safe passages considering Pitcairn was initially chartered incorrectly. Using modern equipment is not enough, either; you also need great navigation skills – this was confirmed by a supply ship hitting a reef not that long ago, en route from Norfolk Island to Pitcairn.

The island chartered in the wrong place was beneficial for Christian's plans to hide away and recreate a sexually-liberated way of life – a similar ethos to the lifestyle he enjoyed in Tahiti. The women provided pleasure and offspring, while the Tahitian men supplied the labour. But jealousy, revolt, resentment, and murder were the by-products. And not only did Christian's descendants live on the island, some maintained his way of life with young islanders.

I had to put this black cloud of horror out of my mind, relish the opportunity to step onto Pitcairn, and concentrate on what we needed to accomplish during our short stay.

* * *

Relentless white water had washed our deck and us en route to Pitcairn, causing the laundry to pile up. With thoughts of the drought in the Gambiers, we were keen to find a way to clean our clothes here.

'Can we get some laundry done? Should be only two loads,' I asked the group that had gathered around us.

'Sure, we'll do it for fifty dollars,' one woman offered. I didn't know what to say; the silence hung in the air.

I gathered my wits. 'We have a Dorado for exchange.' Noel held up the large fish.

The lady frowned at me. 'We caught one of those yesterday.'

An uncomfortable silence hung in the air. We were guests here but fifty dollars!

'Okay, what about thirty?' She relented but wasn't happy about it.

'Well, okay then,' I said. I wasn't happy, either, but checking in fees were cheap, and they were doing a lot to help us.

The lady took our bag of laundry and headed off on her mission.

'You could've used our washing machine for nothing,' a quiet voice said. A couple, witnessed the negotiations, stood by, too timid to jump in to save us when we needed it.

As Noel and I digested this information, a decisive voice brought us all up short.

'Right, no more discussions on laundry. That's settled. The fruit and vegetables are sorted, fuel and water arranged; let's get you two off up the top to have a look around.'

We were all glad Heather took charge.

We sensed a little unrest, heightened by offerings and negotiations, between families. Heather straightened out the deal and told everyone, including us, what would be happening. It settled us all back down. We only had one day on the island, and I didn't want to spend that doing the laundry.

And some lucky soul ate our large Dorado! But two enormous loads of washing were cleaned and dried – well, almost dried.

Heather took us under her wing and arranged brief Internet use, lunch, touring, and anything else we could think of. En route to a peak where we could meander back at our leisure on foot, she stopped at her house. Instantly, everything slowed, a calmness settling on our shoulders. Looking out across the ocean through dangling Spanish moss, we could witness the entire form of a squall out at sea – end to end. Fresh aromas tickled our noses with salt, the season of spring, and home grown vegetables. A bewildering array of careless colours assaulted our senses, hibiscus and frangipani in bloom making sharp dabs of colour against the lush greens, yellow sands, ocean blues, pearly white cotton clouds, and soft jade moss; Heather's genuine mirth encompassed all in this private corner of the earth, which must surely neighbour Heaven. Unsure of the isolation and constant, unchanging company a lifestyle like this offers, we found Heather's house to be tranquil, spiritual.

I get it now.

But the recent sordid history played on my mind.

With brief instructions and flippant flaps of hand, Heather dropped us off from the fun-park buggy ride at Pitcairn's peak. We made our own route back down the Hill Of Difficulty, finding most of the recommended lookouts, where the sky's immensity soared above our heads. Mucky, muddy roads trickled through the hills, obvious rain erosion giving thoughts to potential problems with torrential down pours. The simple houses, dotted within the emerald meadow land, illustrates that everyone has plenty of their own space.

Heather had already telephoned the two cafés on the island for lunch. One was closed, so it was an easy choice.

'Are you happy with sausages and chips?' she asked. Our wet grins from salivating glands confirmed the affirmative.

'We'd love a bit of salad, too.'

At 11:30 a.m., we staggered down the hill into the café, a home, and sat on an enclosed veranda, perched right over the Pacific Ocean. Hundreds of carved wooden dolphins were piled on tables. Our hosts explained that cruise ships visit the island. While the passengers stayed on ship, the islanders boarded to sell their wares. This is how many of them make their living.

Pitcairn is unique in many ways, but more so in that they want cruisers to visit. Waypoints, information, and any advice are available on the Internet and from Heather herself. Sadly, we can't imagine more cruisers heading there; it's necessary to put a lot of ocean in your wake to reach the island with the prospect of not being able to stop. That deters many people – and rightly so. A good harbour would change that, but that is not going to happen.

Back at the dock, we were met by children playing in the surf – surf we had to cross – and islanders cleaning out a large lobster pot. Our water and diesel jerry cans had been filled and were waiting on the quay. A lady named Carol arrived with a dazzling selection of pumpkin, spinach, bananas (one stalk green, one yellow), eggplant, passion fruit, and grapefruit; beautiful food and a perfect selection and quantity. We usually spend a day or two in port lugging around these items via our legs, taxi, or pushbike, so we felt like royalty having everything ready at the dock for our departure.

Carol and her partner stood and chatted with us for several minutes. They were bright, funny people. We were making friends in such a short time. As we lingered with the islanders, some men hauled our gear in the taxi-boat, laundry, food, diesel, and water – all it needed was us. We felt the pang of farewell, strangely born within a few hours. *How can people touch our hearts so quickly?* I was not sure but felt the loss of departing.

By this time, *Pyewacket's* decks were heaving in a hideous, sickening motion. My gut twisted; a slip, a simple mistake, and it could be nasty. I didn't even notice the breaking waves that Andrew negotiated, though I witnessed his furrowed brow and deep concentration. However, I did notice our enormous fifteen-metre boat lurching ungainly.

'Don't think about it. Get your timing right, feel it, and just go. No hesitating, no turning back.' Noel instructed me in his no nonsense way. I vaulted on board; there was no time to rejoice. The jerry cans came next. These mighty men hung on to *Pyewacket's* lurching hull with grim determination and flung our gear on board. I have no idea how they managed to do so without breaking their limbs; it made the fifty dollars an extremely fair price. We were grateful for their herculean effort.

Back on board, we stowed what we could. By this time, we were tired from the travels, last night's lack of sleep, and spending the day walking.

Emotional farewells lay heavily atop sentiments. We knew *Pyewacket* would settle once freed from the bound restraints of her anchor and away from waves and swell that bounced relentlessly off the land.

The last job remained, and I pulled out the laundry from our enormous sail bag and found the clothing and sheets damp; we'd only been on the island a few hours, so we couldn't expect miracles. Efficiently, I pulled shirts over coat-hangers and tied rope around *Pyewacket's* interior, hanging the washing throughout the boat. The homely smell of laundry powder wafted through our accommodation, and we looked like a busy laundry shop!

Underway, we hauled the sails and turned to watch Pitcairn shrink over the horizon.

We are not good at making instant friendships. It's a good skill to have in this lifestyle, but Pitcairn's people wriggled under our skin immediately. Altruistic and kind, friendly and tranquil, but with something more; we admire their chosen lifestyle – one that isn't simply luck. Living off the land is hard work. We realised it was a life similar to cruising: self-sufficient, constant work, evolving, enduring, and compromising. As with cruising, they reap the rewards, living within a settled calm, clean air and enjoying the fruits of their own labour. Like cruising, it is a choice, not simply good fortune; perhaps, also, it is a little bit of a historic echo rolling down the years? Pitcairn and its islanders have enriched the harvest of our adventures; that is why we will return someday.

11

Alien Forms, Rotten Cheese, and Chooks

Iles Gambier had been on the edge of our thoughts for many years since we traversed the Pacific Ocean on our last boat, *Mariah*. Back then, after circling the globe, we were happy to head the easiest route across the vast pool of water back home to Australia. Now, we were adventuring back in our favourite playground, the South Pacific, and keen to try our luck at the Gambiers.

Neptune had allowed us to stay in open roadstead anchorages at Easter Island and Pitcairn, and from there, Mother Nature served up winds of anything from fifteen to thirty knots – beam on or nothing. Along the way, via the radio, we listened to other cruisers traversing the 'milk-run' route that we'd accomplished on *Mariah*. Farther north, they were becalmed and motoring all the way. At the time, we were smugly enjoying a fifteen to twenty knot breeze on the quarter that carried us along smoothly. We had around 370 nautical miles to sail.

During the last twenty-four hours, the wind died. We reefed the sails to prevent them flapping and then fired up the engine. We wanted to make port before dark. The waves calmed; although, the swell still kept us company.

I noticed Noel frowning, watching the engine's exhaust.

'What's up?' Both of us were in tune with the boat and each other. Something was happening, and it wasn't good.

'There's steam in our exhaust.'

'That's not good. What do you think it is?'

'Could be the head gasket.' Noel pondered; meanwhile, a little animal in my stomach gnawed on the edge of my gut. I'd worried about this all the way, especially while puttering through channels, relying on the engine one hundred percent.

Frustration, exhaustion, and simple 'sick of sailing' sentiments were shed upon arrival. Though as we poked through numerous reefs to a safe anchorage, the engine worked fine; although, time was spent diagnosing and repairing.

Our electronic charts were spot on and matched the paper version that we always kept as back-up. A few markers were absent, but daylight, vigilance, and several double checks of various sources meant a safe passage into the bay. It's not only good seamanship to use everything at your disposal navigation-wise, but it also made the journey interesting by challenging our navigation abilities. And it kept our skills current.

On entry, the deep purple ocean casually transformed to sapphire; shadows of sharp coral lurked nearby. We left behind the enormous pulsing swells of the vast ocean; the boat stood up straight, and we finally remembered what it was like to function as normal human beings and stand on our own two feet without tensing every muscle. With little fanfare except stomachs flipping in anticipation of a cold beer and a complete night's rest, we anchored in clear water.

Lying over 860 nautical miles south east of Tahiti, the Gambier Archipelago (aka islands at the end of the world) comprise fourteen small, rugged islands – the largest and most populated of which is Mangareva, where we anchored. They abound with fruit trees and a lush landscape due to the tropical climate that is tempered by the ocean's trade winds. Hundreds of coral stone buildings from the nineteenth century, and its ties with Catholicism, are scattered through the islands, including churches, convents, schools, and watch towers. Mangareva is the centre of the region's pearl industry, and the lagoons are known for their pearl oysters.

Humble, pastel-painted homesteads border the small bay where green meets blue, wet meets dry; sporadic pallid patches of sand are fringed with palms. Mangareva Island has an abundance of brown-tinged trees that cover the vertical backdrop behind the one road village; the seven month drought was evident in the crackling dry land. We knew as soon as we arrived the drought would break. Skimming the skies, great wagging weather fronts streamed east care of the New Zealand born lows. The warm days kept cool, and soon, rain gushed into our water tanks.

Anyone nearby would have heard the sighs from both our lips: contentment? Relief? Tiredness? Amazement? Achievement? Yes!

The South Pacific Ocean is not kind; squalls relentlessly march across the skies. Whirling lows spin off vast lines of fronts that whipped us with instant forty-five knot gusts, settling to a mere thirty-five knots for some days.

After a night of blissful slumber disturbed only by our body clocks awakening us through the night, ready for the next watch shift, we rode our dinghy ashore. Great umbrellas of shade from statuesque pines lined the deserted street. Within a five minute walk, we found the Gendarme office closed for the day. On returning to the shop, we found it had closed, too. We meandered back to the boat and did the same: closed down and slept some more.

The following morning, before lunch, we strolled back to the police, filled out one simple form, and sat expectantly in the office, waiting for the bill. In accented English, the handsome Gendarme said, 'That's it. Enjoy your stay.' There was no fee.

With seventy dollars in our pockets, we searched for a bank to exchange currency. Locals directed us to the post office.

'Can we change some money here, please?' I asked tentatively and in poor French.

'*Non*,' the worker said abruptly.

'Okay, can we draw some money on our credit card then?'

'*Non*. No more, no more money this way or exchange.'

A few weeks ago, the post office had made the decision to cease this kind of service.

Instead of being worried, I was happy. If we didn't have money, we couldn't spend any. Eventually, the proprietor of a dusty, three-sided shed that sold food exchanged fifty American dollars into French Polynesian Francs.

Vegetables were scarce due to the lack of rain, but we had an enormous pumpkin, piles of potatoes and onions from Panama, and some spinach from Pitcairn. I am adept at keeping potatoes, onions, and most fruit and vegetables. Most cruisers say you can't keep potatoes and onions together. I did. If you find a cool, dark, aerated place and start with good quality produce, they can keep for weeks on end. Bananas need to be kept separate, because they release gasses that cause other fruits to ripen quicker. Tomatoes were kept in cartons that kept them separated (like cardboard egg cartons but for tomatoes and apples – without the lid); the cartons prevented them from rolling around and bruising each other. Eggs were, of course, in their cartons and turned each day. Some people swear by covering the shells in Vaseline. I couldn't stand the thought of trying to handle slippery eggs. Besides, they are porous! On long trips, I checked the fruit and vegetables every day and always used the items that were going soft first. I had a whole gamut of tricks and tips for storing fresh produce, which was the inspiration for my first book, *Cruisers' AA (Accumulated Acumen)*, which I was compiling during this journey.

We had dried food and fruit left from Pitcairn.

Mouth-watering aromas waft across the boats each morning via the bakery. Bread was baked daily and frozen chickens were reasonably priced – hence why we ate chicken, interspersed with lentils, pasta and rice, for three weeks. Although vegetables were scarce, fruit ripened in abundance. Locals welcomed us into their gardens to collect their excess that plopped onto the ground and went to waste.

During long walks, we found sagging branches adorned with wild grapefruits and mangoes. They seemed happy to be relieved from their weighty crop. Chickens scratched around the grey dusty pathways and locals offered them up, saying, 'If you can catch one, you can have it.'

Often, food was fuel while underway. Simple recipes with lentils and rice were easy to create and warm up. When in port, we enjoyed finer fare like cheese and biscuits – things that were difficult to keep on your plate when at sea.

'Hey, look what I found!' I said to Noel, holding aloft a jar of preserved cheese that I unearthed during a food stock take.

'Yum, I'll unwrap some crackers. Where's the pickle?' Our tummies were looking forward to a treat. Saliva moisturised my mouth.

'Oh, for goodness sake!' I groaned. Removing the jar lid had released the stench of rotting cheese into the boat. It was enough to curl nostrils towards earlobes!

'Plan B, then?' Noel asked with his hand covering his nose. I am sure his eyes were watering.

I preserve feta cheese in olive oil. It lasts for months and months. I tried the same formula with local white cheese in Ecuador; the rubbery, tasteless cheese turned into a sharp, cheek-sucking fetta-type after several weeks in the oil.

With confidence, I purchased the cheapest *queso blanco* in Panama and utilised precious supplies of oil. That particular cheese obviously doesn't lend itself to preserving! I didn't know plain old white cheeses could be so different.

In town, the locals were indifferent to us salty travellers. It's a wealthy island, and they don't need tourists' money. The pearl-diving and monetary support from France meant our paltry shopping added nothing to their coffers. But they were welcoming, with friendly *bonjours* and cheerful waves.

Wrapped around these escapades were three hours of cleaning *Pyewacket's* bottom. In the clear water, the shark-like fish soon flicked away when we dived in. However, aliens live here. Thousands of see-through globs of jelly float aimlessly in these waters. So thick are their population, it is like swimming through lumpy jelly. Within the protection of wet suits, we could still feel them bumping into our limbs as we brushed over *Pyewacket's* hull, sucking on air lines via the dive hookah. Leaving a slimy residue as they slide into our hands, it made me squeak and squirm like a little girl. They didn't sting... much. Only a little tingle on my face as one tucked its underside to my chin. I dealt with that with all the grace of a two-year-old.

Beneath the glorious surrounds of the pacific island, mundane, but imperative, jobs such as engine maintenance still had to be done.

'I'm sure that steam I saw in the exhaust is to do with the head gasket,' Noel called out from the cramped engine room, preparing to carry out some routine maintenance.

'Will it be okay?'

'Yeah, probably, we'll keep an eye on it. It's not too bad. Somewhere we'll need a new head gasket.'

'Oh, hang on. The supply ship is coming in. Before you start work, we'd better move.'

'That was good timing!' The supply ship sailed in every few weeks, and we were anchored in its path. Feeling under pressure to move quickly, Noel switched on the engine without checking the oil first.

'What was that?' The engine usually fired up without hesitation, but this time, it sounded, what can only be described as, fluffy. Noel turned it off immediately. It had barely run.

He leaped into the engine room and pulled out the dipstick.

'Oh shit, the sumps full of water!'

'We've got to move.' Hearing what Noel said, the stones of dread shifted in my gut. We'd both completed a marine engine course back in Australia and looked after our own engines for many years. We knew water in the sump could be serious, and we'd tried to start it, pumping that water around the engine!

The supply ship glided nearer.

'I'll jump in the dinghy.'

I left the fore and aft lines of the dinghy tied to *Pyewacket's* starboard quarter. Firing up the engine, I pushed *Pyewacket* over. A small boat with a little engine can do this if it is positioned in the right place; it's impossible to tow a larger vessel with a dinghy, but I could push her easily. Noel jumped on the bow and wound in some anchor chain to help move us forward. The supply ship eased passed.

'I don't believe I did that,' Noel said, looking down at me in the dinghy. 'That's the first time in my life I have started an engine without the normal checks.'

'The ship will be here a while. Let's have a look now.'

On inspection, we found that the oil heat exchanger had corroded and allowed salt water into the oil ways; overnight, it had flooded the sump.

'The good news is. I turned the engine off quickly enough, so there's no damage, I think.'

'And the bad news?'

'Lots of work this afternoon.'

And, indeed, there was. Fortunately for us, an oil dump receptacle neighboured a grassy area on shore in a public's work department, so we collected every container that had a good lid and started the process of emptying the engine of the saltwater and oil mix.

Upon starting the engine, the oil/saltwater mix had also been pumped out of the dipstick aperture, causing the fluffy noise; it had blown about three gallons onto the walls of the engine room, and consequently, into the bilge; it bypassed our newly fitted oil-drip tray under the engine!

We spent the afternoon up to our elbows in sticky black goo, taking great care to avoid any spills. All the dark liquid was ferried ashore to be disposed of properly. Folding myself in half and then quarters, I could squeeze beneath the engine; cleaning the walls, engine, and bilge was a long, back-breaking and uncomfortable job. I suffer from cramp, which made the task painful when I couldn't straighten my limbs to counteract the contracting muscles!

That evening, we started the engine.

'Ah, sweet as a nut.' Noel leaned back on the bulkhead, oily, tired, but relieved.

'Thank goodness we have two coolers.' Noel had bypassed the corroded cooler, and the secondary one coped fine.

'We may need to do some more work on it in Tahiti, but we'll see how it goes. For now, we're out of trouble.'

If a drama unfolds, I have two hundred percent faith in Noel; we'll figure it out together. Good decisions and great teamwork. That philosophy accompanied us during our travelling years together, and remained still. We'd made some mistakes along the way during this trip – the un-rated plastic fuel-return lines had escaped our attention, as had the odd plumbing set up. Neglecting to dip the oil sump in the engine before firing up was a one-off, and we paid for it! Despite the possibility of encouraging judgements, these were useful stories we could share, eventually, with our maritime students and other sailors. It's good to discuss your mistakes; it gives others confidence to open up. These were lessons to learn. Murphy's Law anticipates such events – all cruisers have to ready to tackle whatever is thrown in their path. Besides, learning is part and parcel of taking on a challenge.

Murphy was still lurking, though.

From the hull cleaning and the engine repairs, we had that delicious heaviness of spent energy after a good job done, the repairs holding. We tested the engine lightly, with no need to put it under duress yet. We'd do that when we regained some of our energy.

The following day, we took up the offer of borrowing fold up bikes from another boat for a twenty kilometre island circumnavigation. Leaving the boat and the pungent smell of oil was a welcome relief.

Feeling like clowns perched on tiny wheels, the exhaustion became insignificant compared to the rewards: pristine views and an abundance of wild, juicy fruits begging to be picked; only a couple of cars broke the serene silence.

But that was all about to change, and serenity was about to be shattered.

12

Occluded Fronts and Associated Stunts

If you think Gin and Tonics on the aft deck in a protected anchorage are part of life within the Pacific Ocean, you would not be alone. However, witnessing the terrific splendour of unrestrained nature may distort this view; it did for us.

During our second time in this ocean, we were experiencing, shall we say, more 'testing' times – even in 'protected' anchorages. This led to serious thought regarding seeking out islands with airports and yacht brokers instead of island hopping to places of beauty, history, and charm!

Anchored at Iles Gambier in the southeast corner of the Society Islands, we compared alternative weather sources with other cruisers.

Lena and Henrique from *Dana* had caught up with us, and like us, they monitored the weather carefully.

'To the north, strong north west winds are coming,' Henrique said.

'To the south, there are strong south east winds,' said Noel, peering at paper printouts from our weatherfax.

'Funny, isn't it? We're right in the middle.' Noel joked, but it wasn't in jest. I could see his eyes scrunch in anticipation.

Although the unstable whims of nature and Neptune are tricky to predict, there was obviously something afoot; but we were in a protected anchorage... and there lies the problem: a lee shore in every direction; the bay was chock full of chillingly beautiful coral heads.

That night, we maintained anchor watch. At 9 p.m., the wind and thirty of his mates were exposing Poseidon's anger. At 11:15 p.m., I could see the lightning through my closed eyes. Suddenly, a huge gust barrelled through the anchorage and swung us violently. Stumbling into the cockpit, with my night vision still in infancy and pulling on a jumper, I found an oft calm Noel dancing on his toes.

'I was about to yell for you,' he said. The last few words were snatched away by the noise of the wind generator flying at high speeds.

'Turn off the wind generator,' yelled Noel.

'Turn on the engine,' I screamed as *Pyewacket* was slung over onto her gunwales.

Three long, terrifying hours ensued within the jaws of nature's opponents, where rules were their private notion. Regularly, we clocked gusts in excess of fifty-five knots, which nearly knocked us over. Heart action sped, blood vessels contracted, and gusts grew; a steady forty-five knots persisted interspersed with the brutal gusts.

So what's the big deal? These aren't pleasant winds at all, but they're not horrendous. Many sailors have suffered fiercer fights with windy and his mates – as have we. The problem was the vortexing wind that clutched us in its vicious fist and the fact that we were trapped. The wind backed countless times, orbiting in full three-sixty degrees, in a gut wrenching, horrifying lurch from one direction to the next. The cruel gusts pinned us one way, eased to forty-five knots, and then the next great barrelling wall of wind would smack us on the opposite side! Nature put on a performance of ear-splitting music, the beating halyards and howling winds clashing together, reaching a cliff-hanger crescendo. The only light to navigate by was the occasional glimpse of a local house lamp. Our solar panels were vibrating along with my knees.

Mangareva sits on a crescent-shaped island, allowing the wind to whip along the inside curve and build speed – another ingredient in the following fracas.

Viewing the chart plotter, it showed the kaleidoscopic winds pick up *Pyewacket's* fifteen tonnes and propel her and her wide-eyed crew straight over the anchor, pulling it clear of its sandy restraints and tossing us into the realms of chaos. We were no longer tethered to *terra firma* for a few heart-stopping moments. Of course, this took place on the blackest night in history, and most of the markers that highlighted the hidden reefs were unlit.

With the engine on and to hold us in clear water, Noel concentrated on the chart plotter. I staggered to the bow to gather an idea on the situation. Haunting visions of carnage romped before my eyes. Neptune took another swing at us with what felt like a giant cricket bat. I returned to the cockpit and Noel's expectant face; the only answer I had was trembling knees.

Buying time before my next foray onto the bow, I trained the spotlight on two nearby cardinal markers around the nearest reef and *Dana*, who was moving closer (we soon realised we were moving not them). They, too, were dancing around their anchor. All ten boats in the anchorage had switched their navigation lights on. The VHF radio carried a distress call into the void; the disembodied voice filled our cockpit, and the French language did not soften the anguish hanging on the words. Noel's eyes were glued to the plotter, his white knuckles on the wheel, manipulating the motor to hold us within our original circle of anchoring, previously made while swinging over the last few weeks.

Would the repairs to the engine hold? I wondered about our repairs after our oil cooler drama; the possible head gasket problem added to my worries. I nearly convinced myself the engine would stop.

'We'll have to get the anchor up,' shouted Noel, amid the clanging of wind beating everything in its path. I took a hard swallow and looked up towards the bow. *How am I going to get up there safely?*

Twenty terrifying minutes of confusion reigned.

Admittedly, I was petrified of lifting the anchor and finding the engine not coping. *Would our propeller bite? Will the jury-rigged motor hold?* I'm sure I heard Murphy snicker.

I had not grasped the fact that the anchor had become unburied by *Pyewacket* propelling right over it. We had moved by the wind's hands, and the anchor had re-bitten. Now, if we pulled back on the anchor, we would hit the reef. Noel tried to drive us forward into clear water, but the anchor was stopping us!

Noel stayed on the helm; he had a good handle on keeping the boat off the coral reefs. I dithered between a running commentary of where we were located in relation to rocks and other boats, flicking my eyes to the engine gauges, and running up to the bow, trying to haul up the stuck chain.

I am usually great at anchor management, but fear had its steely grip on my innards; I couldn't grasp what was happening. Sitting next to the windlass, I whimpered several times. My overly excited brain had me thinking that, at any moment, we'd be on the coral; my unruly imagination had me catapulted into the water, squished between rocks and fifteen tonnes of boat or floating off into the black void.

In a momentary lull, Noel ran forward to help, letting go the other anchor with the hope it would hold and give us a bit of time while we assessed the situation. We had stopped spinning at this point; the second anchor dug in. For a few seconds, we managed to regroup before facing the unpredictable character of Mother Nature and her whimsical mate Neptune.

What was happening dawned on me and sickness lurched through my innards as I knew for certain the anchor had to be lifted; we had two anchors to pull up now! I swung the search light around again. We were too close to *Dana*; if our two boats swayed differently, we would hit. Jagged rocks glared back at us beneath the illuminated beam. Everything was rattling, sliding, and clashing within the boat; my teeth were clattering in time with everything else.

The end of the spotlight's eerie beam lit a cardinal marker inches from off our stern. I don't know how we didn't hit the reef. I shrieked (in a lady like fashion). *'Forward now! We're about to hit!'*

Noel powered forward and brought me to my senses.

'We have to pull the anchors up.' There was no time for me to gain a handle on the helm. I'm the anchor expert on board, and there was no getting out of it.

Our second anchor, which was shackled to ten metres of heavy chain and rope, was caught between the two bow rollers. I could not free it. I fought for slack to wrap around the warping drum. *Come on, girl, you have to do this.* My determination clawed back. Isolated on deck and at the mercy of the elements, I had to snatch back my wayward emotions and keep them under control. Anger rewarded me with confidence when a gust galloped across the deck with the might of a hundred horses. 'You bitch!' I yelled.

Terror wrapped itself around me again, and I wished we were out in open sea – away from hard things to hit! I tied off the main anchor chain to free up the gypsy (wheel that pulls up the chain) and the warping drum for the second anchor. In a brief lull, I hauled up some slack in the rope, wrapped it around the drum, and pushed the button on deck to start the winch. The power of the windlass pulled the rope free of the bow rollers and on board.

Noel kept us into the wind, relieving strain to the anchor chain and ropes. The process of driving forward and falling back took us sideways, losing steerage. He'd reverse into the wind, and the wind would overtake that momentum, and the process would start again.

Within the storm's full fury of fifty-seven knots, I concentrated on the task at hand. I hauled in the entire rope part of anchor two; the last part of chain (attached to the rope) was stuck fast where the connecting shackle had wedged itself into the rollers. Noel must have been wondering what I was doing; it felt like I'd been fighting on the bow for hours.

I could instantly see the solution. With my focus now on the problem, I no longer heard the wind or felt the lurching deck. I looped another rope over the caught chain, the other side of the bow roller, and slid that rope along the chain, pulling it up to the side of the boat;

this allowed me to grasp the chain and haul it and the anchor straight up over the lifelines on starboard side, free of constraints.

The storm shook my emotions, pouring a cocktail of confused fears and anger into my core. I was also angry from being bullied for so long – this mixture boosted my strength.

I lashed the anchor to the deck and stumbled back to the cockpit.

'The first anchor's up and on board,' I said breathlessly.

'Bloody brilliant, well done!' His words awarded me the courage I needed to get back out to retrieve the main anchor.

We left the deck lights off to maintain our night vision; our communication was by torch light. Once the main anchor was raised above the seabed floor, I would flash three times. Noel would motor to a clear area and flash me three times with the signal to let go the anchor again. The wind had eased to a comfortable forty knots, still gusting something horrid.

I never put our windlass under severe load, but that night, I begged and cajoled it in all sorts of ways, soothing, swearing, and pledging lifelong allegiance to fresh oil and tender strokes to its innards.

I placed the chain links of the main anchor chain back over the gypsy wheel and started the anchor winch once again. The words of an old sailing friend, who has sadly left this world, always came back to me when I operated the windlass: 'You can repair the equipment and boat but not your fingers. Keep them clear!'

The twenty metre mark on the chain passed over the winch, indicating that the anchor would be clear of the seabed. I flashed my torch three times. Noel moved us to the middle of the bay, into safe water. He flashed me three times, and I let go of the anchor. Suddenly, we had re-anchored with the wind abating to below forty knots, still gusting, but with less fight.

We stayed up all night. Noel was outstanding on the helm. For a while, I terror paralysed myself, but prevailed in the nick of time. We missed the reef by seconds. We suffered only bruises, and one jerry can broke.

'The chart plotter helped save our arse,' Noel said over a steaming cup of tea.

I broke a Snickers bar in two. It was 5 a.m., and while we could relax, the adrenaline – easing back from a frantic dash to a mild sprint – fended off any chance of sleep. Breaking out the chocolate bars was as soothing as a Band-Aid.

'Having the anchor spot marked on the plotter meant I could see that we had left our radius from our original anchor position, so I had somewhere to steer back to.'

'Thank goodness,' I said, enjoying the reward of thick chocolate and crunchy peanuts.

'Yeah, otherwise, we'd be lost in the thick black night. I don't want to think about what might have happened without it!'

The wind had alleviated to a 'gentle' thirty-five knots beneath the comfort of dawn.

Between chewy bites, I said, 'I took my time. I don't think I've ever been that scared before.'

'Do you remember what you said?

I looked at Noel. 'I didn't say anything.' *What's he on about?* 'I remember tasting the acidity of bile, though.' I raised my eyebrows as I sucked the melted chocolate from my unwashed fingers. 'Nice.' Noel laughed. 'Your eyes were wide, and when I said we had to get the anchor up, you said, "I'm not fucking going up there. You can forget that idea!"' He chuckled into his tea.

'Cripes, I don't remember saying that at all!'

Later, we learned within the melee, *Dana* had thought of helping us and prepared fenders alongside their boat.

'If you couldn't stop yourselves going, we were ready to catch you,' they said, which brought tears of gratitude to Noel and me.

We were feeling too far south and craved settled latitudes and distance from the occluded fronts and high pressure ridges that tail off from the perpetual lows born from the Antarctic and arrive via New Zealand, travelling east. We considered setting up a yacht brokerage. We would have had several customers. As our lovely British friends on board their catamaran, *Pacific Bliss*, said, 'We wanna go home!' A few days later, we felt better; ironically enough, we were walking on land at that point.

After many weeks enjoying a flat anchorage, the protected aspect nearly caused us to lose *Pyewacket* on a moonless night, while we did battle with a vortexing wind. Our relaxed bodies were now tensing with every gust above fifteen knots during the night. So we caught the next weather window to make way for the Tuamotus.

Iles Gambier was a delight, a rest full of natural beauty, and it held the scariest night of our lives. It was a great achievement to sail to and a good place to arrive; it was also a good place to leave.

* * *

Momentarily, we did consider sailing farther south, though. The Austral Islands are the southernmost Archipelago in French Polynesia and benefit from extraordinarily rich marine ecosystems; and it's possible to anchor in a flooded volcano. But, we decided to head north.

'I'm weary from the fickle winds.' A gaping yawn escaped from my lips. 'And the hard sailing.'

'Yeah, I'm feeling a bit like that. This morning on the radio I heard of another boat experiencing strong winds and other dramas south of us.'

We decided to revisit Tahiti on our way through to new islands that called to us, including Suwarrow.

En route to Tahiti, we pulled in at Tahanea Atoll (around 965 nautical miles from the Gambiers). We could achieve over two hundred nautical miles a day in perfect conditions. More likely, we'd cover 150 to 175, making this a six day trip.

Traversing the Pacific changes you; you talk about five hundred nautical miles as 'around the corner.' You 'pull into' atolls and islands at whim. Don't get me wrong, the research, weather, and safety of these unique, remote anchorages are still studied and pondered upon. But the vastness of the Pacific becomes home. Anything over a week is a 'voyage'; anything less is a 'pop across' to another island. That's the nature of the beast. You become acquainted with the limitless stretch of sea and sky. It's home; it feels right.

We are always twitchy to make landfall and have a full night's sleep, but we're often ready to be released from the restraints of land and spread ourselves out in the lonely, calming, sometimes challenging and terrifying, ocean. We are always ready to move and always ready to stop.

Tahanea Atoll is part of the Tuamotu Archipelago in French Polynesia. For an atoll, it is large, measuring almost thirty miles in length; the maximum width is just under ten miles. There's a narrow entrance and a wide lagoon to anchor within. It's uninhabited but visited occasionally by islanders from neighbouring atolls for fishing.

We anchored in clear, turquoise water a fair distance away from shore and the other three boats already there. We declined the offer of joining the other cruisers on a shark dive in the passageway – sharks weren't my thing; I noticed Noel wasn't that keen, either.

'They won't hurt you,' they said. 'The sharks there have no teeth; they can only suck the flesh off your arm!'

We weren't sure if this was a joke or reality; either way, the outcome wasn't endearing.

We took time to assemble, pump up, and off load our large rubber dinghy; we wanted to snorkel on a reef, but first, we had to float our anchor chain. Finding a sandy patch to anchor in was a little tricky; between the anchor and the boat, the chain would snag on coral heads. The sharp coral can wear chain over time but, short-term, the chain causes damage. Our boat fenders were ideal floats. Every five metres, we lashed a fender to the chain to keep it floating above the living structure of the reef and to prevent snatching where the chain had been shortened when snagged. I kept one eye open for sharks.

With that job done, we puttered over to a coral patch, where we thought we'd be safe. This is where I learned I could walk on water.

There we were, having a jolly good time drifting along with the gentle current, watching colourful fish flash alongside vibrant coral. Noel swam about twenty metres in front of me, and something made me turn around. As I swung my head over my left shoulder, I practically touched noses with a black-tip shark. A cold rush of terror gushed into my belly as if a sluice gate had been opened.

Noting its teeth and bulky length at almost twice my height, I screamed, spun around, and flailed my way towards Noel. Running on pure adrenaline, I didn't make the decision – fight or flight didn't cross the wreckage of my mind, but clearly, flight had won the day. I can be calm when in immediate danger; meeting a shark so intimately had proven this wasn't always the case.

As I thrashed my way towards Noel, I forgot to breathe, but my mind conveniently decided to voice its opinion.

You're never going to out swim a shark! My thoughts tormented me; they were at odds with my physical emotions as if they were sitting back in a deck chair enjoying the show.

Any moment sharky is going to be enjoying lunch care of your left thigh.

But I couldn't stop. I had leaped into sheer panic mode. I had no control of my actions, and it appeared that I couldn't control my thoughts, either.

As I flogged my way nearer to Noel, he was blissfully unaware of my stress as he silently snorkelled in peace. He jumped two foot clear of the water as I grabbed his leg, clawed across his back, and sat on his shoulders.

'What the.... what're you doing, gerrrooofff!'

He pulled me down beside him.

'Shark, there's a shark!' I scanned the area. Sharky was hiding somewhere, clearly having a good titter at my expense.

'It grinned at me. It was so close I nearly kissed it!' I said breathlessly. 'I think we upset him by not going to see him with the diving excursion, and he decided to pay us a visit.' Fear makes me ramble.

Noel laughed. 'It's okay. Let's go over there. It's a bit shallower, and we can regroup.'

We stood on a reef, where the water came to above my knees. I peered at *Pyewacket* way off on the horizon.

'At least the dinghy is nearby.'

'Well, it's a few minutes swim to reach it,' Noel said. My heart did a little flip.

'Will you let go of me now?' Noel said as he tried to unpeel my arms away from his neck. I'd become a remarkable human form of Velcro.

'Oh, that's interesting,' Noel muttered as he managed to free himself, and I turned to look. I knew his cool demeanour didn't always mean the situation was cool. And I was right. My mate with the sharp teeth circled us, clearly revelling in our situation. He had us surrounded. Round and around he swam; his black beady eyes watching.

'Shit!' I can be so eloquent.

'Let's head back to the dinghy,' Noel suggested.

'And how do you propose we do that?' I asked with my knees knocking. I had found the thing scared me silly. I didn't like any of it – the thumping adrenaline or trembling limbs. Blind panic and tremendous fear wasn't something I experienced often; now it was becoming frequent!

I searched around the area and found two three-foot sticks to carry. I am not sure what I could have done if the blacktip fancied a munch. Perhaps poke him a bit and give him the hump? But it made me feel better.

Much to Noel's amusement, I swam back to the dinghy in circles, so I could keep an eye on anything that lurked behind me.

That moment changed my enjoyment of dipping in the oceans forever, but I didn't know I'd be gleefully jumping into shark infested water again... soon.

That afternoon, Noel caught fish for dinner. Throwing in a few crumbs of bread, he used the net to scoop up two large fish. We were unsure of their type, and having a touch of ciguatera, the stomach vacuuming illness, before (on *Mariah* in Sri Lanka), we were cautious.

'I think they're okay.' Noel flicked through fish identification books.

'That's good, then. You try them, and after an hour, if you're still alive, I'll have some!'

With warm, freshly baked bread, we ate a hearty fish soup.

We became twitchy at this spot. The large lagoon was littered with shallows, and the breeze started to pick up. By nature of a narrow and shallow entrance, it didn't take much for the passageway to become impassable. We didn't want to be stuck inside the atoll, and with growing winds, we became tense and out of sorts. We didn't want a repeat performance of the Gambiers.

'If we leave at dawn, the wind'll be less. I'd be happier if we're out there.' Noel said, hopping from one foot to the next, looking out to the open ocean.

We stowed all our gear, lifted the dinghy and motor on board, and prepared for departure. With the engine checked and a prepared meal on the stove ready to be heated up, the following morning, we bounced through the channel but were soon free in the wide, deep, and comforting ocean.

Dotted along this route are several atolls, but not all of them are easy to enter – some are impossible. Sitting on clear, protected water within an atoll sounds heavenly. It was away from modern man, machines, and shops, but it's difficult to find such a place, and no matter where we were, we always watched the weather.

Our taste buds and tummies were ready for a supermarket, which made the next destination choice easy: we made way for Tahiti.

'Who sails into Tahiti twice?' Noel said.

We felt honoured to have this chance. We both adored the French islands; not only were they a stunning feast for eyes, but they had copious fresh bread, succulent chicken, and tasty red meat. The bland, easy meals on board, while traversing many ocean miles, were becoming a little tiresome.

13

Taking Stock of Locks with Smoking Clippers

The 835 nautical mile sail to Tahiti meant steering a north west course, so the south east trade winds didn't ruffle the surface too much and, instead, gently drove us in the right direction.

At Fakarava, we turned to port, and for the last couple of days, we headed in a south west direction, still enjoying the trade winds. We opted for this route as the clearest, safest way through the scattered atolls. The angst of fighting the head winds to Easter Island soon forgotten.

Even though the engine needed a few repairs, it worked well, never missing a beat. We relaxed; we'd been on board about a year, enjoying *Pyewacket's* good points. She had plenty of living space and manoeuvred with responsive ease despite her length. She sliced through water, chomping through the miles, and with us sitting in the centre cockpit, it made for effortless sailing when the winds behaved themselves.

* * *

'Where on earth are we going to anchor?' Four years earlier, on *Mariah*, the vastness of the area provided many options to set-down our gear near the marina in Papeete. Now, it was littered with mooring buoys – all with boats swinging within cramped space. It was disappointing. We wanted to rest and relax, but we couldn't find anywhere to go. Finally, we nestled into a tiny spot but couldn't let out as much chain as we would have liked to.

The usual check in routine proceeded without a hitch, despite my having to inform the officials that we didn't have to pay the deposit.

'Remember,' I warned Noel, 'you stand there and keep quiet. I'm the skipper, and I'll do what's necessary.'

'Okay, I'll be on my best behaviour.' Noel could become a little impatient with officials.

'You will need to pay the deposit,' the stern faced customs man announced.

'We don't.' I tried not to be smug. 'I have a European passport, and we're married.' I indicated to Noel and pulled out our marriage certificate.

'You still have to pay it,' he said again, but he hesitated.

'Really?' I said in my smoothest voice. 'We have sailed here before together, and we didn't have to pay it then.'

The official stared at me and looked at his colleague, who shrugged.

'Wait a moment.' He dialled a number on the rotary phone, fired rapid French into the mouthpiece, and waited.

My heart thrummed. I knew we didn't have to pay, and I'd stand my ground.

Carefully, the man replaced the receiver on the black, dusty phone. 'Okay, you don't have to pay it,' he announced, as if it was his idea all along. He stamped our passports, issued us with documentation, and off we trotted on our merry way.

If you have a European passport (like me), you do not need to pay the deposit and whomever you are married to doesn't, either. All foreign visitors via sailboats were required to open a bank account and deposit the amount equivalent of airfares back to their country for all on board.

'I thought that coming to Tahiti again would be disappointing,' said Noel one evening as we danced smooth pirouettes on anchor while watching the pink and orange of dusk sweep along the still water. 'When, in fact, it feels like a miracle to be here again. It's always risky to revisit a place as you have certain expectations, but I'm enjoying it as much as the first time.'

I felt the same. We do tend to compare trips and events. Our trip on *Mariah* was different – it was easier. Of course, we had sailed a more straightforward route. But we both felt Tahiti had welcomed us back, and we were glad to be here.

But it was hot! So very hot. Our new boat cover we sewed together in Panama was helping, but it wasn't enough.

Inspired by a friend who shaved her head during an Australian summer, suffering in heat that could dissolve earlobes, and armed with enough years to marshal plenty of pluck, I introduced the hair clippers to my mane. In Tahiti, I was melting, especially beneath the fur-coat-mop that hung, limp, down my back.

Should I? Shouldn't I? I dithered. I'd cut my hair short before, and the fine, but many layered brunette strands, changed the shape of my face from long to round, feminine to masculine. But the heat was winning the battle.

'I look like a boy when I have short hair.'

'Don't be ridiculous,' Noel said. 'It'll look fine. You always look lovely.'

Armed with red wine, a carefree attitude (*It will grow back, right?*), and plenty of sweat, I clipped, snipped, and lopped. Not as brave as my friend, I left a few inches on top.

It wasn't as pretty as my long locks (and stuck up like a startled Gazelle in the mornings), but it was cool – both in temperature and a funky sort of mess.

With reduced temperature came a better temperament and a happy boat. However, Noel did offer one comment when I proudly showed off my hair-cutting ability.

With a sheepish expression, and known for his brutal honesty, Noel said, 'You're right. You do look like a boy!'

* * *

The rules had become stricter. On *Mariah*, we had anchored – for a few days – in the main port to help arrange some repairs (we didn't want to carry the heavy anchor winch on the bus). On *Pyewacket*, as we anchored in the same spot, Tahitian marine police moved us on.

We snuck one night in on anchor right next to the airport runway. The wind howled, and we found a site with some protection. We anchored in the evening.

'I wonder why other boats haven't sought sanctuary here?' Noel asked.

At dawn, an enormous shadow slowly crept over *Pyewacket*, and Noel's question was answered. The Tahitian police ship ordered us to move immediately. But by then, the wind had died, and we'd already enjoyed our peaceful night.

Our engine repairs from the Gambiers were holding well. They'd survived the demands of a storm and many more miles, and we felt that no further repairs were needed. Instead of boat jobs, I spent a delightful afternoon shopping with Judy from *SV Chantey*. We had met Judy and Barry on our last sailing trip, when we were on *Mariah*, and they were on board *SV Theta*; Judy had great shopping sense, whereas I did not!

Anchoring back near *SV Periclees* (purposely spelt this way), we stayed a few days before sailing over to revisit the neighbouring island of Moorea, where we had an altercation with a whale last time (on *Mariah*).

'Well done, that's great work,' Angus called out from *Periclees*.

I was convinced our anchor was under his boat. But as we slowly crept up on them, as I winched in the chain, there was more room than I thought.

'We may see you over in Moorea?' I called back.

'Probably. Safe trip.'

Moorea is one of the more stunning, peaceful islands, and a short while later on the same day, we anchored next to an explosion of green and soft blues; the lagoon resembled an artist's palette of vibrant colours. The vertical mountains that hug the poetic scenery reawakened our belief in the magnificence of nature.

A unique event came together here without planning or forethought. Four years ago, we'd been here on *Mariah*, and in company with Barry and Judy on *Theta*, Rob and Elyse on *Iron Mistress*, and Alim and Kian on *My Chance*. Now, at the same anchorage, all on different boats, most of the group was back, except Alim and Kian.

Barry and Judy were now sailing on *Chantey*, their new boat; Rob was skippering a friend's boat, and we, of course, were on *Pyewacket*. We spent an afternoon reminiscing, catching up, noting each other's changes in life and appearance; whatever the conversation, we managed to retie the threads of friendship as if it hadn't been years between seeing each other.

Over the years, we'd often talked about a reunion in The Netherlands, but this was close enough; although, it would have been superb to have the rest of the gang there.

The Pacific Puddle Jump Rally was in full swing on the island, and we were able to join in some of the festivities, but at times, we sat on the sidelines – we hadn't sailed with the fleet, and that was the difference.

A collection of boats were waiting to leave; the winds kept tugging at the seas and churning them into a frothy mess. By the fourth day, Noel and I lost our patience, and viewing the seas outside the reef and studying long-term weather forecasts, we decided they had calmed enough to make a run for the next destination.

All the boats watched us leave. *Pyewacket* bucked and reared, the engine groaned and our stomachs heaved. In the unprotected, shallow parts, the battle was on, but once we hit deeper water, *Pyewacket's* decks levelled out, and though it was a bumpy ride, it wasn't too boisterous. With only a little over one hundred nautical miles to our next stop, this leg was a mere drop within the ocean.

* * *

Huahine is thriving with coconut plantations, banana groves, bread trees, vanilla, and orchids. Apparently, many sacred temples are hidden throughout dense vegetation. But we didn't see any.

Noel and I were both reluctant to get off the boat. Despite other cruisers encouraging us to go for walks, we were happy tackling jobs on board, swinging on anchor, viewing the lush hillsides and sandy shores.

We'd seen many similar islands. That's not to say we were complacent or bored with the beauty, but we were nearing home, and that meant new challenges, a change of pace, earning money; while here, we wanted to enjoy the boat.

One of my projects was piecing together a portfolio on the boat to try to convince Australian customs and immigration that we were a clean vessel. I downloaded official forms; I scoured websites and blogs gleaning notes written by other cruisers who had already brought in overseas boats; I compiled a list of everything I could think of that the officials would want: equipment on board, islands visited, time at sea, people on board, illnesses, etc. It grew into a thick, impressive report.

We'd visited a different part of Huahine before: a quiet bay anchored near a church filled with a haunting chorus of harmonised voices. Back then, we had painted *Mariah's* topsides and enjoyed the solitude. Noel's sandals had been stolen from the dinghy!

This time, we had entered at Avamoa Pass near the north west tip of the island and followed the lagoon to the southern part. We marvelled at Tahiti's great navigation buoys, compared to the Gambiers, with their ambiguous system of bamboo sticks, all the same colour, only a variation in height. Here, the red and green markers were clean, lit, clear, and bestowed a feeling of safety; you knew you were in the right bit of water.

Huahine is easy on the eyes; the sparkling beaches and flourishing forests appear better than the brochure. Although we weren't energised to view the island, we still took great pleasure in hosting other cruisers on board. A delightful evening of shared drinks and stories flowed over *Pyewacket's* deck; no dress code, no shoes, no rules – just relaxed company and many laughs carrying over the still water.

We were looking forward to something different. On our previous crossing of the Pacific, we'd stopped at the Cook Islands, and Aitutaki stole our hearts. Now, we had our eye on Suwarrow. We knew little about this atoll, except it had two caretakers that checked in and managed the boats. We both had visions of cranky old guys reading the riot act. But we had to see for ourselves.

'They appreciate any gifts of food.' This information came over the radio on a regular sched.

'It's not obligatory, but these guys are there for six months, and to a certain degree, they rely on cruisers to help keep stocks up.'

Noel frowned. 'How can the government put people on the island with insufficient supplies? All sounds a bit suspect to me.' I had to agree.

14

No Strangers Here

'We know they've been here, murdering animals. We witness the evidence of scorched bones washed up on the beach.' This was one of countless stories divulged to sailors who drop anchor at Suwarrow Atoll; around 100-140 boats furl their sails here each year.

This particular story is about the illegal fishing that occurs when the caretaker's six month stint finishes, and the island is left uninhabited; the unwanted fish are killed and thrown back – senseless cruelty even in paradise, and that's what it is here: paradise.

Previously, we've visited a handful of islands without airports, cars, and supermarkets, but Suwarrow (pronounced sue-warh-row) has its own unique, harmonic constant.

The north-facing entrance has a low reef extending east of the wide bar that does a fantastic job of fending off the deep rolling swells. These pulsing lumps of sea had grown into mountains during our five day sail from Huahine, among the Society Islands. The 3 p.m. sun dangled high enough to reveal the coral-fringed entrance; between the frothing white caps and scorched sand, we puttered into a symphony of blues.

Tucked safely behind Anchorage Island, the waters smoothed, and the dreamy scene of tranquillity was broken by squealing birds, crying a welcome. The island's coconut trees spill out onto the white beach and tilt at exotic angles; the pale blues of the shallow water captures the sunlight, accentuating the contrasts of lush green flora, bone white sand, and soft blue water.

The allocated anchorage area is small – if you want to sit in shallower depths of ten to fifteen metres. Tattoos of coral make finding a spot a challenge; by our third attempt, the anchor buried into sand.

'Cheers.' We smiled, at peace. The chilled Panamanian beer from our stores tasted especially delicious.

The next day, we took our sea legs to land and expelled a train of contented sighs. Following the frond hemmed path with its shadowy light to a clearing, we found two buildings, old and new. The timber, two story structure is the caretakers' home during their stay. The ground floor is open, and a large banquet lunch was taking place. Having declined an offer to join the group (we'd just eaten breakfast), James, the seasoned caretaker, suggested we walk around part of the island and return after their lunch for formalities. The blustery but beautiful windward side confirmed the island's name, bringing relief to travelling boats from the strong trade winds, deflecting them a good ten knots less in the lee.

'Stand by that sign,' I said. 'I want to take a picture.' Noel stood against the SHARKS! NO SWIMMING! notice while I continued to click on our camera.

'They should've finished lunch by now. Shall we head back?'

'Yup, oh, look, just climb along that palm tree. That'd make a great photo.'

Noel obliged, and I snapped off more memories. The gorgeous location could be used in any famous photo shoot.

With four straightforward forms to fill out, rules to read, and our wallets fifty American dollars lighter, we could sit back and absorb the tales of history, wildlife, and survival, leaving us with a thirst to hear more. The payment allowed cruisers a two week stay.

A chronicle of cruelty and greed is the atoll's initial history. Originally named Suvorov after the Russian explorer Lazarev (also spelled Lazarov), who found the atoll in 1814, it was later renamed Suwarrow, in keeping with the Cook Islanders' language (apparently, they do not have words ending in 'v'). Sadly, the Russian admiralty took little notice of Lazarov's discovery, and many whalers were wrecked on the low reefs for some years after the find. Discovering an island is a funny thing. As the caretakers say, 'The Cook Islanders never lost it!'

The stories of shipwrecks, murder, buried treasure, and evidence of a former population all stir within the island's history; men were lost when their ship struck the reef, and pearl divers were left on the island for six months, with a promise of payment if and when they were collected.

Pearlers mixed with shipwrecked folk; fights and murder broke the island's peace. Later, the history calms and reveals that the atoll was leased to various large companies to gather pearl shells and plant coconuts. In 1914, a hurricane ceased all pearl shell operations.

Mr. Tom Neale is the one most of us identify this island with. He wrote *An Island to Oneself* about the time he lived in solitude, on and off, for six years. At times, he left the island for a while, due to Rarotonga authorities deciding to evacuate him; he saved his pennies and simply returned. Unconfirmed knowledge is passed along in this land that at some point, while Tom lived on one end of this 'deserted' island, the other end was inhabited by sixty Cook Islanders! The written word is a wonderful thing.

We haven't read Tom's book yet but are keen to do so, especially now that we have stood in his house, which was left over from the military occupation in WWII.

* * *

When at Tahanea, a black tipped shark, one and half metres in length, circled us for fifteen minutes. That's where I found out I could scream under water while wearing a snorkel! Here in Suwarrow, blacktips commonly circle the boat on anchor. A cruising highlight for me is swimming in pristine water at my whim. Apparently, blacktips are curious about humans but not dangerous.

'I can't believe I'm jumping into a shark infested pool!' I never leaped in alone. Noel came, too. *You look tastier than me!*

Learning is an everyday occurrence when cruising: at Suwarrow, I learned two lessons in harvesting cynicism in the written word. The revelation (and maybe only gossip) that Tom was not on a deserted island leaves me miffed. But the written advice for fending off sharks leaves me mystified.

In one of our 'identify sea creatures' books, I read that if you slap the water with your hand, sharks will be scared off. So, that was the great plan…

'This is lovely, the perfect temperature.'

'Yes,' I agreed. 'But there's a large shark down there.'

We peered at a fat blacktip as it sauntered twenty metres below the surface, passing us by but swimming nearer in doing so.

'I'll slap the water. That'll make you feel better.'

Noel straightened out his hand and slapped the surface three times.

Like a torpedo, in less than a second, the shark turned and made a beeline straight for us.

'Shit!'

'Nice one!'

We were at the bow and both clung to the anchor chain, hoping sharky would only nibble our flippers and not our soft flesh.

The shark was upon us. We were scrabbling up the chain, looking pathetic, but all sophistication vanishes when sharp teeth in a wild predator are part of the deal.

As the shark moved within stroking distance, it veered off. I'm sure I saw a glint in its eye.

'That was dumb,' Noel said, trying to scrape back some dignity by treading water calmly. I remained on full alert and look out. 'Of course the shark is going to think that it is a fish in distress. Who wrote that book!'

Two days later, after the sickening terror had petered out and we'd forgotten the fear levels, we snorkelled on the reef. Drifting with the dinghy tethered to our waists and a knife strapped to our thighs, we coasted along a reef for two hours. *I'm armed and dangerous.* With the little boat so close, I could relax. Vivid fish didn't flick away in a flash, but they swam just out of reach. Colourful coral stole our attention and helped us forget about sharky and his buddies.

That night, at the potluck dinner, the scraps of fish were fed to the sharks at the island's entrance on the opposite side – strictly in that area only, not the anchorage site, to keep swimming safe. As James whistled, twenty blacktips came charging into the shallows liked trained dogs. Amid the frenzy of fins, two greys followed at a speed I simply could not comprehend. One blacktip became intimate with James' feet, where he stood in just inches of water. I sensed my low place in the food chain, unsafely perched on a little rock. I now know that it is a waste of time having an escape plan for sharks. If there's a feeding frenzy, there's no hope.

James and John spend May to November on Anchorage Island to check cruisers in and out, and they are present to protect the wildlife and beauty. For non-obligatory donations of food and/or money, they take you diving, which is said to be some of the best diving in the entire Pacific; introduce you to other islands within the atoll; and arrange coconut crab and lobster hunting and excursions to bird breeding areas. But their expertise lies in entertaining. Within the setting of an oft deserted island, privacy is valued, and it is as though James and John own the land, and we all have an exclusive invitation to spend some time there.

At the potluck dinner, the international flags in a myriad of colours flap lazily in the breeze. This zephyr spirals through the coconut trees, enough to keep cool, not too much to bluster. Haphazard international bodies recline in the makeshift benches. The food supplied by all has exclusive flavours and flare that cruisers are famous for. The atmosphere brings several elements together, which creates an environment free of politics, judgement, and opposing opinions. We were all children on the planet, no country of origin better or worse. We all marvelled at this tiny corner of a world that is ours for the briefest blink in history. Kindred spirits are finally content, and that is the key ingredient.

This was the second season here for James Mataa as a park ranger.

'I've left my family behind in Rarotonga,' he explains, 'but I enjoy the solitude of this island.' With equal relish, he plays host to all the cruisers. 'I love the whole job.' And you can clearly see that he's passionate about everything he does. When pushed for a downside of his responsibilities, he said that, occasionally, he has to ask a cruiser to leave. Embarrassingly so, most recently, an Australian cruiser became a little high on rum and lost his friendliness. James had the responsibility to ensure he left promptly.

'We want cruisers here,' he explained, 'but the right type of cruisers, those who will respect the island and our rules.'

James has a neat affinity with Tom Neale – both born in Wellington, New Zealand, travelling the Pacific in their youth, and living on Suwarrow. As a delightful touch, from the Yacht Club, every evening, James would escort each cruiser to the dinghy dock via torchlight and bid us all good night.

John Rouruina Gerald Trego, the assistant park ranger, was on his first season.

'I've left behind my wife Rose-Lee and three children, Jonelle, Elijah, and Silas, in Rarotonga, too'.

John (aka Boo Boo – he's built like a bear, but not a baby one!) was finding his time on the island a great pleasure.

Amongst a myriad of other skills that hold him in good stead for his responsibilities, he has a background in agriculture, marine, and cooking in the army. 'I miss my family, but that is the only downside.'

John had set himself the task to ensure everyone returned back to their boat with a smile on their face. He made a complete success of this responsibility, too.

Both caretakers have all the skills required to maintain this slice of heaven. But they also have a warm welcome and passion for their land. Their knowledge of flora, fauna, and history is exceptional and passed on with immense enthusiasm; they are true ambassadors for their country. They work around the clock, helping, guiding, and hosting all cruisers at all different times of the day, while carrying out their other tasks – tasks which include report writing. The National Government Services require them to map out what fish are where.

As for the family atmosphere, which Suwarrow fosters, James and John truly were a pleasure to meet and created an overall charm that's hard to describe. I hoped this would never change; it would mean the end of some special magic.

* * *

Lobsters and crabs are in abundance, if you can catch them. The first attempt, now known as the 'reconnaissance,' netted us only the knowledge of when *not* to go lobster hunting. Walking along a low reef in the middle of the Pacific Ocean is mesmerising. Crashing barrels of white foam sat on one side, calm pools of trapped, flickering fish on the other. That same night, though, we did catch three coconut crabs, letting one go as it was too small.

'Look under their tails,' James explained, turning a small crab on its back. 'If they have eggs, or a sac, they are female and should be returned. Males are okay to catch.'

Coconut crabs walk forward and run backward, so with a large bucket and a little scare at their heads, they run back into the bucket. Sounds easy, except their mighty, bone crunching claws cling on the edge of the pail or grab your stick, crushing it to splinters. Their beautiful blue-tinged shell turns vivid red once cooked. With two males, we were happy; our buddies, Jenny and Randy on board *Mystic*, shared a delicious lunch with us.

We'd not made as many friends as we had on our trip on board *Mariah* – part of that was the result of sailing to remote destinations. We'd zig-zagged a few times with *Mystic*, and we were both keen to spend more time with Jenny and Randy. Their enthusiasm for keeping their footprint as small as possible was contagious. Sinewy and cheerful, Randy often sailed to and from shore in their timber dinghy; with no wind, he rowed. Jenny kept fit with boat tasks and positively glowed with health; she embraced each adventure with such passion. She possessed great enthusiasm for sharing her skills, even if she first learned a skill hours before teaching others!

The dozen boats swinging on anchor had arranged a workshop: beading, drawing, painting, and all creative talents were welcome. Jenny taught herself palm fond weaving in the morning so she could share her expertise in the afternoon!

Randy and Jenny ran into each other in a café. They were both ready to escape when they met. Jump forward several months later, and here they were, sailing the world on a ten metre boat. Both Noel and I loved *Mystic*. With many similarities to *Mariah*, it was simple, small. Jenny grew herbs on board, and often, yummy baking smells wafted from their companionway – it was a bit like looking back on ourselves fifteen years ago.

The fun didn't stop on Suwarrow. Cruisers are renowned for making their own entertainment. Angus declared he would be holding a workshop to present his favourite culinary dish, entailing a cooking demonstration with noodles, coconut, and prawns. The idea grew. John (Boo Boo) would show the group how versatile coconuts were in the morning; everyone else would bring along a few drinks, and we'd enjoy a feast in the evening.

I learned many things that day. Not one part of a coconut (and much of the entire tree) goes to waste; the white fleshy part is, of course, edible; the water and milk is drinkable; the fibre from the husk is called 'coir' and is used in ropes, mats, brushes, caulking boats, and compost; copra is the dried seed used in coconut oil; the trunks provide building timbers; the leaves provide materials for baskets and roofing thatch; and the husk and shells can be used for fuel and are a good source of charcoal. My learning continued: a small, basic kitchen can cope with half a dozen people cooking different dishes at the same time; everyone has knowledge to share and a fascinating back-story, and most importantly, life was best when kept simple.

The bountiful day culminated in a delicious banquet and a show. Young girls cruising with their parents put on a fine display of island dancing. They taught the women some moves, and we put on a hysterical, short show, wriggling in our sarongs. That night, I learned a dozen new ways to tie sarongs.

'I think Suwarrow has become one of my favourite places,' I said to Noel as we walked along the beach that stretched out just for us.

'It certainly has a special magic.'

We have our favourite places that we've sailed to over the years: Aitutaki, Moorea, and other far flung places of great memories for lots of different reasons. Suwarrow is now one of our lead destinations; this is the most unique, beautiful, welcoming place we have ever been to. Simple tasks, such as going ashore to swap books, thank our hosts for the previous night, and connect with new arrivals, became a pleasure; the calmness of the island affected us all. When I thought of these moments ending, it made my eyes sting.

So what makes this place different? There's no airport, no cars, no town (no shopping!), no tourists, no loud music on the beach, no phones, and no Internet. There is only nature and beauty and friends; that's just it: there are no strangers here.

You have to embrace and value certain times and places in your history; we do this with Suwarrow. But it's not just about the appreciation after the event; it is the awareness and gratitude *at the time*. We spent each and every day in our short stay on the atoll in wonder, mesmerised by the beauty, the solitude, the camaraderie, the support, and the friendship.

Sadly, when it came time to leave, we didn't want to. It felt as though we'd arrived, taken a breath, and then it was time to go.

James held brief radio scheds each day to alert the small cluster of cruisers to the day's activities. On our day of departure, he made me cry.

'It's a sad day today, folks, as we say farewell to the lovely Mr. and Mrs. *Pyewacket*.'

With that, Noel and I hauled our sails and tried not to look back.

* * *

We were both looking forward to seeing Pago Pago at Samoa.

A tsunami had raged through the harbour the year before. We were hearing of many boats snagging supermarket trolleys, a kid's pram, and all sorts of sad debris on anchor.

The two night trip was uneventful sailing-wise, but chock full worry-wise.

On the second night, Noel became ill. He thrashed in the aft-double bed, writhing beneath sweat glossed skin. He moaned, hot, cold, clearly in pain, and with half-closed eyes darting back and forth. I worried over his condition and spent the night alone in the cockpit.

Every fifteen minutes, with stomach clenched in worry, I'd nip below decks, wondering if Noel's condition had worsened.

Mostly, he'd relax enough to relay the message that he's okay. Clearly, he wasn't.

The bed became sticky with sweat beneath him; I tried to mop his brow with a cool cloth, but he fidgeted and ached. 'Everything hurts,' he said; he's never one to complain.

While the pain buffeted Noel below decks, *Pyewacket* sailed beautifully in near perfect fifteen knots of wind aft of the beam; as if the wind, waves, and boat had conspired to make my night easy. I only had to watch for other traffic; check the lines, sails, rigging, radar, course, speed; and then navigate and download weather maps to ensure nothing horrid lurked nearby.

'Do you need me to radio for some help?' I asked Noel at one stage during a lucid moment.

'No, it's a fever. I'm fine.' I watched him closely.

What could anyone do via radio anyway?

The night dragged for us both; Noel in the grip of an unrelenting fever, and lack of sleep threatened my skills with each passing minute. At times like this, I was thankful I could manage the boat myself. Noel and I made a point of us both understanding, handling, and managing every aspect of sailing, weather, navigation, and the boat as a whole. We always feared and prepared for the worst case scenario: something happening to one of us, leaving the other single handing.

Through the night, I became starkly aware of my responsibilities, my power. *I'm in control.* I had sole responsibility. I wallowed in a sense of achievement for a while.

Yes, this is 'enough.' I answered my long asked question.

My little piece of self-indulgence didn't last long with equipment checks, patient examinations, and a foreign port to enter in the morning.

I pulled the large scale chart of the Pago Pago harbour to the top of the pile and studied it carefully. We'd already put waypoints into the GPS for the safest route. I checked the latitude and longitude of each one and opened up the electronic charts, too.

The bright computer-based charts were simply amazing, with the ability to zoom in and out all over the world. We could plug in our GPS and watch us move along the screen. But we didn't trust them.

We didn't trust the paper charts, either. And not to sound like conspiracy theorists, neither did we trust the GPS entirely (not for narrow waterways). Inherent errors exist in every piece of equipment, chart, paper, and electronic. Not one item must be solely relied upon. So we utilised everything at our disposal, as well as our ears, eyes, and all those yummy, fun, imperative navigation exercises the best boat skippers employ all the time: deduced reckoning (DR), distance speed time calculations, running fixes, set and drift, double the angle off the bow, three bearing fixes, and at times, in calm weather, utilising the sextant – celestial navigation.

When we had returned to land after our nine years on *Mariah*, at a loss of what to do next and feeling out of kilter with society, we'd studied maritime. Both of us had achieved Master 5, a ticket enabling us to skipper commercial vessels up to twenty-four metres in length with no limitations in distance off shore.

We'd learned our trade well, having not only the experience but also the qualifications and working on ships in Papua New Guinea, where every morsel of text, picture, practice, expertise, theory, and knowledge was put to use.

A year later, I began teaching coxswains (skipper – up to twelve metres) and, after that, Master 5, as well; Noel taught building and carpentry, but later, he joined me, and we ran the maritime classes between us both. It was a hugely responsible job, vastly rewarding, littered with challenges, but taught us more every day. Some students taught us more about the oddness of people than several decades of living would!

The stimulating and demanding work ensured we had these skills ingrained in our minds; they were second nature. This went a long way to aid Noel's recovery. He couldn't get up, but he didn't have to worry, either. He knew I was in command; we were safe. He only had to worry about himself.

The pre-dawn soft blues arrived hand in hand with my relief. I needed something to help me stay awake, and the promise of daylight delivered the necessary shot of energy.

Noel managed to sip a weak cup of tea and sat heavily in the cockpit; his fever started to ease, but he was pale, weak. I creased my forehead in concern and watched him carefully and unobtrusively. He's so rarely poorly and hates fuss.

As we neared the wide, well-marked channel, his spirits lifted, and together, we discussed the anomalies of oddly placed markers and the winding route on the electronic charts; we eased in, and the new vista made us both feel better.

A funky, dirty fishing fleet lined the outer harbour. Opposite, off-white buildings lined the shore beneath the backdrop of fertile hills. We puttered into filthy water, along the top part of the L-shaped harbour, before turning ninety degrees left into a natural-inner harbour. Within the exotic port, twenty boats hung in the limp breeze; abandoned rusted vessels suspended on fraying rope were scattered between the travelling fleet.

We were worried about dropping the anchor because a lot of debris, including household items, sat on the seabed floor after the tsunami. We'd nearly lost *Mariah* many years ago when her anchor had picked up a sheet of metal. The anchor dragged the metal along; fortunately, someone had saved her as we were off the boat at the time the wind picked up.

As we puttered in, we watched another sailboat leave; there was a mooring free. Usually, we trust our own anchor gear rather that of an unknown mooring. But we were staying on board mostly. The weather was fine, so we'd be doing anchor or mooring watch whichever way we tethered ourselves.

Noel, almost back to his old self, listened as I chatted to friends on other boats via the radio, collecting details of local doctors. Other cruisers listened in, as we all did via the radio, but I was taken aback when a forceful American lady insisted we go to hospital right away.

I wanted Noel to be checked out, but Noel is stubborn.

'I feel better. I just want to be left alone.'

He rested on board, half snoozing, half keeping an eye on the boat, while I joined with other cruisers to buy galley supplies. The local shop's shelves carried more dust than supplies. A few out-of-date items sat forlornly alone, but I was glad to take a walk along the dusty, poor streets, even beneath the humidity of the day.

The lack of secure moorings and trustworthy anchor sites meant we couldn't leave the boat at the same time. Noel recovered nicely. I tried to catch up with sleep, but neither of us felt compelled to explore. The harbour was fascinating, with its esoteric mix of island green and industry yellow, but the next stop was Samoa, the land of giants and a marina to stay at so we could re-group without further concern, and we could sightsee properly.

The night before leaving, we watched an American cruiser jump in the water to retrieve an item that had flipped overboard.

'I'm so glad we don't have to jump into this fetid water,' I mused.

'You're not wrong there.'

As we sat in the cockpit, both feeling much better, we noticed, as the tide changed, all the vessels swung in unison the other way, except us.

'Oh no,' I groaned.

'That doesn't look good,' muttered Noel. 'That'll teach us for being smug.'

'Well, I'd better suit up. You're in no fit state to jump in.' I found my wetsuit, tethered the knife to my wrist, and kept my mouth firmly shut as I dived in.

Upon inspection, I found a rope caught around our propeller shaft. When we collected up the mooring, we also picked up another rope, an old mooring line. Someone had run over it and cut the line below the surface, keeping it invisible just below the surface.

Armed with snorkel gear and determination, I cut the rope away and hoped it hadn't caused any damage.

'We must've taken it out of gear just before the engine stalled,' I said to Noel as I climbed back on board, the brown water dripping smelly stains on the deck.

'It was well wound around the shaft, but it's all off now.' I was thankful we were free, but anxious about starting the engine and finding damage.

'Where's the rope now? The bit that's left in the water?'

'It's gone. I've cut it all away., There's nothing there to snag us now. I had a good look.' I didn't want to dive back in, and I had made a thorough check for other problems below the surface.

The engine fired and ran smoothly in gear with no hint of rattles or vibration, and I had a long, hot shower.

We decided to leave at dawn. Other cruisers were miffed Noel hadn't sought medical attention, but he promised he would at Samoa. We were both glad to ease out of the packed harbour without further trouble.

Even with all the pollution, Noel reckons this harbour to be one of the most classical, beautiful, and exotic harbours he has entered.

* * *

After an easy overnighter of smooth waters and clear skies, we were in Samoa.

Filled with an overabundance of previous open, untenable, and windy anchorages, we were keen for the luxury of a marina. The journeyed jungle drums told us to expect a reasonable marina in Apia, the main port of Samoa. The marina opened a few years ago, the eagerness of the officials to fill the slips quickly caused boats bunching up at the entrance, running aground – where the dredging was incomplete! Things are a lot better now.

Our friends, Rolande and Angus on board *Periclees*, were already tied in the marina, and they held a spot for us next door to them. The tenseness flowed from my bunched muscles. There's such comfort in tying up securely and not worrying about wind and waves.

Noel ran more lines between the firm structure of the wharf and *Pyewacket*. 'I just can't help myself,' he said with a wry grin. We had administration and medical appointments to take care of here, so we'd be off the boat a fair bit. It was also our first stay in a marina since Ensenada, Mexico!

We arrived on Saturday; the officials wouldn't be available to check us in until Monday morning.

'Can we go into town?' I asked the marina staff.

'If you are very discreet you can. You should stay on board, though.'

'We'll be very careful,' we promised.

The next morning, we couldn't resist the invite to the local church, with their vibrant singing, colourful attire, and a warm welcome, but the generosity didn't stop there.

'I'd like all our visitors to introduce themselves.' Rolande and Noel explained to the finely dressed congregation who we were and why we were there. Each man received a gift of a photo frame, and we were invited to stay for lunch.

'Please join us next door in our hall,' the minister said.

Vast displays of identifiable and unidentifiable food teetered high on plates along narrow tables, with plenty of different cakes to sample. All this was offered to the town's guests, namely Rolande, Angus, Noel, and me.

'We've had some interesting changes here,' the locals explained. 'Just a few years ago, the entire island changed from driving on the right side of the road to the left.' Amusement stretched across brown faces as they remembered the day. 'Fifteen kilometres an hour was the permitted speed for the first day, and if you look around town, many signs and painted arrows still remain, reminding drivers of where they were supposed to be in the road.'

'That would have been fun to witness,' I said. 'I expect the town clock that sits on a roundabout would've been an interesting point to watch from.'

The following day, as the official checked our paperwork on board *Pyewacket*, Noel said, 'The singing in the church yesterday was wonderful!'

The uniformed officer went still, his welcoming smile slid from his face. Before his anger gathered momentum, I stepped in, 'We only heard it, of course, from here; it was truly beautiful.' With my sweetest smile for the official and my best tut reserved for Noel, we got away with it! I cringed a few days later when I heard a crew severely berated by a customs officer, threatening them with a fine, because they had left their boat prior to checking in!

* * *

Apia, the capital of Samoa, is the joint where all the big Samoan football players come from; the ones who flatten the opposition when they run down the field.

Walking along the street, we gave the locals a nice smile and a hello, and if any started to run (which we hadn't seen as it was way too hot for that carry on), we gladly stepped aside, pointed to some other poor bugger coming the other way, and shouted, 'He's got the ball!'

I'd been looking forward to visiting Samoa because a famed author had lived there for a while. In 1889, at thirty-nine years old, Robert Louis Stevenson arrived in Apia and never left. I've read that he suffered with tuberculosis and came to Samoa for the climate, passing away in 1894 from an aneurism. His resting place, Vailima, overlooks Apia harbour with a museum (his home) in his dedication. Our eloquent guide reported that Stevenson's tuberculosis was never confirmed; she doubts the rumour is true. More apt to his profession, the locals call him *Teller of Tales*.

'He made an effort to ingratiate himself with the locals,' explained a local Minister. 'Unlike the other expats.' This observation left me befuddled. Why would you want to live in a beautiful, welcoming island like Samoa and not mix with the locals?

Samoa (formerly Western Samoa) lies 620 nautical miles east north east of Fiji. It neighbours American Samoa and has been proudly independent since 1962. Samoans are said to be the second largest Polynesian group (after the Maoris of New Zealand). They have their own Polynesian dialect that we had no hope of understanding; fortunately, English is spoken widely. Samoans have retained their traditional ways, with a chief heading the family group. Most of the men, young and old, wear lava lavas, but we could see the western influence slinking in; teenagers had better mobile phones than we've ever owned and ear plugs carrying music from the latest iPod. Everyone wore Cheshire Cat smiles, big white welcoming grins, and offered 'good mornings' that manufactures an embracing welcome.

After monitoring power constantly for nearly two years, watching water consumption, and having the ability to count the number of times we had eaten out in that time on one hand, we were ready for a treat. Endless amps and indulgent showers are great comforts for cruisers. Reams of restaurants and cafés rescue us from galley serfdom.

Situated on the edge of town, the marina was quiet – if you could ignore the passionate drumming in the long boats at 5:30 every morning as semi-naked men practice their technique. The town centre is a five minute stroll beneath enough trees to find comfortable shade from the searing heat. Vivid perfume from vibrant flowers leads us into town. Samoans are always happy to see us and help with our bumbling efforts to find what we need.

We were rapidly approaching Australia, and the stocked shelves in the supermarket highlighted our approach. Recognized brands, the beloved Vegemite and freshly baked meat pies carried the smells and tastes that had been sadly absent on board for too long. Of course, none of this helped the waist line, but beautifully designed lava lavas and pāreus wrapped around our waists, hiding lumps and bumps from the effects of scrumptious sins! It wasn't the first time we'd both worn sarongs, but it's a bit disconcerting when your man looks better in a skirt than you do!

We treated ourselves to local tastes: tarro, breadfruit, and coconut milk. During our indulgence, Polynesian and fire dancing mixed with the dining experience – fit males spiralling up into a frenzy of passion, maleness, and pure unadulterated joy with their dancing and singing. The women, beautiful, serene and a little sedate, did not command the fever of the golden skinned males, which may be part of the ritual.

During our stay, we did a comprehensive tour of government buildings. Visiting a private doctor, we were dissatisfied with the consultancy, so a visit the hospital was in order.

'Line up at the records queue,' the receptionist whispered. Twenty minutes later, we had filled in a form, paid twenty Tala (about fifteen dollars), and Noel clutched a piece of card with the number eighty printed on it.

'What number are we up to?' Noel asked a young guy.

'Thirteen.' He grinned a white smile at us.

Four hours later, after dodging hordes of coughing, vomiting, sneezing, crying, and sleeping bodies strewn in the dirtiest place in town, number eighty was called in Samoan. We were now best mates with the town's sick, dying, and whoever sat nearest to us who could translate to English, giving us a good dose of germs with their helpfulness.

Noel had his blood pressure taken in front of an audience of one hundred people.

'Wait again, please,' the nurse said.

We could see cubicles, with the sick prostrate, and figured that many doctors were calling the next patient once they were free. We could hear a soft voice calling numbers in Samoan, but could see not where or whom the voice came from.

Samoan language is fascinating. Reading a translation, I noticed that it is full of vowels, with the odd consonant thrown in for good measure. On hearing the language, it sounds full of Ms, Ns, and Ls. You can guess or understand the odd word in many languages, but Samoan was alien to our ears. We constantly checked numbers with our ailing acquaintances.

The hospital café, with surprisingly yummy rolls and good books combined with short walks, helped retain our sanity during the wait, and you never know who you are going to meet.

'We've been invited for a cup of tea.' Noel returned from a lengthy visit to the bathroom. 'Follow me,' he said without stopping.

'What?' But he was walking off, so I grabbed my book and followed.

'Here we are.' Noel knocked on the door bearing a sign: Assistant Director.

'Come in, ah, welcome, so very nice to meet you.' A handsome, suited man took my hand.

'Tea?' The (stand-in) assistant director had offered Noel his private bathroom and invited us back. We sat in his clean, tidy office and chatted about our lives.

'You must visit my home and family.' He smiled. 'Do you need any assistance while you are here?'

'We're looking for a company that makes vinyl signs. We need some for the boat. The boat name is painted on at the moment, and our paintwork is wearing off.' I'd diligently painted *Pyewacket II* on the hull in Ecuador, but the paint hadn't lasted.

'Well, I own a sign company!'

Vinyl signs were exactly what we needed, and it was fortuitous to meet Amosa. He helped us avoid giving yet another challenge to the information centre, who had so far answered our odd queries with wide grins. Tourists are not known to ask for directions to hardware stores.

After another two hours, we heard number eighty called again. Noel talked to a young lady, who, despite drowning in defective bodies, sitting under flickering strobes, and shouting over the shuddering death moans of a patient who was far too near, was professional and caring. Noel underwent some tests. Much to our relief, he was fine now, but was advised to follow up once back home.

Our next tour of duty was the Australian Consulate. My Australian Residency visa had expired, and I needed to renew it before entering Australia. The Consulate bent over backwards to help us.

During many visits to the pristine offices, we had much fun in the waiting room. Like the hospital (but much cleaner), you are issued with a number and wait your turn. Unlike the hospital, the numbers only reached thirty, so sometimes, as the numbers cycled around, you held a lower number than the person in front of you. It's a bit confusing, but lots of fun creating conversations in the usually silent waiting room. Two young girls had arrived before me. I could see they had number thirty as they fanned themselves with the laminated card. I picked up number twenty-nine; six of us sat in the reception area! Sitting opposite, we smiled at each other and compared numbers. Much discussion and laugher ensued. I tried hard to make them go in front of me.

'You were clearly here before me,' I explained, Being a Brit, I like the order of queues.

'No, please, go first, follow the numbers, and you're our guest here.'

These beautiful young girls were the epitome of courtesy. I suspect they were happy to sit in a comfortable place, maybe away from school or work. But I also know that this type of pleasant exchange does not come from malcontent people; such fine manners are becoming sadly extinct in some countries.

Next to the visa desk sat another enquiry desk for different matters; only opening for a few hours a day, the locals arrived early in readiness. Each person would come in, kick off their dusty sandals next in a line in front of the desk, and sat bare-footed. Once the operator was ready, the owner of the first set of shoes stepped up, slipped their foot wear on, and had their enquiry dealt with – and so on along the queue of footwear.

I looked forward to my consulate visits and exchanging fun dialogue with new people while we waited our turn to talk to the official. Annoyingly, misinformation created a two week process, instead of a two-day procedure, but at last, I was legal to enter Australia.

* * *

My island tour cost me fifty Tala (six dollars) for nine hours, plus lunch and a few cheap entry fees. Noel preferred to snooze – we were both shy of potential illnesses – so I was accompanied by Canadian, American, and Finish cruisers. On the windward side of the island, the previous tsunami had left its mark; only house foundations remained alongside gaping holes where enormous trees had been uprooted; beautiful beaches were stolen by nature's power.

'There was no warning,' explained Chris, our guide. 'Many people died.'

What struck me most was the cleanliness of the island. We had heard that nearby islands had a litter problem; it was blamed on lack of education. Traditionally eating by hand, when plastic utensils were introduced, they were thrown on the ground with the scraps. However, that excuse doesn't exist in Samoa. Colourful houses and fales (thatched huts) are dotted between emerald foliage. Bumpy roads, clear of rubbish, circumnavigate the island, allowing awesome views of both plush land and pulsating sea. Locals waved as our white faces were pressed against the car windows; they wanted to know all about us when we stopped to admire art work, wildlife, museums, beaches, and simply the island itself. The highlight, for me, was Stevenson's house and our guide's home with local fare and the warmest welcome into a simple but homely abode that bloomed with extended family and laughter.

Life revolves around family. From what we understand, land is kept within family relations and cannot be sold, given, or rented. Land is available to buy, but not much. Extended families live together, offering support to help the young grow.

With Noel back in top form, we hired a car with Rolande and Angus and spent two days touring the fertile island. An Australian rugby team flew over to play the Samoans; the power of the locals over awed our players. We left quietly!

The town centre meets every desire. It's safe day and night and extraordinarily friendly. Each morning, the police band marched up and down the main street, stopping all the traffic for thirty minutes, filling the air with cheerful music. The famous Aggie's Hotel is worth a visit, if only to see the founders beautiful sepia photo proudly on the wall, mixing with ornate decor. The buffet meal and colour show of dancing was outstanding in taste and entertainment; descendants of Aggie greet the guests.

Most businesses, taxis, and cafés are priced fairly, and rarely did we feel taken advantage of. The hourly rate here for most people is far below half our lowest wage in Australia; some families are unable to afford education for their young. At the time, school was optional, costing around 150 Tala a year. However, things were about to change. The following year, schooling would be compulsory and free.

By some miracle, we had timed our stay here with a local, week-long festival. Night after night, music blared, hips wriggled, and the dancers giggled, begging us to take their picture. Rich with thick make-up, the performers strutted their stuff on the make shift stage within the park. Everyone was invited; all you needed was a blanket to sit on.

The time came to depart in order to avoid the impending hurricane season. Australia was not far over the horizon. With a heady mix of answering Australia's call to come home and reluctance in ending our aquatic adventure, we cast off to claim the next horizon.

15

Wallis Island – The Beginning of the End

At Wallis Island, we had a bit of time to reflect on what we were doing, where we were going, and why we were going there. We didn't have the answers to any of those questions –
except we knew the same thing that happened on *Mariah* was happening now. We were swept up in the return journey home. Like before, as we sailed closer to home, the urgency to reach the safety of known ports and comfort of familiarity tugged at our emotions.

When compared to our trip on Mariah, this journey had been so different. Whereas everything fitted then, we now felt as if we didn't fit. *Mariah* was a simple, small boat. Though *Pyewacket* was not much more complicated, it was larger. We weren't in the small boat group – neither were we in the salubrious boat group.

We'd entered a new world. The type of boat we had was typically bought by people who've worked all their lives and finally figured out how to escape.

We were now removed from the younger age bracket – people who were inspired with high designs, had innovative ideas and ambitions, but could only afford a smaller boat; we'd now grown out of that group. We sat in the 'buy the biggest boat for the least bucks' faction, and we were prepared to do all the work necessary to upgrade her into tip-top ocean condition.

I'm not sure if it was that or perhaps this time we were not as wide-eyed with wonder as we were before. *Did things change so much after just four years? Did we see things differently now that we were qualified?* I'd like to think we didn't.

With all these thoughts, we still made lovely friends: Jenny and Randy on *Mystic*, a similar boat to *Mariah*, and Angus and Rolande on *Periclees*, who were becoming lovely friends, too. They had a similar boat to Pyewacket, except Angus had started with a good solid hull and refitted the entire boat himself. Jenny and Randy were a similar age to me and Angus and Rolande a similar age to Noel. Age on board boats has never been a barrier.

Maybe it's the memories that made us feel this way; we always remember the good times of previous trips and often forget the bad. When we were on *Mariah*, we did have a few months of despair near the Portuguese coast, when every day something else broke or stopped working. All our buddies sailed in different directions from the Mediterranean; so few travelled to England such as we did. That's the danger of revisiting a trip again; we'd always compare, even though this was a wonderful adventure in its own right. We had proved that we could achieve a great journey the second time around.

* * *

The polished surface of the Pacific Ocean was a new experience on this journey. Flat, calm water, with a little bump of a swell, accompanied us most of the way toward Wallis Island.

We had read little about Wallis. We knew it was French, permission from the Chief was necessary to enter and move anchorages, and, twenty years ago, the population was approximately three thousand on Wallis and Futuna combined. I imagine a lot less live there now, as my old book states that many of the young leave for Fiji or Tonga.

We tried to arrive during the second day of passage, but the lack of wind and lack of desire to use too much diesel meant another night. That was until we picked up some current, and our GPS informed us that we would arrive at 10:30 p.m., which was the worst possible time.

'I think we'll be arriving at night now,' Noel said while pressing buttons on the GPS.

'Well, we'll have to deal with it.' I secretly hoped we would see the leading lights and markers easily with the half moon. 'The French are usually fantastic with their buoy system; you never know it might be marked well.'

'I'm not sure I'd trust it, though, especially through a narrow entrance at night.' Noel was right. I prayed there would be fishermen nearby to guide us in – a forlorn hope.

Sailing is not like driving a motor vehicle; there are no roads to follow into a new town. Some entrances to new ports can be large, well buoyed, and safely traversed at night, but few islands have this luxury. Many people take the risk, and most make it in safely. Tiredness that tugs on your limbs, the desire for a whole nights' sleep, and a bed that isn't moving is hard to resist. But attempting an unfamiliar entrance at night can be lethal for the boat and crew. It's not worth the risk.

So, as darkness turned our eyes to night vision, we reduced sail, scanned the charts, and hoved-to near the entrance, awaiting dawn. Usually, these nights have frightful currents, evil winds, and obstacles to make the wait uncomfortable and lengthy. This time, we had plenty of space, calm waters, and a gentle breeze. We shared a pleasant evening with the cool night time air, and the stillness of dark came and went.

We puttered into the anchorage at dawn. The turquoise waters and sunny-yellow beaches with fisherman waving at us stirred my excitement for exploring a new place.

One catamaran swung on anchor, and we quickly made friends with Don and Denise, who had sailed from New Zealand. They provided the directions to the check in location, and we agreed to share a hire car to explore the island.

Checking in was swift and painless in a drab office with bored officials. Our paperwork received a cursory glance, was stamped, and we were free to roam. We knew we weren't staying long, so we checked out while we checked in. Most islands allow this if you leave within a certain time frame; here, it was three days.

I found the island odd. As we puttered ashore, it had looked like a mini city; on exploration, there was no centre of town. It's oddly sprawled out with small pockets of villages housing large modern abodes. A peculiar mix of showy four-wheel drives and small battered mopeds scattered pedestrians. Buildings were spread out, and the majority were gaudy empty churches made ugly in an attempt to be grand.

We stayed for two days, enjoying brief company with other sailors. Aside from friendly people, there was nothing appealing to make us stay; our hearts had turned to the thoughts of home.

* * *

During the last few weeks, I'd spent an inordinate amount of time working on increasing the intense pain of stiff muscles in my shoulders and neck while doing research. We'd heard horror stories of people importing boats into Australia. We read about the mounting costs, poisonous sprays for vermin and termites, tax loading, and people having a horrid time.

I tied myself in knots, worrying over something I knew little of and had yet to experience.

'It's never as bad as we think it's going to be, is it?' Noel reminded me. 'Everyone loves telling you the bad bits, how hard it is, how mad you are!'

'You're right,' I said, only half convinced.

'We've seen it all around the world, on every escapade we've done; taking *Mariah* around The Great Loop, sailing around the world, the French Canals. Even in our studies, I remember people telling you in particular how hard it is and how most people fail.'

'Hmm,' I said. 'You're right.'

'You came joint top of the class in a room full of blokes who knew it all! Don't forget people love to see others fail.'

I worried about Noel's thoughts on this at times. His reassurance did help me, but to think that most people like to see you fail is a horrible thought. Sadly, it is true. People love a good horror story; they like to hear of other people's failings, it makes them look better. Of course, not everyone is like this – but it is depressingly more common than I thought.

I had compiled a substantial file on our expenditure and what treatments *Pyewacket* had undergone. In America, I'd found some disgusting brown gunk that killed cockroaches; the pamphlet within the packet had noted it killed termites, too. I copied this out, highlighted it, and hoped the health officials would take this as a treatment. I didn't want the interior of *Pyewacket* sprayed with poisonous chemicals; not just because of the cost, but because having my home covered in possibly cancer-inducing liquids was not appealing.

I nursed this file all the way to New Caledonia; despite Noel's calming words, I was still anxious about importing a foreign vessel.

We'd stop cleaning the boat at this point. We didn't live in squalor, but we no longer washed and polished the hull. Previously, we had tried to present *Pyewacket* the best way we could; now, we were thinking of the valuation that the import duty would be based upon.

* * *

We didn't stop at Fiji. We anchored at a remote part in the south. We'd been to Fiji before and felt no compunction to return. The horror stories of checking in, expense, and masses of paperwork did put us off, despite knowing that it would be fine.

As before, we were focused on home and the next stage of adventure, so we enjoyed two peaceful nights in solitude, bobbing around next to sparse rocks that provided a little protection. Thoughts of home bounced and dipped around our minds while we waited for a small blow to pass over.

We'd sailed into Noumea on *Mariah* five years ago. The mix of emotions at that time is still vivid. It was a cross roads. We were with

Americans, Turks, Thais, New Zealanders, and we were all going in different directions from New Caledonia. We'd checked into a marina, sipped colourful farewell cocktails, and bid our sailing buddies farewell.

Now, on *Pyewacket*, we were on anchor with Rolande and Angus. We'd met them in Tahiti when we'd squished in beside them at the tiny anchorage area. Over at Moorea, we'd seen them again, and slowly, we developed a friendship through Suwarrow and Samoa.

This time, we had to wait out weather. So we anchored on the western side, behind the protection of a long reef.

We enjoyed a long exhilarating walk in company, where we lost Noel, became entangled in the bush, and lost shoes and a fair bit of dignity, but we laughed a lot between becoming snagged on the shrubs.

I looked forward to the sail into Australia. On *Mariah*, the nine days from New Caledonia to Bundaberg, Queensland had been perfect, with gentle swells, kind wind, and clear days. This area was renowned for good sailing. I'd love to sail to New Zealand one day, but the spiralling lows in that part of the world put me off. Up here, in the lower latitudes, the weather remained more settled.

Daily, we all downloaded the weather. We still used weatherfax, and Angus and Rolande utilised another system, which listed out more details within a smaller area.

'It doesn't look too clear, but there may be a weather window in a day or two,' Noel said.

Angus agreed. 'It doesn't look too bad the day after tomorrow. I think we'll go then.'

Angus and Rolande hopped on that window. We decided to wait for a sure bet. I must admit, I was the tiniest bit relieved that we'd waited while we listened to their arduous journey of lumpy seas and howling wind. But boy was that going to bite me on the backside!

While waiting, we sailed a few miles from one anchorage to another. We didn't care if we glided at two knots; it just didn't matter.

'It looks good to leave tomorrow,' Noel announced one morning.

'Great, I'm ready to go.'

'It may be a bit bouncy to start, but it looks as though the weather will improve the closer we get to Bundaberg.'

'That sounds good,' I said. 'Let's get ready.'

The following day, we upped anchor and pointed *Pyewacket's* bows towards home. All thoughts of importing a boat, paperwork, and cost were shed. I had to concentrate on the here and now. A safe passage, comfort, weather, food for fuel, night-watch, and sleep were our priorities.

'I hope you're right about the weather,' I said to Noel through gritted teeth. The long channel leading away from New Caledonia was stirring up into a rough texture of lumpy, angry seas. Head winds knocked us around; they were only twenty knots, but it was enough to stir up seasickness.

The seven hundred nautical miles became a battle – a scene of war and torture. Winds stirred, and waves rose to sharp peaks. Half way home, we were tired, fed up, and just wanted to get there.

'There's a gale coming,' Noel said one night after receiving a new weatherfax. 'It doesn't look good.'

'Oh, shit, just what we need.' I sighed and gathered my thoughts. *We can deal with this. Noel doesn't need me becoming despondent.* I decided to lift my game. 'Right, what do we need to do first?'

We spent time double checking rigging and lines. This is a daily job, but with bad weather approaching, we needed to be extra vigilant. We checked everything was stowed well, prepared a simple rice dish that would only need warming up, and hunkered down.

Two days out of Bundaberg, the gale didn't come, but a bloody great – stonking, angry, nasty – storm arrived to pick us up and slam us about.

We spoke to Rolande and Angus daily on the radio. They were snug and safe in Bundaberg. *Why didn't we leave when they did?* They didn't have a great journey, but they didn't have a storm.

Twenty-four hours away from Bundaberg, the seas raged, the winds howled, and we cursed. Fortunately, the wind blew onto our beam, but when driving a boat forward, the side-on winds appear forward. We slammed, bumped, and became accustomed to regular salt spray over the entire boat.

Neither of us could rest; we were tantalisingly close to home, but first, we had to participate in a major fight.

The winds backed to our port quarter, usually our sweet sailing position; however, huge rolling swells, coupled together with the building seas, created mountainous waves that raced up to *Pyewacket's* quarter; they'd lift her stern, and you could hear their effort.

We smiled at each other as we love wind on the quarter, but immediately, *Pyewacket* lurched and broached.

Broaching is where a wave picks you up and forces the boat sideways, side on to the next on-coming waves. It is dangerous; it can be lethal. Boats can roll right over; things can snap – and not only equipment. Boats can be lost.

In the nick of time, she righted herself.

'You bitch,' Noel muttered under his breath.

'That was close.'

'We'll have to take the main sail down and run with just the staysail and a bit of jib.'

We ran with this set up through the afternoon, but as the night approached, the battle commenced once again. Rounding the northern tip of Fraser Island and turning south west towards Bundaberg put the winds forward of our port beam.

As the wind howled through the rigging in a sickening death screech, Noel yelled, 'We have to put the storm main up. We'll need it now that we have turned into the wind.'

The storm sail is small and tough; it copes with strong winds and bestows a better chance to reach port.

'We still may not make it into Bundaberg,' he added.

'What? Oh god! Where will we go?'

'We'll look at the charts later; pointing south west is becoming tough. I'm not sure the old girl can do it; we're pinching at our maximum already.' We were now yelling at each other, not in fear or anger, but the crashing hull, tossing waves, and screaming wind was raising a racket.

We stripped off for the sail change. *Pyewacket* bucked and reared. Not for the first time, I thanked the previous owners for installing bum bars or fanny bars – stainless steel rails near the mast to lean on while the boat heaved and moaned beneath us.

We both fought on deck; ropes and canvas stretched, creaked, and slapped. Icy salt water sprayed over our shivering bodies. I wasn't sure if the fear, cold, or effort made me shake. We clung on tightly, working like a well-oiled team. Both of us knew what had to be done; there was no backing down or wimping out – it was up to us, and no one else, to get us home.

We stayed clipped on via our harnesses for the entire time. We watched out for each other. We never rushed – the most important thing was our safety.

I hated the thought of not reaching Bundaberg. If we couldn't push the boat that hard, then we'd have to anchor off an island farther north. That meant anchor watch for a few days, which meant more dried food and little sleep. I wanted to get home – a powerful emotion that was uncomfortably at odds with our usual ethos on safety.

Cajoling our limbs to pull, push, and fight harder, slowly, the storm sail worked its way up the mast. We'd lashed the big mainsail to the boom, only just managing to yank it back from the gusting winds. Thankfully, our self-steering Aries wind vane held our course.

As we finished the final touches, I ran back to the cockpit to heave on the mainsheet. I flicked a glance at the windometer. Fifty-five knots flashed up, and my stomach dropped.

'Argh!' I yelled at the sky in frustration, fear, and defiance. 'Come on, old girl,' I pleaded to *Pyewacket*, 'you can do it.'

We huddled in the cockpit, neither of us could eat. Occasionally, we'd manipulate the lines and try to pinch up another degree. The boat jolted like a fairground ride; we clutched the handholds all the time, even while sitting. As darkness surrounded us, we could only hear the waves towering and breaking – and sometimes witness the white water as it gushed passed.

The radio constantly crackled with chatter; several boats were making a similar crossing. We were kindred spirits not by sight, but by experience. We heard one boat make it safely into port. The selfish pang of jealousy tweaked my tummy. *I should be happy for them!*

A collective groan travelled over the radio waves from the boats behind us as the weather guru announced, from the solace of his office, that it was getting worse, not better. I joined in the chorus of doom.

Night thickens and takes on an evil heaviness during bad weather. The clouds wiped out all the stars and any hope of light from the moon. Our watery ride was the greatest rodeo that ever lived. My throat scratched with fear and dehydration.

Noel did battle below decks and re-appeared carrying two bottles of water. It was too tough to repeatedly clamber up and down the steps. We clung to the wheelhouse, under cover. *The ocean is right there, just a couple of feet away.* The sipped water only unsatisfyingly teased our thirst. My face ached with worry lines; my limbs groaned under the tense clinging.

The epic night became exhausting and terrifying. We sat in silence, trying to block out the ferocious sounds of banging and crashing, trying to ignore the boat juddering and bucking.

'I can see a marker!' I yelled several hours later; my voice burst through the misery. 'There's the entrance!' I was as happy as if I'd just won the lottery. But I'd won so much more, because we were going to make it.

Bundaberg has a fantastic entrance. It is large enough for commercial ships, well buoyed, and once within the channel, it offers reasonable protection from the pounding waves.

As we eased *Pyewacket* forward, the swells died down. A pang of regret stirred my emotions for the boats behind us as the radio squawked into life, revealing that the storm was set to continue.

Pyewacket sat up a bit straighter and slowed; we could unclench our white knuckles and tight buttocks. The entrance lights lit up like a celebration, flashing red and green, so welcoming – home.

We drank more water and managed a small bite to eat, but we had to be vigilant; the wind still wailed, and we were close to land. We were tired but still alert with adrenaline, checking our position, equipment, and monitoring the conditions.

Finally, with relief that hung across the entire decks, we puttered into flat water at 3 a.m. and dropped the anchor.

'I'm not comfortable here,' I said, glancing up the channel; we sat right in the middle.

'It'll be okay.'

'No, I want to move.' I turned around and headed for the bow to haul up the anchor. I had heard what Noel said, but the engine started.

We anchored twice more, my dear husband with the patience of a saint, until I felt comfortable. At last, I was satisfied, and we opened a bottle of wine.

'I just can't relax until I know we're safe,' I explained.

'I know, but after the second time...'

But it didn't matter; we let our shoulders drop and worry lines smooth. Moving anchor isn't hard; it takes but a few minutes. We smiled at each other, in the simple comfort of being safe, being together. At last, home – for now.

Epilogue

I've included the nitty-gritty on the process of importing *Pyewacket* into Australia in the next part of the book. Needless to say, it went far smoother than we envisaged.

Upon arrival, we accepted the valuation amount and paid the ten percent tax before anyone could change their minds. The rules stated that we had to pay it within twenty-four hours.

We were required to have a termite inspection, which was all clear. The rest was pretty much the usual checking in procedure.

The trip south along the NSW coast was pleasant and quick. Our thoughts of revisiting places we had sailed into on *Mariah* were washed away with the thoughts of earning money and settling back into our little house.

Pyewacket sold quickly, for she's a fine boat. Before we listed her for sale in our home port, we shaved the engine head, replaced the head gasket, and had new valve guides fitted; the engine was perfect – now that we had finished our trip! She suited her new owner well; a highly qualified mariner with all the right contacts for boat trades. He's talking of voyaging the oceans now that he has the right boat to do it.

I realise now that Suwarrow was the pinnacle of this journey – what it was all about. It was where we picked up the threads of our previous life – to me, it made sense.

After Suwarrow, we were focusing on the next town and the best way to get home. It is extraordinary now to realise we felt that way. We could have found a hurricane hidey hole and spent another season in the Pacific. We contemplated Japan, but after in-depth research, the indiscriminate typhoons put us off – there is no safe cruising season.

Our life of storms of emotions and oceans was now dampened with the thought of work. Freedom has compromises; we still needed money, and at times, we did crave consistency like having the shop in the same place each day...

At the start of the journey, I asked, 'Is it enough?' I now know why.

I must feed my addiction of adrenaline-thumping emotions of electrifying fear and invigorating fright.

Sailing is my drug. When I'm scared, I feel alive; when times are tough, my senses are heightened. Surviving the demands of furious seas enhances calm anchorages.

I do wonder if I made the most of it. Gained all I could. Or did I spend too much in the grips of dread with an unknown boat and an old engine?

Does that make me ungrateful? I wonder, and I know that it does not – and I am not.

I look back in disbelief. *Did we sail down to Easter Island and Pitcairn? Survive a vortexing storm in the Gambiers?*

We battled with Mother Nature and won. We laughed in the face of Murphy – after we'd dealt with his antics!

I had wanted the challenge of a different boat, but it doesn't matter what we tackle as long as tension, terror, anticipation, and elation can have a punch-up in my gut and come out battered and bruised – but, still, mates.

So, yes! It was enough!

I met amazing people who caused my cheeks to stretch into a smile so wide it made my face hurt. I've experienced cultures that caused a tingle of joy to skip through my body; the locals showed me the lightness of life. I've felt the cold prickle of fear run through my veins and the warm glow of success.

The most important part of seizing life by the scruff of the neck and relishing it is learning to love yourself. It doesn't matter if you are living in paradise or a shoe-box; if you don't like yourself, you won't like your life. You must love the boat you have, and love the body (and mind) you have, too. If you don't, a trip won't change that, and it will never be special.

We must all face compromises to move forward in life. Many concessions are our own decision, but there are also penalties in how people perceive you, especially if you are a little different.

But I urge you to be different; step outside the box; allow your light to shine.

We all make career, family, and money decisions. Whatever you do, someone somewhere will judge you.

Have faith, follow your inner compass, and be gracious, because then you can't fail.

If that means standing away from the crowd and making yourself a prime target for opinionated people, then keep this in mind: those who are ostracised, judged, and questioned are remembered.

I learned many things on this trip: my age is more noticeable in my forties, and I can be terrified out of my wits. I've experienced fight or flight. I've also learned that you don't have to act on your emotions, and today is the good old days of tomorrow.

But mostly, I've learned: *This* is it... Right now...

Where Are We now?

Since this sailing escapade, Noel and I taught maritime and studied, too, achieving Master 4 commercial skipper's certificates for vessels up to eighty metres.

We also adopted five horses and trekked part of Australia's Bicentennial National Trail (BNT). This trip was way beyond the hardships of sailing or anything we have tackled before. With those adversities came tremendous rewards that we are both still reeling over.

In June 2014, we purchased a 1920s Dutch barge we renamed Rouge Corsair. We are moored in Belgium for the winter; we've been on board a year and a half as I write this book. Much of that time has been spent renovating and wondering if we are doing the right thing – it's been a rocky road so far. But slowly, we are making positive plans.

I had wondered, again, if this would be enough. And although we face a different set of challenges, they have been, and are currently, plenty. The twists and turns of European laws and the tests in handling a heavy steel barge, sometimes alone, are enough.

My horses are still calling me, too, having left them with friends to be near UK family.

But as I said to Noel the other day, I am so grateful for my life. I'm doing everything I have ever wanted. I have my own business; I write often; I travel constantly; and I am free, independent, and in charge of my life.

I also have the most wonderful friend as my husband. Noel and I are kindred spirits; we have too many ideas, and they show no sign of ceasing. I wonder where we'll be this time next year – neither of us knows, and that's just the way we like it. Perhaps that's what makes it enough?

PART TWO – Bonus Material

Here, I've included articles, information, and further reading.

Not all of these are published articles; although, some are in various sailing magazines around the world. I have also included sections of articles. For example, the breakout boxes that contains details such as costs and visas. I've kept these aside from the main story to maintain the flow of our journey. Of course, you do need to bear in mind that the costs incurred were between 2009 and 2011.

Pyewacket's Particulars

We blew our budget when we purchased *Pyewacket*, though we knew we would. Marinas chock full of reasonably priced ten to twelve metre boats were on offer, but we wanted something different from our last vessel of ten metres.

Built in Langley BC by Huntingford, *Pyewacket* is an Aleutian design similar to a Maple Leaf design, she was launched in 1980. She's a surprisingly modern design for her thirty year age. The vast galley and separate workshop initially caught my eye. With a gas and kero stove, two sinks, and oodles of storage space, *Pyewacket's* galley was larger than our kitchen at home in NSW. The second great appeal was the workshop. Boats are endless work; there are always projects on the go, but we could simply shut the door to the workshop and, therefore, the mess. On *Mariah*, her entire innards turned into a workshop!

Specifications
- Designer: S. Huntingford
- Aleutian 51
- Builder: John Nissen Built in Canada
- Length: Deck – 15.5 metres. Waterline 13 metres
- Beam: 4.3 metres Draft: 2 metres
- Deck/hull material: Fibreglass, Balsa cored above the waterline
- Year of manufacture: 1980
- Interior: Timber
- Hard dodger, canvas enclosure
- Three-quarter keel and skeg hung rudder
- Displacement: 15 tonnes
- Encapsulated lead keel

Engine:
Chrysler Nissan
Model: M6336
Diesel
Cylinders: 6
55 amp and 65 amp alternators
Duel filter fuel system

Tanks:
Fresh water cooling
Max speed: 9 knots
Cruise speed: 7 knots
2 x fibreglass diesel tanks fore and aft
(750 litres total)
864 litres water (two separate, baffled tanks)
60 litres holding tank

Sail area:
1300 sq ft.

Rig:
Cutter

Mast:
Schaeffer, Forespar – Aluminium

Standing Rigging:
316 Stainless steel wire
Norseman fittings

Ballast (internal): 5.9 tonnes

Equipment: 2 x 120 Watt solar panels with Charge Controller for maximum amp output.
2 x Airex, 30 amp max, wind generators.
Teleflex wheel, hydraulic steering.
Wagner autopilot, Raymarine autopilot, and Aries wind vane.

Buying in a Foreign Country

This was much harder than we imagined even after two years carrying out Internet research prior to leaving. Thousands of boats were for sale; most of the boats we viewed had major problems. Here are some friendly tips:

- Have a clear idea of what you are looking for and where you will/will not make any compromises.
- There will be at least one compromise you have to make.
- Budget 30% more than you plan for expenses and the purchase of the boat.
- A lot of boats already have a survey of a varying age; most brokers/owners will let you read them – this could be a great time saver.
- Many chandleries give discounts if you have just purchased a boat or you spend enough – if you don't ask, you don't get.
- Hire a document agent – be aware of fraud; check and compare engraved numbers to document numbers and use an insured and certified document agent.
- Research, research, research! We joined several chat rooms on the Internet for lots of different types of boat owners. This led to a day out sailing on a Pan Oceanic 43 on Sydney Harbour! (Prior to our trip to America.)
- Ensure you extract the construction of the boat from the broker prior to viewing. One broker avoided this question for nearly a year. Just before flying to Mexico, he told us the boat we were interested in was fibreglass/ferro build-- something we did not want. Fractured fibreglass can be a big problem.

Our Costs (US dollars)
- Car hire: $320 per week ($AUS394)
- Value motel rooms: $70-$100 a night ($AUS86-$123)
- Food ($ dependent on where/what you eat)
- Fuel ($ dependent on how far you are prepared to travel)
- Mobile phone (charges for making and receiving calls)
- Free WiFi (own laptop)
- Document Agent: $500 minimum ($AUS615)
- Surveyor: $500 minimum ($AUS615)
- Hauling costs: $250 ($AUS307) haul out/in +$102 per day ($AUS125)
- Australian Import duty: 15% of value of vessel. (10% GST and 5% duty)
- Inspiring movies!

Mexico: Costs, Checking In, and Supplies

We were told that cruisers had to have liability insurance, specifically purchased from a Mexican company. Insurance can be purchased through an agent in San Diego or Mexico. We later heard regular (not of Mexican origin) insurance was accepted.

Most boats of around ten to twelve metres were paying about $190 for one year of insurance. Our quote (for a 51' boat) was $365. You could buy one or three months. Three months cost more than the year! We had good WiFi access on board at this point, so I scoured insurance options and finally found a company willing to insure us for $175.

On arrival in Mexico, vessels must go to the nearest Port of Entry, with the Q and courtesy flags flying. Immigration, customs, quarantine, and finally the port authority must be cleared.

As well as the ship's papers, six crew lists in Spanish are required (If you hire an agent or have help from a marina such as Salinas, they will prepare these crew lists for you.).
Our total checking in costs for Mexico came to around $300.00.

America is the only country we have come across that does not check vessels out of their country. Mexico is ready for this and does not request the usual Zarpe (clearance paper from last port of call).

In Mexico every boat must check out of the port with the Port Captain, *Capitania de Puerto,* every time it leaves for more than twenty-four hours.

Checking in Costs

We spent $300 checking into Mexico. This includes immigration, customs, quarantine and two fishing licences at $48.50 each.

On departure, we paid two fees: a $60 exit fee and a $20 error fee (Our initial immigration paperwork was filed incorrectly.)

Ecuador: Fees, Cruising Guides, and Visas

Total costs are around $250*, including our three month visas, health, immigration, customs, agent fee, and taxi fares for officials.

Ecuador's currency is American dollars. Prices quoted are in US dollars. At the time of writing, the Australian dollar and American dollar are on a par.

Customs took our passports away to have them stamped, returning them several days later.

Supplies
With a great daily market a five-minute walk away, shopping was easy. The carrots were straight out of a Bugs Bunny cartoon!

Boat parts
Parts are few and far between in Ecuador; importing is enormously expensive.

Eating out
Lunch (*almuerzo*) is cheap ($1.75 - $2.50), including soup, main dish (fish or chicken with rice), and a soft drink.

Mooring
Puerto Amistad
For $6 a day (if on anchor), you have a safe dinghy dock, showers, Internet, and a nice place to sit. A range of moorings are available, varying in cost up to $350 per month. The hard working employees at Puerto Amistad were simply fantastic.

You can download an Ecuador Cruising Guide at:
http://yachtpals.com/cruising/ecuador.

Visas

Rules and regulations for visas in Ecuador are as clear as Bahia's coffee-coloured river water. Generally, most people can stay six months (three months on arrival and renew for another three months). We were granted our three months on arrival and obtained, from the Ecuadorian Embassy in Lima, another six months (for $180 each). This rule changes for different ports within Ecuador.

Pitcairn: Communication and Information of Interest

Pitcairn Telecommunications provide broadband Internet and telephone service to every home on the island. They share New Zealand's country codes.

Pulau School offers both pre-school and primary education.

In the main square is the Government Treasury and Post Office, where stamps can be purchased. Money can be changed at the Treasury. Pitcairn's official currency is New Zealand dollars.

The Pitcairn Museum contains many artefacts most notably from ancient Polynesia and The Bounty.

Basic supermarket supplies are available at the Pitcairn store; a warehouse supplies hardware items. Both shops are open three days a week.

The main source of income for the Islanders comes from souvenir sales. Other services provided are cafés, bakeries, hair salon, massage, take-away meals, and accommodation.

Pitcairn has a health centre run by a doctor contracted on an annual basis. The facilities are designed to manage minor emergencies and general health. Serious cases require medical evacuation for treatment overseas.

Gambiers: Anchoring: What We Could Have Done Differently

- A heavier anchor maybe? But dragging wasn't the problem; being propelled straight over the top of the anchor will often lift it.
- Head/mic sets for us both, so we could talk while I was on the bow. Lighting my hand signals with the torch did work okay, though.
- We paid a lot of attention to the weather (and two different weather forecast providers predicted gusts of thirty knot winds only), but we'd be more aware of opposing winds on either side of us and pronounced dips in isobars.
- Anchor in a place where we can escape. We both felt that being at sea would have been better – still no fun-park ride but fewer things to hit. You can reef down, go with the wind with the wind vane controlling (instead of fighting it), and have control of the boat. It would have been impossible to leave this anchorage during the storm winds. Rikitea has a windy, narrow, coral strewn channel that would not allow for a gust of fifty-seven knots of wind pushing you sideways (the channel was not lit).
- We mostly maintained *Pyewacket* in a ready to go fashion; this prevented gear breaking. The jerry split because it wasn't put away properly.

Other boats: One boat dragged up to a wharf. He was hitting bottom, hence the distress call. As far as we know, he did not suffer any major damage. All the other boats in the anchorage faired okay. Some anchors held; some didn't. Some cruisers decided to pull up anchor and circle the anchorage. This made for a busy little bay, but we all lived to tell the tale.

Suwarrow: Formalities and Costs
Formalities
Checking in is informal; however, there are rules to follow that all cruisers are required to read as they check in.

It cost $50 for a two week stay.

No pets are allowed on shore, and no picnicking around the island, except at the Yacht Club. (There are more detailed rules to adhere to.)

James and John gratefully received donations that supplemented their diet. If sailing to Suwarrow, tune into the Pacific Cruiser's Net at 16:30 (02:30 Zulu) on 6Alpha (6224 MHz) for up to the minute details of Suwarrow.

James and John are growing a plethora of vegetables and appreciate any live matter from the cruisers that they can use for compost.

Australia: Checking In and Importing A Foreign Boat – Costs, How It Works, and Contacts

Article published in Cruising Helmsman magazine (costs in Australian dollars). Please note that Bundaberg Cruising Yacht Club no longer run the rally. It is now hosted by John and Leanne Hembrow. The rally is now called the Down Under Rally (2015).
More info: http://www.downunderrally.com.

Article:
Here we are, folks, the big game: Australia vs. New Zealand. Who's your money on?

The competition is hotting up. New Zealand is the clear leader, but Australia has a new secret weapon which may disrupt the league. Boy, are we in for a good game. Is the contest of check in destinations about to become a victory for Australia, or will the perennial favourites continue to dominate?

The teams
Team New Zealand is currently top of the league with benefits of a beautiful country, friendly, welcoming people, and great cruising ground. No fees to check in and smooth procedures on arrival. The chink in their armour? The sail south from Vanuatu or Tonga (two most popular departure points) is a challenge. The trip is over one thousand nautical miles, so the chances of meeting one of those vortexing lows that are regularly spat out from between Australia and New Zealand are high.

Team Australia has many of the same benefits: great country and people, spectacular cruising, and a relatively easy sail from

New Caledonia (popular departure point). They have a double-whammy holding them in second place in the league. The penalties: cruisers pay $330 to check in during a weekday, adding landfall on the weekend another $288! It's also been revealed that cruisers prefer to play ball with a possible low weather system en route to NZ than to tackle Australian officials. Rumours have been kicked about in a scrum, launched, caught, and thrown world-wide; horror stories of fines and court appearances abound within the cruising community crossing the Pacific.

Level pegging
Both teams have a minimum notification period for checking in. Australia requires ninety-six hours, and New Zealand requires forty-eight hours. Officials just want to know your boats ETA; a simple email from your last port is enough. Both teams remove certain foods. This isn't to annoy cruisers; it's to protect their fair lands. If you are unsure about any items onboard you simply declare them – the officials take care of the items and this action will avoid fines and/or court appearances. It is straightforward, and both teams are level pegging in this criterion.

Will Australia win?
Revealing a new secret weapon, there is hope. In Bundaberg, Queensland a group of people, are introducing new tactics. The Bundaberg Cruising Yacht Club organise the Port 2 Port Rally* and *Gateway* magazine for cruisers at the end of their Pacific crossing. The Club rolls out the red carpet, smooth procedures, entertainment, and hands out goodies. In their twelfth year, they have upped the anti – watch out team New Zealand. This

year, they refunded the entry fee for all cruisers arriving into Bundaberg (conditions applied). Eighty-four boats joined the Rally this year and only twenty-four last year.

Sadly, they can't keep doing this. The joining fees from previous rallies over the years paid for the refund (Thank you one and all!), but the Club does not have enough funds for next year.

Team Australia has flexed their muscles, but are they just a flash in the pan? Or can they maintain the strength to topple New Zealand for the number one spot?

Catch the ball and run!

The Rally committee are passionate about cruisers arriving into Bundaberg, but what is refreshing is that they are keen to send off the rumours until the final whistle and convince boats to come to Australia. This has inspired the group to publish a magazine *Gateway*. Modelled from New Zealand's existing magazine (outside assistance rule?), the glossy publication is brimming with forms, facts, anchorages from Alan Lucas's cruising guide, and information to help cruisers collect other good experiences – but this time in Australia.

Why bother?

There are 17.5 million *dollars* of reasons to be bothered. On the website of Opua Marina NZ, it boasts that last year 438 boats spent $NZS17.5 million in the port of Opua, New Zealand. I wonder how much the three hundred boats that checked into Whangheri and elsewhere brought in.

No brainer
It's time for Australia to come in first place. The world is in financial ruin; wouldn't several million help? It's a no brainer. Eighty-four boats paying $330 to enter creates a fine $27,720, but 438 boats entering for free coughed up 17.5 million. Why are we dithering along the sidelines?

Team leaders
NZ captains (aka 'the government') knows which side of their bread is buttered. Forget asking cruisers for money upfront; welcome them with open arms and reap the rewards as they repair and maintain their vessels in the country; say nothing of tourism and the foreign visitors hauling out their boats to fly home. Most cruisers avoid repairs and updates while crossing the Pacific (unless essential). After several thousand miles of driving our vessels to full potential, both boat and crew require much physiotherapy.

NZ has their eyes on the ball.

Australian captains have dropped the ball. The facts are there; businesses throughout Australia are losing out, the country is penalised, and the reputation that abounds around the cruising community is sad and embarrassing.

Head coach
The lead appears to be starting in Bundaberg. I have spoken to cruisers who checked in at various Queensland ports, and they all received a warm welcome. But the Port 2 Port Rally has stepped up to the plate. Their magazine *Gateway* is not Australia-wide – yet. Lesley, the Club's President, has sent a

copy to The Marina Association to show them and, hopefully, other ports what is possible. The Yacht Club wants to turn the view of cruisers on its head and steer boats into Australian ports.

Team effort
I've canvassed several international and Australian boats from Bundaberg and other ports about checking in. I received the following resounding response: 'The actual event is nothing like the rumours.'

Phrases such as 'helpful,' 'so easy,' and 'professional' out match the negative comments such as 'giving ninety-six hour notice is inconvenient,' 'finding information is difficult,' and 'the termite inspection is ridiculous.'

Andy on board SV *Chinook* sums it up perfectly: 'Immigration and quarantine were a helpful friendly lot in Brisbane; it's just the rubbish they have to enforce.'

This is our second go at checking in, and it has, on both occasions, been a simple, efficient, and trouble free.

Rumours
The rumours have not grown from thin air. I expect mistakes have been made by both officials and cruisers. However, the game is straightforward: follow the rules, and you will not receive penalties. The officials at Bundaberg do admit that some of the information is hard to find on the website, but it is there. And now we have the *Gateway* magazine that tells us all

we need to know. Contacting officials direct via Internet produces reams of speedy answers.

GOAL!
We joined the Port 2 Port rally for the refund. The assistance and welcome were a fabulous bonus. Clearly, the savings encouraged boats to come to Bundaberg this year, and the magazine was like finding treasure – an equal score according to the referees *Pyewacket II* and other cruisers.

Serious prize
Team games aside, there are enough cruisers to fill the grandstand of both Australia and New Zealand. To make landfall at one means a trip to the other; both are must see destinations. The cup holders are Team New Zealand; they have it all – stunning cruising and a warm welcome – all for nothing. Let's see if someone in Australia, with the clout, has the *foot*balls to score a try and help our ports become serious contenders.

Additional information - support
Bundaberg Cruising Yacht Club received support from the Port of Bundaberg and local businesses. With more support and advertising in their magazine, they hope to pay the fees again for next year's rally participants.

Port 2 Port Rally
Without doubt, the information and support provided from the Rally smooth the way into Australia. This year's participants say that the refund helped the decision to come here, but was combined with the support from the Yacht Club. Most cruisers

found the magazine in different ports in the Pacific, which steered them into Bundaberg.

What they offered:
> Refund of $330 (may not continue next year).
> Club's ambassador to meet and greet you.
> Forms, information, rules and regulations contained in magazine, as well as good anchorages (from Alan Lucas's Cruising Guide), local discounts, and freebies.
> Free BBQ.
> Guarantee of notification of impending arrival to Australia Customs.
> T-shirts.
> Radio schedule... and more.

The compromise:
> Pre-paid cost of $200 per vessel.
> Arrival in October and November only (from any Pacific Port).
> If the wind blows you elsewhere, you do not receive a refund (but you still receive the radio/Internet support).
> If you arrive at the weekend and after hours, they will not refund the additional overtime costs.
> All the events and socialising is exhausting!

Customs/Immigration/Health
The professional officials that checked us (and many other boats) into Bundaberg were extremely professional and welcoming. They asked the pertinent questions, and I knew they were listening to our answers, as well as watching our body language. But we never felt under

interrogation, powerless, or scared. *Pyewacket* received a thorough looking over.

Termite inspections
This was a relatively new ruling. Vessels are classed as high or low risk. High risk are those that have spent three months or more in Pacific Islands and/or have 10% or more of timber on board. These vessels will be required to have a termite inspection at the boat owner's cost. This creates a bone of contention; cruisers on foreign vessels – who are not importing their boat – receive up to twelve months to complete the termite inspection. (I didn't know termites could read a calendar!)

Our checking in fees
$330 AQIS (Australian Quarantine and Inspection Service) fees.
$363 termite inspection (discounted for Port 2 Port Rally members).
$180 per hour AQIS fee (if you do not hire their 'approved' supplier, which costs in excess of $1,000 and an AQIS officer has to be on board during the inspection).
$200 Rally fee.
$330 REFUND from Port 2 Port rally.
TOTAL $743.00 (Australian dollars).

*2016: The Port 2 Port Rally is now called the Down Under Rally and hosted by John and Leanne Hembrow.

Steering by a Star: Fitting an Aries Wind Vane to a 51' Boat
Article printed in Australian and USA sailing magazines

I suspect that if it is your personal aphrodisiac to hand steer, you sail for short periods. Connecting with nature through steering gear is admirable. From time to time I like to hand steer... out of port. Once clear of land Roy takes over. Roy is our Aries wind vane, named after my dad who assisted Noel in scraping off the decades of salt, lubricating and fitting new bearings; allowing the $US300 ($AUS347) seized Aries to flex his muscles and get to work.

While Roy attended fittings, fellow cruisers tossed a few sceptical looks our way, which we refused to catch.

'You think the Aries will steer a 51' boat?'

Admittedly, a little doubt had wormed its way into my thoughts. The enigma compounding these concerns was connecting the Aries to hydraulic steering and operating the vane from the centre cockpit.

With Roy fully limbered up, Dad and Noel measured up the required Aries support frame out of tubing. Noel and I commenced search by phone and many miles on pushbike to find a fabricator to help fabricate the frame. A week later we changed tack and embarked on an oratorical fiesta searching for an electric welder large enough to handle our proposed projects and small enough to afford (in both dollars and power) and stow.

Noel had pondered the problems of the cockpit position and hydraulics and dialled up his ingenuity. For many moments I caught him gazing at the back of the boat trying to join the dots and ultimately create an interesting overture.

After many hours of Internet searching, hoping someone had simply written up the answer, the emergency steering was the way to go. It meant much welding and weighing up the cost of paying a fabricator. It resulted in a new crew member in the form of an 110v/240v arc welder.

On board *Pyewacket*, the design of the emergency steering places the helmsman in the aft cabin, standing in a dark room, staring at him/herself in the full length mirror; the only visibility to the outside world being the side and rear port holes. The rudder stock is directly below the stairs that lead to the boot (aft cockpit), which is the reason for the obscure positioning of the helmsman. Above the stairs is a hatch. To connect the Aries to the rudder stock we had to extend the length of the rudder stock up through the stairs and through the hatch and to this extension fabricate a 'wind vane tiller'. We also had to find a way to quickly and easily turn the bypass valve, to bypass the hydraulic steering.

Holes were drilled into the hatch to allow an extension from the rudder stock up to the aft cockpit, leaving the sliding door closed (or open if we wished). Noel welded the emergency tiller arm onto the wind vane tiller (that in turn, was bolted onto the extended rudder stock). The emergency tiller is at an angle to allow us to stand on the seat in the aft cockpit. This gives us a much better view of the entire boat.

Our last boat was tiller steered, but this is not the same. The emergency tiller on *Pyewacket* runs aft, instead of forward, it is, in effect, backwards. So to steer to starboard we push the tiller to starboard. Despite a little bit of wandering during practice, we've finally nailed it and are chuffed to have this steering available should the main hydraulic steering decide to opt for early retirement.

The Aries can easily be attached to the 'wind vane tiller'. The ropes that run from the Aries are attached to chains, which in turn, slip over the tabs welded on the arms of the wind vane tiller. It is recommended that where the Aries ropes connect to the tiller in use, they should be 600-900 mm from the rudder stock. The distance on our set up is only 450 mm, in order to clear the liferaft. Adding a block roved to advantage on each line has halved the effort and in effect, lengthened the tiller.

The lines to adjust the Aries (directionally) run into the centre cockpit, so changing course is simple.

The bypass valve was not so simple. Flaunting its conceptual imperfections sitting under the aft cabin stairs is the hydraulic bypass valve and relief valve. All hydraulic systems incorporate these two valves. The relief valve comes into action if the rudder is put under an unexpected load, for example being hit by a large wave or suffering a grounding. The bypass valve is just that, to bypass the hydraulics and must therefore be utilised when using the emergency tiller steering (and, in our case, the Aries). To add to the complexity, once the emergency tiller is in place we cannot lift up the stairs (to access the valve) without a complete dismantle of the system. Also, the bypass valve neatly sits under the hydraulic hoses.

Enter: remote spindle. Noel made a kind of crankshaft to go around the hydraulic hose obstacles, drilled another hole in the stairs and hatch and created a remote spindle to turn the hydraulic bypass on and off. This we can operate from both cockpits. I tell Noel I think he's a genius; he simply shrugs his shoulders and says he is not the first to do this. It is the first contraption of this type I have seen and I am impressed. It means I can sit and write (as I am doing right now) while Roy merrily steers. Any adjustments are just an arm stretch away.

A compromise exists as with most operational systems on board. Catching a fish and hauling it in the aft cockpit does now require a certain amount of limbo dancing and partaking in a boat 'twister' game. Successful cruising is about finding a solution and accepting compromise. Whether cleaning dishes in a storm, reefing the main downwind, or connecting conventional self-steering to an unconventional set up. We are fortunate to have an aft cockpit where all the lines are situated, out of the way (mostly) but easily accessible. We are happy 'wackets' with hands free steering to enable us to pee and make tea at will.

Incidentally, the worm of doubt turned into fish bait. So far we have successfully tested Roy in eight to forty knots of apparent wind. We are in no hurry to try him out in stronger winds and we are confident he will cope admirably as the Aries generally works better in stronger winds.

So, now we steer by a star as the romantics prefer. However our 'star' is the wonderful Roy.

More information
Personal observations: We find it imperative to have reliable self-steering, ideally electrical and wind vane. We are ecstatic that the vane steers in such light winds. Our Wagner electric steering copes with calm seas, it is thirsty on power so it usually means we have the engine on.

The Aries website states that the Aries steers boats up to 50'. Our Aries has no problems with fifteen tonnes and 51'.

Our second hand Aries model is dated, but strong. New gears and bearings were purchased from England, Helen Bell Franklin, (daughter of the Aries inventor, Nick Franklin), whom we had last spoken to in 1998 from a phone box in Southport, Queensland, Australia for our previous Aries parts on board our last boat, *Mariah II*. Helen recommended that we purchase new cast stainless bevel gears. The aluminium gearing we currently had was, to quote Helen, 'renowned for dissolving in mid ocean.'

We always set the Aries up before leaving port. Once set up we cannot open the hatch (we can open the sliding door). To enable fitting of the 'new' rudder stock, the hatch has to be removed in the assembly process. To do this we have fitted removable hinge pins.

An additional compass is now installed should we have to steer from our newly positioned emergency steering.

Maintenance and restoring
When we first brought it home, we laid the Aries on deck and poured penetrating oil on every conceivable, screw, bush, and bearing; turning it over every couple of days to do the same on the other side, ensuring the oil soaked all the way through.

Replacement parts
The replacement stainless steel gears cost over £120 ($AUS205) (there are two), plus £90 ($AUS154) for the standard rebuild kit. But we figured that was still cheap for a working, reliable Aries. Our previous Aries steered us around the world over nine years across oceans and up rivers and canals using a connected auto pilot to the wind vane, and is still going strong with *Mariah's* new owners.

Mounting
Mounting the Aries on board *Pyewacket* meant the transom door would be permanently closed. During long stays in port we can dismount part of the bolts and pivot the Aries out and use the transom door. So far climbing over the transom to the platform is easier. Noel considered mounting the Aries on a bridge over the door, but due to the strength and conglomeration of forces we decided against this idea. The compromises are small and the pay off large. The Aries is easily accessible from our swim platform and from the safety of

behind the transom. Having the radar frame in place allowed us to dangle the Aries in position prior to bolting it on.

We could have mounted the 'wind vane tiller' pointing aft and utilised a number of pulleys each side as a more conventional tiller steered boat (albeit in reverse). But that just clogged up the back cockpit with more ropes and pulleys. This was why we decided to mount the tiller on top of the rudder stock athwartships, having the ropes leading directly from the Aries to the 'wind vane tiller'. The head of the emergency tiller was welded on to the top of the 'wind vane tiller' at an angle, so we could steer from the seat in the cockpit and more easily see where we are going.

Alternatives?
We researched a clutch operated wheel drum for connection to the Aries ropes. They could be purchased for two hundred Euros. This expense, the complexity of running pulleys to the centre cockpit, the problem of progressive creep* and the reliance on our thirty-year-old hydraulic steering, meant we opted for the idea of connecting the Aries directly to our rudder stock. We have successfully tested the transfer from Aries/emergency tiller, back to the centre cockpit hydraulic steering.

*Progressive creep can occur when wind vanes are connected to hydraulic systems. It simply means that you may have to continuously adjust the position of the ropes that lead onto the wheel clutch.

Additional adjustments
On our previous boat, *Mariah II* we connected an electric ram directly to the Aries which steered a fantastic course and consumed little power. The system never failed and continually held us on track

saving us hours at sea in longer crossings. We eventually plan to set the same system up on *Pyewacket*.

Emergencies
Everyone on board a vessel should be aware of the emergency steering equipment, its location, and how to operate it. The time to become familiar with the emergency steering is in a safe port or calm waters, not when you have just lost steerage and find yourself on a lee shore or crossing a bar.

Aries operation (courtesy of the Aries website)
When the yacht goes off course the plywood vane through its connecting linkage rotates the servo rudder from dead ahead. The water flow forces the servo rudder to one side pulling ropes which apply corrective helm to the tiller or wheel. The servo rudder has only to pull the steering lines to steer. It does not steer the yacht directly (the servo rudder does in fact assist the main rudder in its sideways thrust but only by a negligible amount).

The plywood wind vane has to be feathered 'edge on' into the wind by pulling on the course adjusting lines. When feathered correctly the vane is vertical or in line with the gear. As the yacht goes off course the wind comes round on one side of the vane deflecting it from the vertical on its pivot shaft which in turn deflects the servo rudder from 'dead ahead' pulling the steering lines as previously mentioned.

Ecuador: Radio Invigilating in Ecuador – Pilot Testing the New, On-line Exam in Ecuador
Article published in Australia

Witnessing Noel wearing large red knickers over blue tights is not something I have on my must do list. Fortunately, he may have felt a little like a saviour, but his uniform on the 'mission' day was more official and handsome.

Epaulettes do transform a mere mortal into something super. Wearing his maritime uniform to invigilate an examination felt appropriate to us, if only we could stop the candidate giggling!

Sometimes, the planets are aligned just right, and the cosmos lend fate a hand. Between boating, Noel and I worked for TAFE in NSW. Noel taught carpentry/building and, in the midst of all that, Marine Radio (He later moved into marine teaching only.). I taught marine only. Deckhands, Coxswains, and Master 5 classes were filled with professionals, requiring their ticket, and general folk, who were just interested in boats and all that goes with them. Part of the curriculum is the MROCP qualification (Marine Radio Operator's Certificate of Proficiency), which allows the holder to legally operate a VHF and SSB radio. We guided the students through the curriculum and taught them what we knew. Previously travelling oceans for nine years meant we had vast experience on both VHF and SSB radios: installing, programming, and operating.

The OMC (Office of Maritime Communications) issue the radio exams; as invigilators, Noel and I were licensed to oversee the exams on OMC's behalf. Our responsibilities included ordering the correct number of exams and ensuring they were not tampered with (They are all sealed in a clear plastic bag, and the edges of the booklet are stuck together with tabs.). If any exams remained unused, they had to be returned with the exams that had been completed by the students – all within a certain time frame. In the returned package was the answer sheet, the exam itself, a verified passport photo of the candidate, payment, and forms with the candidate's and our details.

The invigilators licence is renewed every three years. Mine had expired; Noel's was still current. But we had no idea it would be useful in Bahia de Caraquez, Ecuador.

We met Sandy and Max in Ecuador. They sail the planet on their sailboat, *Volo*. They built this fine vessel themselves some fifteen years ago. They are true pelagic people, with twice as much sea time as us and no plans to switch back to *terra firma*.

With no time to allow friendships to foster over a long period, they develop them with speed while living this floating lifestyle. Being fellow Aussies, Max and Sandy quickly became friends who understood our obscure humour. After several weeks, they found out that Noel and I were teachers of the nautical sort, and Radio was part of our repertoire. As this information unfolded, I could see Max's eyes light up.

From Ecuador, Max and Sandy were planning to sail south down the South American continent, eventually reaching Chile. Chile requires the skipper to have a Radio Licence. The *Volos* had been contemplating the problem, and suddenly finding an Australian Invigilator, the answer had been provided.

We agreed to try to help Max. He offered to pay all and any expenses we may incur. We assured him there would be none, and as invigilators, we accept no payments or gifts whatsoever.

Staff at the OMC had been incredibly helpful over the time I invigilated exams through Technical and Further Education (TAFE), so I whizzed off an email, explaining the predicament. I pointed out that both couples have Australian Registered boats, where we could hold the exam.

We received a response straight away. The current regulations stated that the exam must be held on Australian soil. The OMC recommended that we find the nearest Australian Consulate or Embassy. The nearest embassy was a nine hour bus ride away (one way), slightly prohibiting. As a last ditch attempt, I told the OMC staff member about an Australian lady in Bahia who owns a hostel; could this slide through the regulations as Australian soil? Unfortunately not, and we explained to Max that we had done all we could.

With the trip to Chile approaching, Max was becoming a little anxious about legally fulfilling the communication requirements. He decided to take the challenge up and contacted the OMC himself. The OMC had just finished internally testing online examinations and had approached external organisations for testing; with Max's willingness to be a guinea pig in this venture and some collaboration between the OMC and the Australian Communications and Media Authority (ACMA), they granted the go ahead. Max is an intelligent man, and I had an inkling he was enjoying the ground-breaking conversations across the Pacific Ocean.

Max and Noel are similar in that all their undertakings must have all the Ts crossed and Is dotted with meticulous care. Max had organised the practice questions over the Internet and the time and date of the exam. At the required time, over the Internet with a password, Noel could access the exam.

Usually the Internet connection on board is good here in Ecuador, but in a stiff wind, the boats move, and the connection can break. On the night of the assessment, it was calm, and while Noel pulled up the exam on the screen and issued Max the instructions, Sandy and I looked after the margaritas in the saloon.

On board *Volo*, they have a small private office where the exam took place, Noel sitting on the steps behind Max, performing as invigilator, while Max silently tackled the questions. Again, the planets aligned, and everything proceeded smoothly, especially smooth were the girls' drinks.

In keeping with super human efforts, once complete, the exam was emailed back, and within a minute, the result was returned!

We'd all like to thank the staff at OMC, who went out of their way to help us make this happen. It was ground-breaking for all parties: for the crew of *Pyewacket II* and *Volo*, for Ecuador, and for OMC.

The pass mark of the MROCP is 70%. Max joined the league of professional radio operators who passed the exam with flying colours.

More information
Under the provisions in the *Radio Communications Act 1992*, governing the use of radio transmitters in Australia, a person is required to have a certificate of proficiency to operate a MF/HF and VHF marine radio; 27 meg radios do not require this certificate – only a class licence (see below). Note: should an emergency occur, anyone can use the radio to hail help.

Snapshot of requirements
27 meg – Class Licence only (set of conditions to follow only)
VHF – Class Licence and Certificate of Proficiency
MF/HF – Apparatus Licence and Certificate of Proficiency. When the apparatus is licensed, ACMA will issue a call sign.

Class licence
A class licence is simply a set of conditions that operators must follow. An actual licence is not issued; you do not pay money or take a test (for the Class Licence only).
Check out the ACMA website for a list of these conditions. The Ship's Station licence that was previously required for 27 MHz and VHF is no

longer required. It is the responsibility of the boat owner/radio operator to read and follow the conditions of the class licence.

Apparatus licence
For our HF equipment, we completed an ACMA form, R057, which found on the AMCA website, and paid $49. For clarification of appropriate forms and costs, contact Radio Communications Licensing and Telecommunications Deployment.

Marine Radio Operators Certificates (Proficiency)
Three proficiency certificates in regards to marine radio operator qualification are available:
1. Marine Radio Operator's Certificate of Proficiency (for VHF and MF/HF radio operations) – MROCP
2. Marine Radio Operator's VHF Certificate of Proficiency (for VHF radio operations) – MROVCP
3. Marine Satellite Communications Certificate of Endorsement – MSCCE (SATCOM)

Ecuadoran Flopper Stopper in a Flap
By Noel Parry
Article published in Australian and American magazines.
(Notes: 'Sheila' is Australian slang for woman and 'barney' is UK slang for an argument.)

Right, all you blokes pay attention: Sheilas turn the page (Well, if you could just wait a little while.); this is for the emasculated males.

The scene is set in early morning on anchor in an open roadstead: the Pacific Ocean. Here, we sit outside Bahia de Caraquez, Ecuador; the day we supposedly finish a 2,800 nautical mile voyage. This odyssey entailed crossing the Intertropical Convergence Zone (ITCZ) with all its associated calms, squalls, lightning, and running before hurricane warnings. After four weeks, the nerves are shattered.

Our hearts slowly sink as the sing-song Spanish lilt carried along the waves to our VHF, informing us that we have just missed the pilot for entrance to a safe harbour by thirty short minutes. This necessitates anchoring twenty-three hours for the next high tide; daylight and pilot need to be synchronised. Okay, then, the *'beepin'* journey is not over yet!

Three dimensional acrobatics have been our life for four weeks, since La Paz, Mexico. Even then, we had wind-over-tide rolls on anchor. The Corumel winds were firing up with the onset of summer and the commencement of Hurricane Danger Time! On anchor at Isla del Coco, we morphed into an immense lurching pendulum, followed by head-butting winds for fourteen consecutive days. Life, recently, has been a tad arduous.

But the real problem, the actual crux of the flap I'm in, the reason I call on my brothers to hear my tale, is because last night the wife and I had a barney. Of course, I was in the right, like all good males invariably are. How-some-ever, Jackie was convinced I was a raving lunatic in need of sleep and external restraints, preferably off the boat and furthermore at a considerable distance from her fair self. Imagine my shock, my horror, to find that my dearest thinks my keen judgement and decision-making skills were shot.

'Just get out of the cockpit, you half-witted dolt; get some sleep and get off my watch,' yelled Jackie.

'Right, all the best, good luck to you then,' I retorted, brilliantly.

The details matter nought, right, guys? It won't matter what you do, say, or venture; you are *persona non grata*. You are the enigma, the ghost who walks, the bloke scratching his head, asking himself, 'What?'

The only thing to do, of course, is retire to the shed. Make something, fix something, lube, file, or adjust. Then maybe, just maybe, the result will be something the wife thinks favourably toward.

By this stage, what the wife 'thinks' is in the too hard basket – something understandable like a nuclear reactor or a way of stopping a fifteen tonne boat from rolling in a four foot swell; now that's something a bloke's got a chance at.

In our dash to convert *Pyewacket II* to our way of life, we had overlooked the essential cruising peacemaker: the FLOPPER STOPPER. For the sake of our sanity and comfort, we needed one right now.

Several versions of the Flopper Stopper exist; some commercially available and the rest are made-up designs. The Aussie and the Kiwi cruisers usually make their own (ingenuity or testament to our Scottish heritage with our reluctance to buy anything we think we can make ourselves?).

Whatever the version, the requirement is identical: to break the rhythmic pendulum-like swing of the vessel's mass about its geometric centre. Bashing up against a wharf can do it; although, that is a trifle harsh. A stern anchor can induce pitching and reduce rolling; however, you may want to have a quick departure, especially on an open roadstead. The best method, of course, is to have the boat propped in a twenty acre paddock.

A successful Flopper Stopper principally has to do two things:
(1) Sink easily.
(2) Resist an upward force.

One simple method is to have a weighted, horizontal door. The door opens on the way down (sinks) and closes on the up lift from the halyards – a bit like a one way valve.

I have plans, in my head, for a stainless steel flopper. Sort of like a flat door in a four-sided door jamb, the whole thing being held by a halyard at each corner. That was not going to happen off the coast of Ecuador today.

What could be achieved, in a flap, is this: A plywood door with halyard on each corner, the 'hinge' side being weighted down with heavy lead sinkers, the opening side having just enough lead to overcome the buoyancy of the door, and the hinges being the flexibility of the rope halyards.

The spinnaker pole set up with fore and aft guys and a topping lift keeps the whole thing in position. The longer the pole, the greater the turning moment (torque); this torque is what your creation is exerting when it is Stopping the Flopping.

Good luck with it gentlemen; maybe one of us can find the perfect solution to our woes. At least whilst in 'the shed,' you can make a better Flopper Stopper!

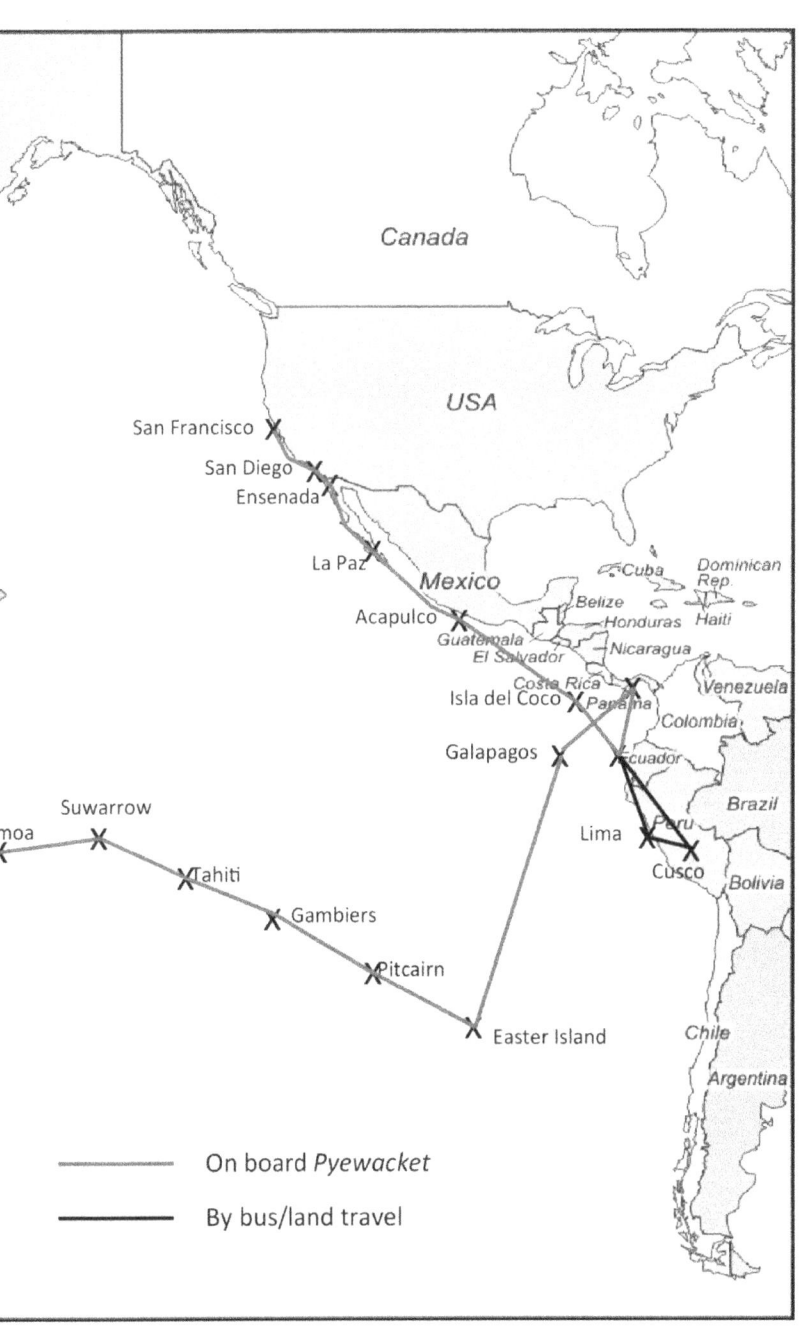

Glossary

Anodes: Where corrosion could be a problem (due to the electrical potential of dissimilar metals in a conductive solution such as seawater) sacrificial anodes protect all ships at sea, underground and above ground pipelines, boilers, hot water heaters, and generally steel structures immersed in water or damp soil conditions where corrosion could be a problem.

Aries Wind Vane: See Wind Vane.

Athwartships: From one side of the ship to the other. In this case, I use the word to explain how Noel is sleeping width-ways in the vessel.

Autopilot: Self-steering gear controlled by electronics operating according to one or more input sensors. Ours was via our magnetic compass. See Electronic Autopilot and Wind Vane.

Bar: Bars form at the entrances to rivers and estuaries because of the drift of sand along the coast.

Bare Poled: No sails aloft; only the mast and rigging driving the boat along – usually used in severe storm conditions only.

Beam: Widest part of the boat (middle). When the wind is beam-on, it is blowing square on the side.

Blocks/Pulley-Blocks: A simple device consisting of a wheel with a grove in which a rope can run along to change the direction or point of application of a force applied to the rope.

Bow Rollers: Friction-free surface to make dropping and weighing anchor easier – rolls as anchor chain passes over them.

Broaching: When a sailing vessel loses control and is forced sideways to the wind and waves. This can become dangerous in heavy seas as the boat will often heel heavily, leading to capsize. The change in direction is called broaching-to.

Brown Booby: A large seabird of the Booby family.

Bruce Anchor: A claw-shaped anchor designed by Peter Bruce.

Cardinal Markers: A buoy or fixed structure used in maritime pilotage to indicate the position of a hazard and the direction of safe water. They indicate (by a sign and/or by a light sequence) the direction of safety as a compass direction (North, East, South or West) relative to the mark.

Ciguatera: Poisoning by neurotoxins as a result of eating the flesh of tropical marine fish that carries a toxic dinoflagellate.

Chart Plotter: A device used in navigation that integrates GPS data with an electronic navigation chart.

Clocked: When talking about the wind, if it has 'clocked,' it means it has changed in a clockwise direction (e.g. from north to east, etc.). 'Backing' means the wind has changed in a counter-clockwise direction (e.g. from south to east).

Cold front: See Weather Frontal System.

Deduced reckoning (DR): In navigation, Ded Reckoning (DR) is the process of calculating your position by using a previously determined fix. You advance your first fix based upon known or estimated speeds over elapsed time and course. You must maintain the same speed, time, and course for the duration (note length of time) or calculate an average. Full details and diagrams in Cruisers' AA here: http://amzn.to/1N8Y968 or http://jackieparry.com/2014/12/12/free-navigation-advice/.

Derrick: A kind of crane with a movable, pivoted arm for moving heavy weights, especially on a ship.

Double the angle off the bow: This calculation, for calculating your position (fix), takes advantage of the properties of an isosceles triangle. An isosceles triangle has two sides of equal length and consequently; it has two internal angles that are also equal. This rule is used when the second bearing between the bow of your boat and the target is double the angle of the first bearing. (See websites above for further details.)

Displacement: In maritime, the displacement (mass) of a floating boat equals, exactly, the mass of the water it displaces. Remember Archimedes principle? *'Any "body" partially or completely submerged in a fluid is buoyed up by a force equal to the weight of the fluid displaced by the body.'* Another way to say it: a floating object displaces a volume of water equal to the mass of the object. As an example, when you get into a bath of water, the water raises a certain amount. Weigh that amount of water (the amount it has risen by), and that would be your displacement.

Dodger: A frame-supported canvas or solid structure partially protecting the helmsman on a sailboat. It covers part of the cockpit and the companion way (entrance) into the boat.

Doodad: My term for 'thingy,' 'wotsit,' etc.

Draft: Maximum depth of vessel in the water.

Electronic Autopilot: Self-steering gear controlled by electronics operating according to one or more input sensors. Ours was via our magnetic compass.

El Nino/La Nina: Complex weather patterns resulting from variations in ocean temperatures in the Equatorial Pacific.

Fales: Traditional, simple thatched huts in Samoa.

Fix: A 'fixed' know position usually plotted on a chart with a time reference.

Flags: A Q flag is a yellow quarantine flag, and a courtesy is the flag of the country you are visiting.

Flopper Stopper: Helps reduce rolling at anchor. See article 'Ecuadorian Flopper Stopper in a Flap.'

Following-seas: Where the wave direction matches the direction of the boat.

Furler: This was our Genoa sail on the furler. The furler is really the pole that the front sail is attached to. With the use of lines, you can spin the pole, and the sail furls around it.

Gimballed (as in gimballed stove): A gimbal is a pivoted support that allows the rotation of an object about a single axis. When you gimbal a stove, it means the top remains horizontal when the boat leans (heels) over.

GPS – Global Positioning System: A satellite-based navigation system.

Gunwales: The upper edge or planking of the side of a boat or ship.

Gypsy (on anchor windlass/winch): A notched wheel that engages the links of a chain. See Warping Drum.

Harmonic Constant: Officially, the amplitudes and epochs of the harmonic constituents of the tide or tidal current at any place. It's used in predicting tides. I am using the phrase in the book as a little play on words – a special phenomenon – harmony, perhaps.

High Pressure Ridge: A broad region of sinking air or a deep warm air mass. It usually brings warmer and dryer weather, but when we've encountered a ridge (prior to the settled weather), often, they bring a band of challenging weather, too.

Hove-To: Heaving-to or hove-to involves backing your jib, releasing your mainsail, and pushing and holding the tiller away. This causes conflicting forces on the boat. The backed jib is trying to push the bow away from the wind and the rudder is turning the boat into the wind.

The flapping mainsail and the backed jib prevent air flow over the sail, and therefore, stops the driving motion. Heaving-to is a sailing tactic that gives you time to stop and rest and wait for daylight for a safe entry into a new port and when conditions are rough.

In-mast furler/furled mainsail: The main sail of a boat (fixed along the mast and boom) that furls within the mast. Similar to a furling jib/Genoa, but more likely to jam in the mast.

ITCZ Intertropical Convergence Zone: The region that circles the earth, near the equator, where trade winds of the northern and southern hemisphere come together. An area of perpetual thunderstorms.

Jib: A triangular staysail set ahead of the foremost mast of a sailing boat. Its tack is fixed to the bowsprit, to the bow, or to the deck. The clew does not extend aft past the mast. (The tack is the lower corner of the sail's leading edge.)

Jerry Cans: A large, flat-sided container used for storing or transporting diesel or water. Usually, they are metal, but we used plastic cans.

Jury-rigged: Makeshift, improvised.

Lava lavas: aka pareus and sarongs.

Leading Lights: Any two objects or lights that, when in line with each other, indicate you are on the correct path to enter port.

Lee Shore: A shore lying on the leeward side of a ship and on to which a ship could be blown in foul weather.

Low (Frontal/Weather System) or Low Pressure System: A low pressure area, or a 'low' for short, is a region where the atmospheric pressure is lower than that of a surrounding area. A low pressure system develops when warm and moist air rises from the earth's surface. Air near the centre of this mass is usually unstable. As the warm and humid air rises, it can become unstable enough to produce rain, storms, and strong winds.

Main or Mainsail or Mains'l: Usually, the most important sail, raised on the aft side of the main (or only) mast of a Bermuda rigged sailing vessel.

Mainsheet: The mainsheet is attached to the boom (pole attached to mast) and is used to control the mainsail.

Nautical Mile: A nautical mile is a unit of distance set by international agreement as being exactly 1,852 meters (about 6,076 feet).

NSW: New South Wales State.

Occluded Fronts: See Weather Fronts.

On The Hard: Where a boat has been hauled out of the water and is placed in a yard.

On The Quarter: See Quarter.

Outboard: An outboard motor that is towards or near the outside of a boat.

Pelton Wheel: An impulse type water turbine invented by Lester Allan Pelton in the 1870s. The wheel extracts energy from the impulse of moving water. Many variations existed prior to Pelton's design, but they were less efficient.

Port/left side – Starboard/right side: In the early days of boating before ships had rudders on their centrelines, boats were controlled using a steering oar. This oar was placed over or through the right side of the stern. Hence sailors began calling the right side, the steering side, which became Starboard.

With the oar on the right side, the boat was docked on the left side, which was known as larboard or the loading side. Larboard was too easily confused with starboard, so it was replaced with port, as that was the side that faced the port.

Puddle Jump Rally: The rally supports and reports on the annual migration of cruising sailors from the West Coast of the Americas to French Polynesia. Boats from many nations register with the rally and depart any time between late February and early June.

Pump-Out: Equipment that will pump out the black and/or grey water from your holding tanks on board.

Q-Flag: Yellow quarantine flag. Always aloft when entering a new foreign port. Officially, it means: 'I am a healthy vessel and request free pratique.' The flag remains up until quarantine has cleared you. (Pratique is permission to use a port, given to a ship after quarantine or on showing a clean bill of health.)

QLD: Queensland State.

Quarter (on the quarter, starboard, or port quarter)/on the quarter: If the wind is on the boat's quarter, it is said to be on a direction of forty-five degrees or less from the stern of the boat. (Not directly behind and not on the beam (side) of the boat, but in-between.)

Radios: Marine Radios: VHF (very high frequency), short range. Maximum range is usually when aerials are in line of sight. HF (high frequency), long range radio works by a radio wave signal that is transmitted; it then bounces off the ionosphere and reflects down to another point on earth (the ionosphere consists of layers of ionized gas situated a few hundred miles above earth). This means that the range of the HF radio could be thousands of miles, with good equipment, set-up, conditions, and propagation (behaviour of radio waves). (HF can be referred to as SSB, which means Single Side Band.)

Raw Water: Natural water like rainwater, groundwater, and water from bodies like lakes and rivers. Water is considered to be raw until it is treated by a potable water treatment process. In this case, it refers to the water we were sailing in, primarily salt water.

Reef: A ridge of jagged rock, coral, or sand just above or below the surface of the sea.

Reefing sails: Reducing the area of sail.

Rode: I've removed this word from the story. However, the rode (also known as anchor cable) is what connects your anchor to the boat. It could be the rope or chain or a combination of both.

Running fixes: A running fix is a fix using two bearings, and it doesn't matter how far the course line is from the bearing object; therefore, it is used when you have no means of measuring the range.

Full details and diagrams in Cruisers' AA here:
http://amzn.to/1N8Y968 or
http://jackieparry.com/2014/12/12/free-navigation-advice/

Scheds/Nets: Radio Scheds and Radio Nets are 'Schedules' and 'Networks.' This just means that they are a planned meeting of people on the radio at a set time and frequency.

Set and drift: Drift is the speed of the current (in knots) and set is the direction it is flowing.
More here: http://jackieparry.com/2014/12/12/free-navigation-advice/

Shifter: An adjustable spanner.

Southerlies/Easterlies: Also westerlies and northerlies. This is referring to the wind. The wind blows *from* the stated direction (e.g. when you have a northerly, it is blowing *from* the north, which is unlike currents because they run *to* the north, south, east, or west [and anywhere in between]).

Spinnaker Pole/Whisker Pole: A spinnaker pole is a spar used on sailboats to help support and control a variety of headsails, particularly the spinnaker.

Staysail or stays'l: A fore-and-aft rigged jib sail whose luff (forward leading edge of the sail) can be affixed to an inner forestay (aft of the forestay), running forward from a mast to the deck. Triangular sails set forward of the foremost mast are called 'jibs,' 'headsails,' or 'foresails.' The innermost such sail on a cutter, schooner, and many other rigs having two or more foresails is referred to simply as the 'staysail,' while the others are referred to as 'jibs' or 'flying jibs.' The inner jib of a yacht with two jibs is called the 'staysail,' and the outer (foremost) the 'jib.' This combination of two jibs is called a 'cutter rig.' Differences between European and American terminology exist; however, a sailboat with one mast rigged with two jibs and a mainsail is called a 'cutter.'

SSB: See Radios

Starboard: Right side. See Port.

Stem: The most forward part of a boat's bow and an extension of the keel itself.

Snubbers/Strops: Lines used to prevent transferring the shock load from the anchor chain to the boat. They have stretch.

Storm Main: A sail of smaller size and stronger material than the corresponding one used in ordinary weather.

Stuffing box: If a boat has an inboard engine, it is most likely to be fitted with a stuffing box to provide a watertight seal for the propeller shaft. In principle, a stuffing box is the same as a packing gland on a common tap (faucet).

SV/MV: Sailing vessel, motor vessel.

Swell (Ocean): Swell in an ocean wave system not raised by the local wind blowing at the time of observation; it has been raised some distance away due to winds blowing there. The swell can travel for thousands of miles before dying away.

Tender: Small boat (dinghy) used to travel from your boat on anchor or mooring buoy to land.

The Great Loop: The circumnavigation of eastern North America; a continuous waterway connecting inland lakes and rivers with the Atlantic Intracoastal waterway and the Great lakes. It touches the shorelines of America and Canada.

The Intertropical Convergence Zone (ITCZ): Also known to sailors as the 'doldrums.' From about five degrees north and five degrees south (depending on land temperature), the north east trade winds and south east trade winds converge in a low pressure system; this is the ITCZ. In this region, solar heating forces the air to rise (convection), causing plenty of rain and lack of horizontal movement of air (wind). Thunderstorms are prevalent in this area; they are normally short-lived but plentiful.

Three bearing fixes: This is a great way to double check your position. On your chart, select three conspicuous landmarks to use. To avoid large errors when underway, take a bearing with your hand compass of the landmark closest to your stern first, then closest to your bow, and, finally, the one that is abeam (090° from your bow). Convert to True bearings by applying Variation and Deviation, and then plot them on your chart. Your fix (position) is where the lines intersect.

Tricolour: Combined port (red), starboard (green), and stern (white) light at the top of the mast.

VHF: See Radios.

Warping drum: A small drum on the side of an anchor winch (windlass) that is used to haul in ropes and sometimes chain. Usually, a gypsy wheel is on the windlass to haul in the chain. See Gypsy.

Waxing: Referring to a moon phase. Waxing essentially means growing or expanding in illumination. Waning means shrinking or decreasing in illumination.

Waypoint: A stopping (or noted) point on a journey.

Weather frontal system: This is a boundary separating two masses of air of different densities. The air masses separated by a front usually differ in temperature and humidity. Cold fronts often feature narrow bands of thunderstorms and severe weather with unpredictable winds. Warm fronts are usually preceded by rain and fog. Fronts invariably cause wind shifts. The weather usually clears quickly after a front's passage.

Occluded fronts are where a cold front overtakes a warm front. Typically, a developing storm or cyclone has a preceding warm front and a faster moving cold front. As the storm intensifies, the cold front rotates around the storm and catches the warm front; this forms an occluded front.

Windlass: Anchor winch.

Wind Vane: Wind vane self-steering gear is an entirely mechanical device which senses the apparent wind direction and holds the vessel on a course relative to it. The power to steer is provided by the force of moving water over the water vane part of the wind vane apparatus

Zarpe: Boat exit papers administered when you leave a country.

From the Author
Thanks for purchasing and reading *This Is It* I hope you enjoyed it.

A lot of people don't realise that the best way to help an author is to leave a review. So, if you did enjoy my story, please return to the site you purchased it from and say a few words. It doesn't need to be long; just saying what you thought is fine – and much appreciated!

Do feel free to contact me on: Facebook or drop me an email:

www.jackieparry.com
www.noelandjackiesjourneys.com
FB: Noel and Jackie's Journeys
FB: SisterShip Training
www.sistershiptraining.com
www.sailingeden.com

Acknowledgements

A huge thank you to the following people for their feedback and support during the writing process for *This Is It:* Alison Alderton, Roger Harrington, Valerie Franks, Brenda Parry, Philip Hodson, Phil Sherwood, Carole and Barrie Erdman-Grant, Roger Brown, Susan Jackson, Pat Ellis, and Nancy Utterson Lynch.

My deepest gratitude and respect goes to my editor Danielle Rose at Narrative Ink Editing LLC.

To my family and friends – thanks for all your support in whatever form you've provided it. I love writing and appreciate everyone for giving me the time I need to do so.

To everyone who's left reviews and connects via social media, I sincerely thank you, too. Your positive messages and marvellous reviews mean more to me than you'll ever know.

Our Other Adventures

Of Foreign Build: From Corporate Girl to Sea-Gypsy Woman

Reviews:
"This is a literary masterpiece."

"This book reads like a mystery novel."

"I couldn't wait for the next chapter."

A Standard Journey: 5 Horses, 2 People, and 1 Tent

Reviews:
"Special and unique."

"A hauntingly beautiful book."

"Will tick with readers for a long time."

Cruisers' AA (Reference Book)

Reviews:
"Probably the most comprehensive reference book designed for preparation for a cruising life."
"A remarkable reference, there is a depth of information that beggars the imagination."
"This is a new and fascinating insight on how to go cruising."

www.ingramcontent.com/pod-product-compliance
Lightning Source LLC
Chambersburg PA
CBHW061733070526
44585CB00024B/2657